Socia
Gene

CW01082265

Social History in Perspective i₅   nany
topics in social, cultural and r   o give
the student clear surveys of   ·cent
resear

PUBLISHED

John Belchem *Popular Radicalism in Nineteenth-Century Britain*
Simon Dentith *Society and Cultural forms in Nineteenth-Century England*
Harry Goulbourne *Race Relations in Britain Since 1945*
Tim Hitchcock *Sexuality in Britain, 1690–1800*
Sybil M. Jack *Towns in Tudor and Stuart Britain*
Christopher Marsh *Popular Religion in the Sixteenth Century*
Hugh McLeod *Religion and Society in England, 1850–1914*
Michael A. Mullett *Catholics in Britain and Ireland, 1558–1829*
John Spurr *English Puritanism, 1603–1689*
David Taylor *Crime, Policing and Punishment in England 1750–1914*
N. L. Tranter *British Population in the Twentieth Century*
Ian Whyte *Scotland's Society and Economy, 1500–1760*

FORTHCOMING

Eric Acheson *Late Medieval Economy and Society*
Ian Archer *Rebellion and Riot in England, 1360–1660*
Jonathan Barry *Religion and Society in England, 1603–1760*
A. L. Beier *Early Modern London*
Sue Bruley *Women's Century of Change*
Andrew Charlesworth *Popular Protest in Britain and Ireland, 1650–1870*
Richard Connors *The Growth of Welfare in Hanoverian England, 1723–1793*
Geoffrey Crossick *A History of London from 1800–1939*
Alistair Davies *Culture and Society, 1900–1995*
Martin Durham *The Permissive Society*
Peter Fleming *Medieval Family and Household in England*
David Fowler *Youth Culture in the Twentieth Century*
Malcolm Gaskill *Witchcraft in England, 1560–1760*
Peter Gosden *Education in the Twentieth Century*
S. J. D. Green *Religion and the Decline of Christianity in Modern Britain, 1880–1980*
Paul Griffiths *English Social Structure and the Social Order, 1500–1750*
Anne Hardy *Health and Medicine since 1860*
Steve Hindle *The Poorer Sort of People in Seventeenth-Century England*
David Hirst *Welfare and Society, 1832–1939*
Helen Jewell *Education in Early Modern Britain*
Anne Kettle *Social Structure in the Middle Ages*

Tittles continued overleaf

Alan Kidd *The State and the Poor, 1834–1914*
Peter Kirdy and S. A. King *British Living Standards, 1700–1870*
Arthur J. Melvor *Working in Britain 1880–1950*
Anthony Milton *Church and Religion in England, 1603–1642*
Christine Peters *Women in Early Modern Britain, 1690–1800*
Barry Reay *Rural Workers, 1830–1930*
Richard Rex *Heresy and Dissent in England, 1360–1560*
John Rule *Labour and the State, 1700–1875*
Pamela Sharpe *British Population in the Long Eighteenth Century, 1680–1820*
Malcolm Smuts *Culture and Power in England*
W. B. Stephens *Education in Industrial Society: Britain 1780–1902*
Heather Swanson *Medieval British Towns*
Benjamin Thompson *Feudalism or Lordship and Politics in Medieval England*
R. E. Tyson *Population in Pre-Industrial Britain, 1500–1750*
Garthine Walker *Crime, Law and Society in Early Modern England*
Andy Wood *The Crowd and Popular Politics in Early Modern England*

Please note that a sister series, *British History in Perspective*, is available
which covers all the key topics in British political history.

CATHOLICS IN BRITAIN AND IRELAND, 1558–1829

Michael A. Mullett

Senior Lecturer in History
University of Lancaster

First published 1998 by
MACMILLAN PRESS LTD
Houndmills, Basingstoke, Hampshire RG21 6XS
and London
Companies and representatives throughout the world

ISBN 0–333–59018–X hardcover
ISBN 0–333–59019–8 paperback

A catalogue record for this book is available from the British Library.

This book is printed on paper suitable for recycling and made from
fully managed and sustained forest sources.

10   9   8   7   6   5   4   3   2   1
07 06 05 04 03 02 01 00 99 98

Printed in Malaysia

 Published in the United States of America 1998 by
ST. MARTIN'S PRESS, INC.,
Scholarly and Reference Division,
175 Fifth Avenue, New York, N.Y. 10010

ISBN 0–312–21397–2

For my brothers and sisters,
in memory of our parents

CONTENTS

PREFACE

This book is offered as a contribution, in the area of religious history, to the 'British' historical approach that has become popular in recent years; this is not a work of 'English' history but of history in the 'British archipelago', of which England was and is an integral part. England shared the experience of her sister nations, or regions, within the islands of the archipelago in being a Catholic land at the beginning of the period of this survey, in 1558: indeed, English Catholicism underwent a strong revival under Mary between 1553 and 1558.[1] In common with her neighbours in the component entities of the pattern of islands that we (generally) call British, England retained a Catholic element in her population for the whole of the remainder of her history down to the present day.

Even so, to treat England in the story that follows as no more and no less than one of four component parts of these western European off-shore islands, equal in weighting as an historical force with the others, would be to betray the facts of the situation. Though some might see the Union of the Crowns of England and Scotland in 1603 as a successful political take-over of England by Scotland, I prefer to view England, with her demographic, economic, military and political preponderances over the duration of the period covered by this book as the driving force of historical decision-making within the islands; as an example of the way in which policies adopted in England ushered in change within the rest of the cluster of realms, in Scotland it was English intervention in 1559–60 that was decisive in securing the Protestantisation of the northern kingdom. Indeed even the mismanagements of English rulers were crucial to outcomes, as they were in determining the alignment of so much of Irish society to religious tradition, to Catholicism, within the critical Elizabethan decades. As for Wales, not only were her fortunes largely forged after 1536 by decisions made on the banks of the Thames, but as a member of a binary 'perfect union',[2] the little Principality was treated constitutionally as simply a western extension of England. Therefore, because of England's key role in religious evolutions within the group of kingdoms and a principality that made up the 'composite kingdom' which arose in these islands between the sixteenth and the nineteenth centuries, her part in our essay in Catholic history is given primacy within each chapter; likewise, the chronological divisions of treatment – the periodisations from c.1558 to c.1642, from c.1642 to c.1745 and from c.1745 to c.1829 – take their significance chiefly from the political events and decisions that arose or were made in England at those junctures.

Though England thus sets the pace in my account, religion obstructed the achievement of her total hegemony, whether in the cultural, linguistic or political fields, within the British composite. As Scots nationhood was squeezed in linguistic and constitutional terms following the Act of Union of 1707, the northern nation's identity was expressed all the more vociferously through its Calvinist Presbyterianism; when Wales adopted Methodism at the same time – in the eighteenth and nineteenth centuries – that its possession of its language was threatened, a Christianity different from England's set the Principality apart as a people. Above all, it was in its Catholicism that Ireland, the Poland of the western world, found not only a talisman of difference from its imperial overlord but, by and large in the nineteenth century the very vehicle of a nationhood otherwise threatened with extinction.

The survival of Catholicism in Ireland forms an extreme paradigm of its survival elsewhere in our archipelago. Irish Catholicsm endured as a majority creed within the island emphatically against the odds. But that is true also of the Catholic survivals in English regions, in one Welsh county and in parts of the Scottish Highlands and Islands. By about 1715 the British state was the most powerful and effective in the world, and yet was incapable, either before or after that date, of crushing a religious minority traditionally and legally regarded as treasonable.

Some, then, might regard our story of the survival of Catholicism as falling within the genre of sagas of the victory of the human spirit and perhaps of the virtue of fortitude. If that is so, the durability of other forms of obduracy against the odds, of the splendours of human dissidence, quirkiness and difference – whether Quaker or Unitarian, Muggletonian or Independent, Methodist or Jewish – also represent human victories. Whatever might be the case with other systems of religious co-existence, our British tolerance has been achieved over time less through the influence of theories of toleration than as a result of the invincible persistence and obstinancy of obstreperous minorities. Time after time, and above all at the cruces of Nonconformist toleration in 1689 and of Catholic Emancipation in 1829, often reluctant law-makers have had to concede that what could not be exterminated must be tolerated. The beloved Church of England itself has gained immeasurably from the legacy of recalitrance insofar as it has been cheated of or spared the fatal inheritance of the status of a monopoly church.

Acknowledgements

The research for and writing of this book were made possible by Lancaster University's generous sabbatical provisions. My head of department, Ruth Henig, has provided constant encouragement, as have my colleagues, especially those with whom I share more immediate academic interests, Eric Evans, Joe Shennan, John Walton, Bob Bliss, Angus Winchester, Sandy Grant, Marcus Merriman, David Allan, Sarah Barber and Harro Höpfl. The late Ralph Gibson, a great historian of Catholicism, stimulated my enthusiasm and listened to my ideas. Bob Bliss, Marcus Merriman, Sandy Grant, Mike Winstanley and my wife Lorna provided patient help with my inadequacies at the computer. Marcus Merriman was also kind enough to lend me his set of the indispensable journal *The Innes Review*, for which I thank him most warmly. Bishop John Brewer of Lancaster recently set up a library of Catholic and religious studies and history, the Talbot Library in Preston, where I have had the pleasure of many hours of study preparing this book under the care of the librarian Fr Robbie Canavan, who was generous with wise advice, with friendly encouragement, with the fruits of his own rich scholarship and with an endless supply of biscuits and potent Irish tea. The ever-helpful Lancaster University Library staff, especially John Illingworth, have made my tasks so much lighter and I am deeply grateful for the special efforts of Thelma Goodman and her staff in the Inter-Library Loan Office.

I have received encouragement from the many scholars in Catholic history who live and work in the North-West – including Bishop Brian Foley, Cyril Hall, Leo Warren, John Giblin, J.A. Hilton, Tony Noble, Fr Paul Harrison, Margaret Pannikar, Anne Parkinson, Derek Longmire, Emma Riley and many others. My editor Jeremy Black has been a constant fund of encouragement, close textual guidance and wise advice. Jonathan Reeve and other publishing staff have been patient, understanding and helpful in every way My wife Lorna and our sons Gerard and James and daughter-in-law Rhiannon and my family in South Wales have been loving supporters of my efforts.

MICHAEL A. MULLETT

1

CATHOLICS IN ENGLAND AND WALES, c. 1558–c.1640

England

This chapter surveys the emergence of Catholic recusancy and its con-solidation in Elizabethan and early Stuart England and Wales. We begin with a study of the early English Catholic recusant community and its emergence in particular regions as minority groupings, largely rural in location and with Catholic aristocrats leading a predominantly plebeian rank and file; this community was, at the best of times, marginalised and in the worst periods actively persecuted on political grounds, for in the course of Elizabeth's reign from 1558 to 1603 England's Catholics were to become linked in the official and the public mind with treasonable conspiracy in alliance with Spain. The Catholic-inspired Revolt of the Northern Earls of 1569 against Elizabeth led to the excommunication and papal deposition of the queen in the bull *Regnans in Excelsis* of 1570; this was followed by the Ridolfi Plot of 1571, a conspiratorial version of the 1569 rising, sharing its programme of a Catholic marriage between Mary Queen of Scots and the Duke of Norfolk backed by Spanish and papal military and financial assistance. The Throgmorton Plot, exposed in 1583, involved French as well as Spanish and papal support for another bid to dislodge Elizabeth, while the Parry Plot of 1585 indicated a high degree of papal intervention in English affairs, and the Babing-ton Conspiracy in 1586 once more centred on the violent substitution of Elizabeth by Mary. The survival of an English Catholic community was thus threatened by its association with conspiracy backed by foreign

1

powers to endanger the very existence of Protestant England and the life of its queen. Yet despite the political perils attending its survival, the Catholic community in England and Wales managed to endure over the first 80 years of its existence as an endangered minority and did not undergo the fate of annihilation of the Catholic Church in Scandinavia: the English and Welsh Catholic Church lived on to become the Catholic community of post-Reformation England and Wales and experienced, indeed, a revival during Elizabeth's reign.[1]

One of the tasks of this chapter will be to evaluate the right balance of emphasis in a discussion of whether what came into existence as recusancy in Elizabethan England was predominantly a continuation, necessarily in an altered form, of the religious life of pre-Reformation England or whether it represented a largely new amalgam inspired by innovative elements coming out of the Tridentine Counter-Reformation which was launched by the Catholic Church's Council of Trent sitting between 1545 and 1563.

On the face of it, it would seem obvious that what arose as Catholic recusancy in Elizabethan England was in direct descent from the medieval past. Elizabethan recusants themselves were conscious of preserving such a tradition intact. The recusant Cecilia Stonor, speaking in 1584, typified the view of an unbroken continuity which the Tudor state had sought to sever: 'I was born in such a time when the holy mass was in great reverence, and brought up in the same faith ... I hold me still to that wherein I was born and bred.'[2] Stonor's perception that Elizabethan Catholicism was the authentic heir of the medieval English Church typified Tudor recusants, their traditionalism justifying in their minds their obduracy. However, one of the most influential of historians of English Catholics, the eighteenth-century Vicar Apostolic Bishop Richard Challoner, helped in his *Memoirs of Missionary Priests* of 1741 to shape and perpetuate an alternative historiography according to which Catholicism under Elizabeth was in effect re-made, creating the model of the kind of Catholic community to which Challoner himself ministered, high in zeal, low in numbers and in many ways severed from its medieval moorings. As the pioneer martyrologist of post-Reformation English Catholicism, Challoner gave rise to a view that the English Catholic Church was re-created under Elizabeth in two particular closely linked ways. In the first place, he tended to treat somewhat dismissively the priests who survived into Elizabeth's reign from the previous Catholic regime and whom some more recent writing has seen as important bridgeheads of continuity from Catholic past to recusant future: for Challoner, these were simply 'the old priests daily dying off,' and urgently needing to be replaced. Secondly, this provision of replacements was made by the new breed of martyrs whose heroism it was Challoner's task to chronicle. Their blood was the seed of a new Catholic Church, founded in the 1570s and 1580s. Richard Challoner's concentration on 124 priests martyred under Elizabeth, in 'fortitude and courage, joined with so much meekness, modesty, and humility', operated alongside his silence over 44 Catholic victims of the Tudor state between 1535 and 1539 to accentuate the impression of a new-made Elizabethan Catholicism.[3]

Within the present century, too, historians have tended to discount an assumption of a chain of continuity linking pre-Reformation Catholicity with post-Reformation recusancy. For example, writing with particular reference to Yorkshire, A.G. Dickens described a lingering medieval Catholic tradition that was extinguished during the first decades of Elizabeth's reign, to be replaced by a new form of the faith as a result of a determined campaign conducted by Jesuits and seminary-trained priests, agents of the new Catholicism of the Counter-Reformation which began in the second half of the sixteenth century. Dickens claimed that

> shining out most clearly from our study of Yorkshire recusancy is it lack of organic connection with medieval tradition . . . [O]nly the slenderest of threads connect the old reaction with the new . . . [S]urvivals of medieval religion which came to light in . . . 1567–8 . . . had already almost vanished before the seminary priests got to work in the later seventies. Between survivalism and seminarism little or no connection existed; arduous proselytism, not the weight of tradition, accounted for the romanist revival.

A vague religious conservatism, Dickens argued, found expression in the survival of essentially medieval devices and devotions and took temporary shelter under Elizabeth's Protestant Church of England for a few years following 1559. As far as Yorkshire was concerned – one of the northern counties in which the recusant tradition was nourished after 1559 – an official crack-down exterminated this weakening traditionalism after 1570. A new Catholicism, that of the European Counter-Reformation, was engendered by the seminary priests and rapidly acquired a separate existence apart from the Church of England.[4]

Turning his attention to Lancashire, which became the heartland county of post-Reformation English recusancy, J. Stanley Leatherbarrow pointed to a revival of Catholicism in the 1570s and 1580s, rather than its simple lineal continuation during the crucial first decades following the Elizabethan settlement of religion of 1559. Leatherbarrow suggested that the English Reformation was not (as generations of English Protestant historians had viewed it as being) 'a popular uprising against a corrupt clergy and a body of erroneous doctrine', but rather 'the imposition of an unpopular new religion by a clever and powerful bureaucracy upon an unwilling and rebellious people'. Out of a strong preference for continuity English Catholicism was bred as an essentially conservative set of values. This religious survivalism flourished in Lancashire in particular because poor communications and weak leadership inhibited the enforcement, which elsewhere in the realm was overwhelmingly successful, of Protestant change driven forward by a powerful and autocratic government in London. More specifically, the agents of Catholic survival were the Lancashire priests Laurence Vaux and William Allen. Their work was subsequently reinforced 'by a new generation of missionary priests...trained during the 70s...They represent the impact of the full force of the Counter-Reformation.'[5]

John Bossy is more sceptical than Leatherbarrow about the religious quality of the English Catholicism that obtained before the arrival of the seminarian and Jesuit missionaries from the 1570s onwards. True to its roots in medieval rural and agrarian society, traditional Tudor Catholicism was involved in 'a set of ingrained observances which defined and gave meaning to the cycle of the week and the seasons of the year'.[6] From the 1570s, Bossy argues, there arose a new English Catholic community, concerned not with the communal rituals of a whole society but rather with promoting personal morality and religious conversion. In contrast with the zeal and high professional calibre of the new English priests coming from the 1570s out of the Continental seminaries set up at the behest of the Council of Trent, the surviving priests who represented what links there were between pre- and post-Reformation English Catholicism were, Bossy claims, sadly defective: the surviving priests did not adjust mentally to the harsh fact of a Protestant hegemony after 1559 and were trapped by their own nostalgia for a vanished Catholic England, as well as being legalistic in their thinking and incapable of taking up the new ideals of the priesthood emerging out of the Italy and France of the Counter-Reformation.[7]

Christopher Haigh has written in much more positive terms about the Catholic priests who maintained the faith in years of essential continuity following 1559, years which witnessed 'a continuation of traditional English Catholicism shaped by the circumstances of the Reformation'.[8] An unflattering image of the traditional Church was, Haigh alleges, deliberately put about by the Jesuit Robert Parsons as a means of highlighting the success of the mission carried out by the seminary priests and above all by the Jesuits. Haigh saw Parsons as standing at the headwaters of an influential but essentially erroneous historiography which depicted the pre-Counter-Reformation Catholic Church in England as being incapable of generating an English Catholic renewal out of its own resources: according to the historical overview propagated by Parsons in the first instance, the restoration of Catholicism under Queen Mary between 1553 and 1558 had been merely formal and neither spiritual nor profound; Haigh summarises Parsons' kind of depiction of the old Church as 'spineless, moribund, hierarchical and monopolistic', succumbing without real resistance to 'a fast and easy reformation' – up to the point, that is to say, at which seminarians and Jesuits of Parsons' own order rescued the seriously weakened patient, converting the old Church into a militant outpost of the Catholic renewal set in motion by the Council of Trent.[9]

Haigh rejects that kind of view of the old English Catholic Church. In particular, he maintains that the traditionalist priests who refused – markedly in the North – to accept the Elizabethan religious settlement were neither supine nor inactive:

> In upland England, where government was weak and the parochial structure of the established Church ineffective, recusant Catholicism was created in the 1560s and 1570s by local clergy who led their people into separation.... Sacraments and religious services were provided by Catholic priests unreconciled to the Church of England with which they competed so successfully that there was a real chance of setting up a separate, popular Catholic Church in the western and northern regions.

And all this took place 'before the mission from the seminaries had any impact' – that is to say, before the main waves of seminary-educated priests began to flood out of the Continental seminaries in Douai, Rome and elsewhere from 1574 onwards. Indeed, that later mission was, Haigh argues, a failure in terms of a mass mission since in its concentration on the pastoral care of gentry households it lost the allegiance of many of the lower orders who had been attracted by an emotionally and liturgically rich Catholicism: 'The grand enterprise which some saw as a mission for the conversion of England from heresy became an agency for the provision of private chaplains for the gentry.'[10]

There are good grounds for accepting the proposition that the older, pre-Elizabethan styles of English Catholicism, with their roots in a vigorous late medieval devotional tradition, remained extensively alive in the decades following 1559. After all, whatever the extent of 'revival' in early modern Catholicism, whether specifically in England or in Europe at large, it stood for essential continuity with medieval doctrines and practices. Indeed, there is evidence of nostalgia amongst representatives of Counter-Reformation revival for the Catholic England of their recent past, overlooking its deficiencies. Thus, for example, the ex-Jesuit Thomas Wright was full of regret for the charitable, artistic and liturgical riches of pre-Reformation Catholic England as he surveyed the

> heate of charitie exiled, the fluds of almes and hospitalitie . . . which in former ages ranne amaine . . . frosen with . . . solafidean erroure: while all the churches are hoary white without Image, Taper, Altar, priest, sacrifyce, piety or de-votion.[11]

And if – as we are led by Eamon Duffy and J.J. Scarisbrick to believe – English Catholicism before the Reformation was essentially vital, creative and popular, there is no reason to disbelieve that its vigour should have continued on an upward curve in the, admittedly restrictive, circumstances following 1559. Haigh offers the late medieval Catholic resurgence in Lancashire as part of his explanation for the county's continuing Catholic preferences under Elizabeth. More generally, and beyond Lancashire, the early sixteenth-century reformist English Catholicism that welcomed Erasmus and produced the early Tudor Catholic reformists Colet, More and Fisher may well have had a late flowering in the retention of Catholicism by appreciable numbers of English people following Elizabeth's accession – in the same way, for instance, that a late medieval and early sixteenth-century Catholic renewal provided inspiration for the Tridentine Counter-Reformation from the 1540s onwards.[12]

Indeed, it was late medieval piety that fed the devotional life of the Catholic remnant in Elizabethan England. A manual on praying the Rosary, *Instructions for the vse of beades* . . .(1589), which targeted not the recusant gentry and nobility but 'the husbandman in the fields . . . the labourer with his toiling . . . the simple . . . the woman . . . the poore . . .', had its roots in the confraternal religious life of medieval England and Europe, in the form of an urban sodality which was founded in Douai in the Netherlands in 1470 and spread in 1486 to England. Its ethos, formed in the medieval Netherlands that had produced the *devotio moderna* and the *Imitation of Christ* (whose influences were disseminated in England by the Carthusians) was still being fostered a century after its implantation in the country.[13]

The way in which types of collective piety originally formed in a late medieval urban ambience acted as a continuing source for post-Reformation English Catholic spiritual life, independent of the gentry households, can be confirmed if we look at York, the county city of a shire with an exceptionally rich late medieval tradition of religious theatre designed for religious teaching; it is an extraordinary fact of Catholic survival in an Elizabethan urban environment that ten years after the Elizabethan settlement the city's traditional Corpus Christi play, the expression of a distinctively Catholic eucharistic theology, was still extant.[14]

Even so, it would have been politically difficult to retain for very much longer such an overt survival of public Catholic didactic religious theatre. What did survive in York, more quietly than street theatre, but as a bridgehead between early Tudor urban piety and the persistence of minority Catholicism after 1559 was a York sodality centred on a 'middle-class' urban professional, Dr Thomas Vavasour. The Vavasours nourished Elizabethan recusancy in York and to do so drew on the resources of a surviving and continuing civic tradition for, though they were 'in touch with the new springs of Catholic piety on the Continent . . . in their case continuity with the past is especially strong'. In the Vasasour circle the Mass was at the centre of a type of group piety familiar in the towns of late medieval Europe. In York it was not a country gentry that protected and provided patronage and employment for priests but an indigenous urban group which in 1580 adopted the Jesuit Edmund Campion as its sodality chaplain. Richard Rex comments that the York circle fits the continuity 'model of development of Haigh's thesis according to which the seminary priests were able to build on a solid foundation of dissent of varying degrees of articulacy and commitment'. Thomas Vavasour's religion was no mere unthinking traditionalism or 'set of ingrained observances' but a cogent faith grounded in the earlier Tudor age of Catholic reform in the Cambridge that had welcomed Erasmus: 'he was living testimony to the connections between the Catholicism of the Henrician establishment and that of the beleagured recusant minority under Elizabeth'. Such continuities initially made it difficult to enforce the Elizabethan Reformation in the northern city but also eventually gave rise to York's small but deeply engaged and well informed Catholic group, one already identifiable 'two years before the first seminarists reached the city'.[15] In this regional and urban case, survival looms far larger in our overall picture of what happened to Elizabethan Catholics than does a picture of sudden transformation and 'revival' under Tridentine, clerical and gentry auspices.

Religious traditionalists who were neither priests nor squires played a key role in maintaining the continuities of a Catholic presence in England after 1559. Born Catholics, they were typically – and often truculently – attached to the old ways. Where they were influential in their local communities, they might make life difficult for a browbeaten Protestant incumbent struggling to introduce the changes commanded by the queen in Parliament. One such parson recalled how he had, as required, denounced the Mass and the elevation of the Host as 'Idolatry':

> Whereat old Thomas Whyte a great rich merchant and ringleader of the papists, rose out of his seat and went out of the church, saying, 'Come from him, good people; he came from the devil and teacheth unto you devilish doctrine.' John Notherell ... followed him, saying, 'It [the eucharistic Host] shall be God when thou shalt be but a knave.'[16]

These were typical voices of early Elizabethan lay Catholicism – loud, aggressive, unafraid, fluent and abusive, and above all confident in the imminent vindication of tradition and continuity.

Especially in those areas in which regional popular culture permitted it to happen, notably in Lancashire, lay Catholicism remained vibrant in continuity with the past within identifiable districts, allowing families to remain Catholic 'without flouting convention'. Yet this enduring Catholicism amounted neither to unthinking and obstinate habit, nor to near superstition, nor to blank rural rejection of all change. Typically, the religious traditionalists were liturgically and ecclesiologically knowledgeable, consciously Roman in their allegiance to the pope and insisting on the retention of the Mass; they were to be found amongst the laity in town and country. Indeed, lay people played a key role in the continuing persistence and survival of Catholicism in England after 1559.[17] Though the new-style priests of the Catholic revival later in the reign overwhelmingly led the ranks in Elizabethan Catholicism's army of martyrs, lay folk suffered imprisonment in large numbers: for instance, in the London Clink in 1586 eight lay people outnumbered five priests among those imprisoned for their Catholicism, while in the Gatehouse two priests were swamped by ten laymen.[18]

Even so, and however fully we appreciate the role of the laity in maintaining the continuity of Catholicism in Elizabethan England, we remain confronted by the inevitable indispensability of the priests, without whom Catholicism simply cannot subsist. In this area, debate over the rival hypotheses of continuing survival versus innovative revival in Elizabethan Catholicism turns on the relative importance accorded to surviving 'Marian' priests ordained in England before 1559, as opposed to the new products of the Continental seminaries arriving from 1574 onwards. There is now a widespread inclination to appreciate the work of the surviving 'Marian' or 'Massing' priests – those ordained before Elizabeth's accession who witheld their ministry from the Church of England and who were far less exposed to legal punishment than the 'seminarists'. Regional patterns point up the Marians' achievements: in Lancashire, the county in which Catholic survival was most effective, up to two-thirds of priests serving in the Catholic Church in 1554 were no longer in place in 1563, and we may assume that a high proportion of these continued to serve the recusant laity as priests: at least, the authorities of the Church of England assumed that such patterns prevailed, not just in Lancashire but in areas such as the Welsh Marches, where in 1564 the Bishop of Worcester blamed strong Catholic survivals on

> Popish and perverse priests which misliking [the Protestant] religion have forsaken the ministry and yet [still] live in corners, are kept in gentlemen's houses and have great estimation with the people where they marvellously [astonishingly] pervert the simple and blaspheme the truth.[19]

Though hardly as spectacular in the calendar of martyrs as were the seminarians and Jesuits who came in their wake, but alongside whom they continued to work for some decades down to 1616, the 'Massing' priests were in no way inferior in motivation to their seminarian brethren: Patrick McGrath counted at least 130 Marian priests in prison under Elizabeth and 30 dying in gaols around the country. In the 1580s and 1590s, wrote Professor McGrath, 'the Marian priests shared in some measure in the fierce persecution directed against the seminary priests and Jesuits'. Given the relatively small number of seminary priests once these started arriving, it was inevitable that 'Marian priests would...form a larger proportion of the priests at work in Elizabethan England than is commonly believed and their contribution to the total achievement of Elizabethan Catholicism becomes correspondingly greater.' J.J. Scarisbrick adds that 'later Catholicism had ample ground for gratitude for often heroic Marian priests...Marian clergy had laid the foundations of the Catholic mission.'[20]

Part of the secret of the effectiveness of the 'Marians' lay in their relative legal immunity. The Act of Parliament of 1585 making it high treason for a priest ordained abroad even to be in England exempted priests ordained within the realm – the 'Marians' – who thus operated with a comparative freedom of action denied the seminarians. They enjoyed operational advantages: they were safer for lay people to harbour; they knew their way around their terrain; and they could consecrate marriages which might be recognised by the Church of England. It is true that as a result of the dominant martyrological concerns of post-Reformation English Catholic historiography, the seminarians have always enjoyed the cachet of heroism. The assets of the 'Massing' priests in Elizabethan England lay rather in the appeal, especially the popular appeal, they exercised as touchstones with a familar past, and as former parish priests who had refused to conform to a novel religious dispensation and who covertly provided a liturgy well loved by many. Their conserving role did not necessarily facilitate re-proselytisation back to the Catholic faith, and McGrath commented that 'few of them acted as missionaries' – even though, in Lancashire at least, 'Marian' priests did reconcile some to Rome. Their essential and indispensable role was that, in their own persons representing an unextinguished indigenous Catholic continuity, the 'Marians' were the re-builders of a religious community managing to survive an unprecedented disaster: out of their survival came revival.[21]

Partly for that reason it will not do to differentiate too sharply in terms of their aims and achievements between old 'Marians' and new-style 'seminarians'. After all, Laurence Vaux, who helped draw a clear line under the past and to launch a more embattled recusancy into the future by publishing Pope Pius V's condemnation of attendance by the Catholic faithful at Church of England services, was a 'Marian' priest, as was the father of the English seminarian tradition, William Allen. Indeed, Professor Scarisbrick sees an elision between the kind of priests ordained in England before 1559 and on the Continent after 1573:

> The first missionaries to England were not the alumni of Douai in the 1570s but an extremely interesting mixture of men who had gone abroad much earlier and who came home in the 1560s after exile in Louvain – or... Rome ....[The 'Marians'] worked closly with the new clergy from the Continent.[22]

Our awareness of the connective work of the pre-seminarian priesthood in laying the firm foundations for a subsequent religious re-activation helps us to understand that in the vital area of clerical provision too heavy an emphasis on either of the absolutes of 'survival' or 'revival' can be misleading: the work of the 'Marians' confirmed that continuity was the pre-condition of resurrection. That was also the case with the overwhelmingly conservative bench of bishops that Elizabeth confronted in 1558–9. These were also 'Marians' who, virtually to a man, opposed the new dispensation and were deposed. Individuals amongst them such as Poole of Peterborough, Watson of Lincoln and Bonner of London were to link up pre-Tridentine English Catholicism with the new wave of Counter-Reformation influences.[23] In their defiance of Elizabeth, they maintained the prestige of the English episcopate, in marked contrast with the submissiveness of almost all their predecessors under Henry VIII; in their persons they gave a lead in intransigence for their priests to follow; and in their episcopal office they perpetuated a legacy of England as a province of the Church Catholic rather than a missionary outpost of Rome.

A further area of continuity in English Catholicism before and after 1559 is evident in monastic life. Before the Dissolution of the Monasteries between 1536 and 1540 the English regular orders had had their foci of strict observance, including the Carthusians of Sheen and the Bridgettines of Syon, both in Middlesex. The latter of these represent an extension, encouraged by Cardinal Pole under Mary in the 1550s, of what had already been a flourishing pre-Dissolution conventual renewal; this was developed into a clandestine survival well into the reign of Elizabeth, with a lingering outpost in Berkshire as late as 1581; this establishment subsequently led on to the perpetuation of

English regular life on the Continent, successively in Antwerp, Rouen and Lisbon, bridging the lengthy period from the late middle ages until this order's return to their native land in the wake of the French Revolution.[24]

Late medieval Syon represented a realised vision of austerity rare at that time in English regular life – though it was to find an echo in Tridentine disciplinarianism. The impact of the Counter-Reformation programme for the religious life came to be felt in the English convents abroad, for example in the house of the English Augustinian Canonesses at Louvain where initially upon its exile there prevailed an aura of civilised worldliness, of 'banquets..., comedies and plays...'. All that courtly idyll was to come to an end following the appointment in 1569, as a result of papal intervention under the Dominican reformist pope Pius V(1566–72), of Margaret Clemens as reverend mother: through 'zeal of religious reformation and strict observance of regular discipline ...the good Mother reformed all this at convenient time'.[25] Thus the 'Tridentine spirit' was let loose on expatriate English conventual life, suffusing survival with revival.

Around the time of Margaret Clemens' appointment the nascent English Catholic community came to its first crossroads. Out of an inchoate, if widespread, religious traditionalism prevailing in 1559, an identifiable minority sect hardened out about ten years later and was soon to be succoured by the new seminarian priests trained in Tridentine ideals. As we focus on that key decade on the 1560s, and especially on its closing years, we shall see a shift from survival to revival.

In the course of the 1560s the traditionalist preferences of the majority of English people, as identified, for example, in a report by the émigré priest Nicholas Sanders to Cardinal Morone, were accommodated by a degree of official tolerance of surviving Catholic practices within the Church of England – as, to take just one example, with a taper kept before an image of St Nicholas in Lancaster's parish church. Such retentions within the established Church in various parts of the country as the saying of the matins of the Virgin Mary, the giving of communion, in the Catholic way, in the mouth, the keeping of holy water stoups, tabernacles, engraved copes and the icon of the Five Wounds made overt recusancy largely unnecessary for many religious conservatives. In County Durham, for example, where the bishop's order of 1562 that a communion table replace the altar in the church of the village of Sedgefield seems to have been ignored until as late as 1567, pragmatic tolerance of traditional modes removed much of the imperative for overt recusancy.[26] However, in the later 1560s a local campaign of Protestantisation was stepped up and provoked a traditionalist backlash which hardened, amongst a minority, into formal recusancy, the illegal refusal to attend the parish church. In Sedgefield, when the communion table was eventually set up the action provoked militant resistance when two men entered the parish church and 'after dyverse contemptuous wordes...did forceableye...take up and remove the said table'.[27]

With the Revolt of the Northern Earls in 1569, the scenes in Durham Cathedral in which the communion table was dismantled and the Mass celebrated were paralleled in Sedgefield, just a few miles south of the cathedral city, with unmistakable political connotations. Along with a holy water stoup, the massive stone altar was dragged back into place by a crowd variously estimated at between 30 and 80 people, reclaiming the parish church for the old faith. Mass was said by the Marian priest Richard Hartburn, who preached that 'the doctrine of England was nowght, and that this Realm was cutt off from all other Nacions'; he denounced 'the Quene's religion established in this realme' and reconciled people to Rome. The English Bible and the homilies issued by the government to parsons who could not preach were burned to cries of 'se where the Homilies fleith to the devil' and 'se where the bybles bornes'.[28]

The Revolt of the Northern Earls and *Regnans in Excelsis* lent weight to the calls of Bishop Aylmer of London and Archbishop Grindal of York for an anti-papist crack-down. It was true that Parliament had already passed anti-Catholic legislation in 1559 and 1563, but Catholic justices of the peace were still in place in considerable numbers well into the 1560s. Traditionalist hopes for a reversal of the Elizabethan Reformation continued to prevail, while many continued to pursue an option of ambiguity, 'church papistry' – a tactic of professing Protestantism publicly and Catholicism privately in hopes of the latter's restoration.[29] Pressure on traditionalists, however, both from the crown and the papacy to come off the fence in one direction or another forced these ambidexters to make political choices of allegiance. The question of how determined Catholics would respond to a papally sanctioned invasion was put to a group of 103 recusants between 1581–2. The fact that nearly 50 per cent of those examined admitted that they *would* support an invasion or would not defend the queen if one took place suggests, wrote Professor McGrath, 'the need to be cautious about asserting that Catholics in England were for the most part loyal...except in matters of faith'.[30] Three factors made subversives of English Catholics, reinforcing their enemies' demands for further repression: the first was the extant wish to re-convert England, of which the dethronement of Elizabeth was a pre-condition; the second was the pressure of persecution (arising from a perception of Catholics as traitors), making some Catholics desire or seek release through a change of regime; and the third was the papal bull of 1570 which deeply committed recusants were bound to take seriously. The second two of those motives were expressed in a manifesto composed by exiled Catholics at the court of Philip II of Spain in 1597 expressing 'the universal outcry of the oppressed catholics in those countries' and calling on the Spanish king to enforce the 'ecclesiastical censures' – the 1570 bull – against the usurper Elizabeth.[31]

Cardinal William Allen, the clerical leader of English Catholicism during much of Elizabeth's reign, was haunted by a vision of the re-conversion of England and 'remained loyal to Philip [II]... Both he and Philip continued to hope and pray for a successful expedition against Queen Elizabeth', dreaming of the realm Allen had known in the 1550s, of which Philip was king. Allen's political programme in fact linked the strategy of the Spanish alliance with a high statement of the pope's position over secular rulers and his right,

> being the first and chief prelate of all Christendom of giving his consent that anything be done or attempted by arms and violence against any lawful or anointed prince whatsoever; be it for religion or any other never so rightful or just cause in his conceit [judgement].

The Jesuit Robert Parsons moved radically away from Allen's essentially medieval vision of papal sovereignty and dynastic legitimism towards a doctrine of the popular deposition and election of rulers. Despite these differences of emphasis and strategy, the voices of Allen and Parsons were unmistakably subversive and although they were not the only political tones of Elizabethan Catholicism, they did sound the political alienation of recusants that was made explicit in the bull of 1570. That document and its clear identification of Catholicism with disaffection and treason induced many traditionalists to draw back from the more crystallised minority Catholicism that emerged hardened out as intransigent recusancy in the 1570s – that recusant faith to which the seminarians and Jesuits of the Elizabethan Catholic revival ministered. The number of seriously committed recusants increased as a result of stepped-up official vigilance.[32]

In the year of the papal bull the Bishop of Carlisle (entrusted, in view of the Bishop of Chester's negligence, with conducting a visitation of Lancashire) reported to the Secretary of State Cecil on the state of religion in the county. Though Lancashire had played no active part in the revolt of the previous year, the publication of the Queen's excommunication by Pope Pius had given the strongest encouragement to overt rejection of the established Church, to public Catholic worship and to the holding of Catholic services in gentry homes:

> More great assemblies are Dailie [held] then were fytt: on all hands the people fall from religion, revolte to poperie: refuse to come at churche, the wicked popisshe priests reconcile them to the churche of rome, and cause them to abiure this christs religion and that opêly and unchecked:… since…the excommunication. In some houses of great men…no sv'ce hath been said in the englisshe tounge.[33]

This Catholic upsurge that the Bishop of Carlisle observed in Lancashire at the end of the 1560s was not restricted to that county, with its 'constant fame', in the Bishop's words, as nursing mother of recusancy in England. In London, Europe's leading Protestant city, which had welcomed the Elizabethan Reformation so enthusiastically, smashing stained glass windows and images, parodying the Mass obscenely, Aylmer joined with Grindal to report 'that the papists do marvelously increase, both in number and in obstinate withdrawinge of them selves from the Church and service of God'.[34] There were a number of reasons for this expansion of recusant numbers and assertiveness around the beginning of the 1570s: the drive on the part of the likes of Grindal, through episcopal visitations, to make the services, personnel and building interiors of the Church of England unambiguously Protestant, accelerating a withdrawal of traditionalists; a greater willingness on the part of the authorities to identify recusants by prosecuting them; and the longer-term effect of the declaration from Rome in 1566 banning Catholics from attending church services (being present so as to avoid paying recusancy fines, set at 12d. per Sunday in 1559 and increasing to £20 per month in 1581). Thus around the turn of the 1560s and 70s there arose 'a very small but definite and well-instructed group of catholic recusants, quite distinct from the amorphous and fading mass of more or less conservative conformists and "mislikers of religion"'.[35]

The demography of this more defined recusancy can be examined on a county-by-county basis. Yorkshire had a maximum of 2800 recusants by 1580–2 and 3000 by 1603–4; they were concentrated in specific locations within the shire and became a tiny minority – 80 out of a city population of 12 000 – in York, where the late medieval urban confraternal piety that was a feature of Catholic survival in the city was the matrix from which a highly committed revivalist recusancy emerged. Recusancy was indeed to be found in pockets all around the country – in Sussex and in south-eastern shires already famous for their Protestantism, along the Marches of Wales, in London, sustained by the foreign embassy chapels to which access for Mass was confirmed by the government – but nowhere after 1570, except in some parts of Lancashire, was recusancy a majority preference: Lancashire's neighbour Cheshire was more typical of England as a whole in having a small – only 302 in number – group of recusants, though their religious vitality was intense.[36]

What impact did these low but solid recusant numbers, as they emerged out of a more diffuse religious conservatism from the end of the 1560s onwards, have on the aims, specifically the political aims, of Catholics, and especially those of their priests and clerical leaders? Amongst the strategic options facing the English Catholics we shall consider two, which we shall label the *politique* option and the Allen plan.

We borrow the concept of a *politique* option from the later sixteenth-century France of the Wars of Religion in which the moderate Catholic chancellor of the kingdom, Michel de L'Hospital, put forward patriotic unity as the cure for his country's potentially suicidal religious discords. When the anti-Catholic penal code was being extended in 1563 a crypto-Catholic English *politique*, Robert Atkinson, member of parliament for Appleby in Westmorland, spoke against the legislation in terms that might have been borrowed from L'Hospital, citing the example of Germany which, in the 1555 Treaty of Augsburg, had made a peace of religion, and calling for the unity of the realm to be exalted above sectarianism:

> Let us... leave all malice, and notwithstanding religion, let us love together... let us make an end of division, for fear lest our enemies... might peradventure, finding us at dissension among ourselves, the easier vanquish us.[37]

Atkinson's solution was not adopted in England because there was not an acute problem for it to address. Live-and-let-live arrangements over religion in early modern Europe – in Germany with the Peace of Augsburg, in France with the Edict of Nantes of 1598 – were generally conceded only as treaties of exhaustion following religious wars in which experience showed that dissidents simply could not be subjugated. Though the existence of Elizabethan England's religious minorities was undoubtedly problematic, the problems they presented *could* be contained. In particular, the English Catholics were neither strong enough nor numerous enough to *demand* rights.

They might, though, seek more ambitious goals than the ones set out by Atkinson – nothing less than the reversal of the Reformation, the reconversion of England. This was the 'Allen option', one necessitating political, diplomatic, dynastic, military and naval victories and, above all, Spanish aid. In 1583 Allen wrote to the rector of the English College, Rome, the Jesuit Agazzari, feeding him glowing reports of the prospects for a Catholic restoration based on his own recollections of the situation in his own country, Lancashire, and extrapolating from those to describe the position as he thought it was in England at large in the early 1580s:

> All that part of the country where we were born is Catholic... Nay,... throughout England up and down the hearts of almost everyone are ours, while the outward actions of many persons are the Queen's. And in this respect we seem to have made no small progress, since the minds of men are imbued with the right doctrine, though fear... prevents them from confessing it.[38]

Though his hopes were based on diminishingly realistic calculations of internal support, Allen remained to the end of his life a firm believer in a national Catholic restoration: he bequeathed his vestments to a parish church near his birthplace 'if the kingdom of England should have returned to the Catholic faith'. The goal was to be achieved (1) by means of the close understanding with Spain which was at the centre of Allen's political programme; and (2) through training and sending missionaries to *reconcile* people to Rome and to activate what Allen believed to be an inert Catholic majority of the population, thereby achieving the reversal of the Reformation: Allen rejoiced in 400 reconversions 'in one of the smaller shires'.[39]

High up in the lists of seminaries entrusted with the task of national reconciliation through reconversions was the English College, Rome, opened officially in 1580. Its initial mission, as set out by its visitor

Cardinal Sega, was Allen's one of the 're-establishment of the Catholic religion in England' by means of large-scale re-conversions, restoring what was deemed to be the latent Catholicism of the majority. With this brief, in 1580 the Jesuit fathers Campion and Parsons set out with a team, 'the first of the Society of Jesus whom at the persuasion of the Most Rev. W. Allen, His Holiness sent to England for the conversion of heretics and the assistance of Catholics'.[40] The Allen programme, incorporating the return of a entirely Catholic England with a Catholic ruler and a native episcopate, postulated a Spanish initiative to enforce the bull of 1570; as the Catholic publicist Nicholas Sanders put it, writing to the Spanish Duke of Alba, 'The state of Christendom depends on the stout assailing of England.' Papal thinking under the politically interventionist Gregory XIII (1572–85) was strongly directed at national re-conversion and at the necessary means of large-scale reconciliation – the capital crime in English law, under the Act of Persuasions of 1581, of seducing subjects away from their due allegiance to the Queen. In 1583 Pope Gregory offered a papal blessing and a plenary indulgence 'to all [whom the missioners to England] should receive into the Church' and in 1583 the pope authorised the dedication of the eucharistic devotion of the Forty Hours for England's 'conversion from heresy'. At first, statements of intent made by the English College seemed to underpin this ambitious and politically focused programme; for instance in 1580, accepting Allen's goal of multiple reconciliations of members of a people still assumed to be Catholics under the skin, the College sent alumni 'to England for the help of the souls there led astray'. The missioners were being entrusted with an essentially national campaign directed well beyond the identifiable recusant community at 'the spiritual benefit of the English nation'.[41]

Once those aims had been set out, it may not have been thought necessary subsequently continually to re-state them. Even so, it is noteworthy that later minutes recording the sending of missioners to England were open-ended in what they said it was hoped they were to achieve, and, in particular, that they stopped short of setting a target of universal nation-wide reconciliation: statements of intent included 'to labour in the vineyard of the Lord...sent on the English mission' (1581) 'for the English mission' (1587) 'sent in April to England' (1592).[42] It is possible that these later minutes express a dawning realisation of the need to establish goals lower than Allen's, less political, less comprehensive in their intended reach. His death in 1594 removed the single most prestigious spokesman for an activist Catholic policy aimed at turning the clock back to the *status quo ante* 1559 by means of mass conversions and Spanish aid.

In the meantime, the consolidation of recusancy as a clearly defined minority cast doubts on the viability of any policy designed to restore the Catholic faith to the position it had occupied in English public life before the Elizabethan settlement of religion. The new recusancy was numerically and qualititatively different from the earlier traditionalism. In the towns, because of their relatively close official supervision and the dependence of the recusant community on the protection of rural manor houses, links between the new recusancy and late medieval and early Tudor urban piety were being severely weakened, as was the case in York, though in 1600 there were – admittedly small – Catholic groupings in the county city as well as in Leeds, Richmond and Beverley. Even though London had a detectable recusant presence, one recruited from around the country though institutions such as the Inns of Court, a crucial feature of the crystallisation of recusancy in the Elizabethan period was its settling down in the seven northern counties and in self-protective clusters within those shires. In Yorkshire, for example, by 1604 the majority of the recusants lived within four groups of parishes on the northern border and around the centre of the shire, though even in those districts of heaviest concentration there was no Catholic preponderance. To find that kind of weight of numbers, we have to move across to look at those parts of Lancashire, especially in the south and west of the county, where by the opening of the seventeenth century the Catholics formed 'an open denomination, playing their part in the life of the parish'. However, that pattern was a Lancashire peculiarity within the sociology of an English Catholic community whose size Professor Bossy estimates at about 40 000 (including children and a fringe of sympathisers), within a population of 2.5 million Anglican communicants at the beginning of James I's reign, in 1603; this was below 2 per cent, even allowing for demographic recoveries – as with Yorkshire Catholics' numerical pick-up, from a maximum of 3000 in 1603–4 to a maximum of 4050 in 1640–2.[43] Patently, what this tiny community needed from the Continental seminaries was not a drive to win over the now firmly Protestant majority but its own provision of priestly and pastoral care and of 'labour in the vineyard of the Lord'.

Socially, the gentry and nobility had come to dominate the life of the community before the end of Elizabeth's reign, providing protection from the laws and shelter for priests. Yorkshire is typical, in manifesting an 'all but universal aristocratic domination of recusant society': indeed, the association of gentry with recusancy became more marked within this period in Yorkshire, where one-third of gentry were identifiable recusants at the beginning of James' reign, compared with one-fifth in 1580–2; in certain divisions of Yorkshire as many as ten out of thirteen or eight out of eleven gentry families were Catholic. The English Catholic gentry cannot be economically stereotyped, least of all in terms of financial decline; indeed, it was the 'business-like gentry families', not averse to holding crown and church lands, deriving income from the law, from money-lending, mining and enclosing, that produced the most entrants for the priesthood in the period 1631–40, while the highly entrepreneurial – and pious – Thomas Meynell of North Yorkshire laid out on buying lands and leases the same amount – £1000 – that he paid in recusancy fines, the whole large double expenditure made possible by his intensive agricultural developments and enclosures. Dom Hugh Aveling suggests that finding the wherewithal to pay the fines stimulated Catholic gentry enterprise, and it may also have been the case that the closure of political options for Catholic squires diverted their energies into enrichment.[44]

The linkage between Catholic preferences and gentry status remains striking: even taking into account a process of erosion over time, ten times more Stuart Yorkshire Catholic squires were likely to be recusant than were their plebeian neighbours. However, the long-term prospects were less hopeful, and the Yorkshire Catholic gentry fell back from its high point of 33 per cent of the county's total in 1604 to 20 per cent in 1642. Even though as late as 1780 Yorkshire still had 80 recusant gentry families, and clans such as the Meynells managed 'by great efforts' to survive economically, others, such as the Lascelles, went to the wall. Charges for recusancy, centring on the swingeing fines of £20 per month for non-attendance at church, were the slow assassins of estates. Social exclusion, a shrunken marriage mart and loss of a political role, were strong longer-term disincentives to the persistence of gentry Catholicism, and the wonder is that the period of post-Reformation English Catholic social history associated with it lasted so long.[45]

The other characteristic feature of early recusant sociology – a demotic and rural rank-and-file membership – was a corollary of gentry leadership, as Catholic country squires attracted, encouraged and made religious and priestly provisions for Catholic tenants and servants. Even in London the national picture of membership of the community from amongst the rural gentry along with agriculturally-employed commoners is borne out: eight lay people in the Clink prison in 1586 included a gentleman and his wife and a yeoman and two husbandmen, while of the ten lay people in the London Gatehouse prison in the same year whose rank was given one was a gentleman and two yeomen. The community's social profile of elite leadership and demotic membership may help to explain the sharp contrasts within Catholic ranks between wealth and poverty (though these were also a typical feature of Tudor social life generally): City of London, Middlesex and Hertfordshire recusants showed a dramatic spread, from a noblewoman worth £100 in land, a man possessed of £100 in goods and another valued at £500 in land, to 34 people each described in some variant of the phrase 'a poor man and naught worth' and six bankrupts. In addition, and as we might expect from this relatively early stage in the history of the community – a period in which recalcitrant Catholics had been demoted from former elevated positions – there was a high count of people who had seen better days: a former teller of the Exchequer, a doctor of laws 'littell or nothing worth', a physician, a former provost of King's College, Cambridge, and the royal composer Sebastian Westcott, along with the wife of William Byrd ('one of the gent of her maties chappell', himself several times prosecuted for recusancy). If the community's presence in the learned professions was being reduced, with closer government controls of the universities and the Inns of Court and its intelligentsia being increasingly concentrated in the priesthood, there was at the same time a significant non-gentry sector in the provinces. In Yorkshire, and especially on the north-east coast of the county, this element was especially cultivated by the seminary priests. In County Durham yeomen made up a solid element of the non-gentry majority within the county's recusant community. Looking around the country, at Oxfordshire, Sussex, Essex, Suffolk, Norfolk, Staffordshire and Lancashire, Dr Blackwood concludes that though by the mid-seventeenth century Catholicism 'was essentially seigneurial . . . at least in terms of *influence*', 'in terms of *numbers* Catholicism was essentially popular, for the gentry was in almost every county swamped by plebeians, especially in Lancashire'. This rural plebeian base was also strongly evident in Essex, Suffolk and Sussex, with their yeomen Catholics.[46]

The foremost social challenge of this community of aristocrats, peasants and priests between the 1580s and the civil war was one of adjustment to the permanence of a Protestant regime, a process that induced acute divisions within the Catholic clergy. What sort of body was the clergy and laity of the Catholic Church in England to form?: was it to be a church in essential institutional continuity with the Catholic Church that had existed in the country since Augustine? If so, it would need to be equipped with an episcopal structure and a monastic order in direct filiation from the medieval past; such an institution would form a canonical province of the Church, recognising the ultimate authority of the see of Rome while at the same time preserving its own ancient autonomous jurisdiction centred on Canterbury. If such a prospect was coming in some eyes to seem unrealistic, another vision of an English Catholic community was available, facing up to the reality and irreversibility of the Protestant settlement and adjusting to a missionary status as a minority, its time-honoured episcopal and canonical structures superseded, taking its orders direct from Rome and given its momentum by the Jesuits, missionary cadres for a missionary body.

These issues came to a head in protracted disputes amongst priests locked up in the Bishop of Ely's gaol at Wisbech in the 1580s, with rejection by 'secular' priests (who were not members of any religious order) of the leadership claim of a Jesuit, William West. Cardinal Allen's death confronted the English Catholic Church with the need to regularise its government and the dispute that had arisen at Wisbech was referred to Rome, where in 1598 Clement VIII responded with the appointment of George Blackwell as 'Archpriest'; the novelty of Blackwell's title and the fact that he was instructed to work closely with the Jesuits, offended the conservatives who, from their appealing their case to Rome, were designated 'Appellants'. Under their pressure, the Holy See re-cast Blackwell's commission in 1602: he was to report direct to Rome, not to the Jesuits and to confer with three Appellant advisers. There the government of the English Catholic Church rested unsteadily as the reign of Elizabeth drew to a close.[47] Clearly, the way in which the minority Catholic Church governed itself – in greater or lesser submission to Rome, with a greater or lesser institutional connectedness to the pre-Reformation past – had the clearest implications for that community's relations with the state under which it must live.

In fact, some years before the close of Elizabeth's reign the possibilities of an accommodation between the Protestant state and the English Catholics had become apparent, crucially in the 1580s, that tragic decade of executions of priests, with four in 1581, eleven in 1582 and four in 1583. Those executions were officially represented as the proper defensive measures of the English state against those who would overturn it, a series of strikes culminating in the putting to death of Mary Queen of Scots in 1587. That removal of Elizabeth's rival in fact took away much of the rationale for the conspiracies against the Queen that had spasmodically filled the period since 1569. As would-be heir to Mary's Catholic claim, Philip of Spain sent the Armada in 1588, but its failure further brought home the need for a reconciliation between the English Catholics and the crown. Thus, whereas the ageing Cardinal Allen, in his *Declaration of the sentence and deposition of Elizabeth the usurper* stuck to the earlier intransigent message of his *Defence of Catholics* and called on his co-religionists to join with the Spanish in a crusade of deposition, the secular priest Wright undoubtedly spoke for the majority of the Catholic laity and an increasing number of priests in repudiating assistance to Spain, portrayed as pursuing her own global aims under a mantle of Catholic ideology. At the time of the Armada, 'Anti-Spanish feeling was strong among Catholics, despite Allen's pleas that they should support Philip II'. From the rising generation, English students for the priesthood were now seen openly to 'rejoice over Spanish reverses, grieve over their success'. These voices of youth, implying a much more purely spiritual and politically disengaged vision of what the English mission meant, largely in terms of ministry to a defined recusant community, were joined by that of the Jesuit Robert Southwell and his insistence on loyalty to England and her queen.[48]

In 1603 a group of Appellants put their hands to a Protestation (not an oath) of Allegiance to Elizabeth, a statement which maintained the pope's spiritual, and denied his deposing, power. The queen's death created further opportunities for a settlement, posited on an abandonment of Allen's type of activist strategies which were themselves designed to accomplish a Catholic restoration, of a kind, writes Fr Gavin, in which fewer and fewer Catholics continued to believe, for 'The most they hoped for was some measure of toleration, and to this end their hopes had been raised by James himself both before his leaving Scotland and after his entering England'. James personally confirmed a stop on executions of priests and their supporters; the renewal of the recusants' hopes were evident in a religious resurgence in the north, for James was the son of Mary Queen of Scots, and the Catholics 'weare the only men amongst the English likely to love him in hart . . . they had loved the mother . . . and therefore would with all gladnes have embraced the sonne'. In point of fact, the Catholic revival born of high hopes at the commencement of the reign alarmed Protestant clerics and counsellors, forcing James to crack down on the recusants, as 'the men he would expose to all manner of persecution', banishing priests and re-imposing the recusancy fines.[49]

The disappointment of English Catholics at the thwarting of their over-high hopes issued in the Gunpowder Conspiracy of 1605, which can be regarded as a throw-back to the Catholic anti-state plotting of the period between the Revolt of the Northern Earls and the Armada. James, writes Mark Nicholls, was 'strongly opposed to the idea that the discovery of such a treason should be made an excuse for a general prosecution of English Catholics', and, instead of a hue and cry, attention was focused on a formula of allegiance to reconcile their spiritual allegiance to the Holy See with their fealty to England's crown, the king leaning on Rome to encourage the recusants to come to an agreement with the state.[50] The Oath of Allegiance that emerged in 1606, requiring an abjuration of the papacy's right to depose rulers, was in the event unacceptable in Rome and for that reason deeply divisive within the English Catholic community, though the Archpriest Blackwell took it. The Oath in fact opened up the possibility of taking it within mental reservations, of a kind set out by Robert Parsons in his 1607 *A treatise tending to mitigation*, even though the authorities tried to insist that it be taken 'according to the plain and common sense and understanding of the ... words'.[51]

The Oath controversy also gave rise to a battle of the books involving James whose *Apology* for the Oath, published in 1609, was written in answer to the Jesuit controversialist Cardinal Roberto Bellarmino. James's love of controversy in fact helped to keep open channels of communication, albeit those of polemic, between the crown and the Catholics. When, later in the reign James took on a Jesuit in a theological debate, the king showed courtesy and, as the Jesuit, John Percy, recalled, in just the same way that fencers were 'wont to salute and embrase one another, soe before hee [the king] entered into argument hee would salute me with a speech'. Possibilities for a more positive negotiation between the crown and the Catholics under James were further improved by standpoints such as those of the priests Ralph Buckland, with his patriotic millenarian interpretation of England's destiny – 'to hurt thee [England] is to hurt him [God]' – and William Alabaster (1567/8–1640), whose quietist views emphasised 'the primary requirement of cultivating the theological virtues'. The rise in earlier seventeenth-century England of an Anglican form of meditative piety encouraged a move away from divisive theology and political ideology in favour a a common ground alongside 'Catholic-like Protestants'.[52]

To be over-sanguine about the prospects of the English Catholics under James would amount to a serious error. The House of Commons was the voice of militant Protestantism and its stance was generally to demand stricter enforcement of the penal laws, in this supported by clerics of the Church of England, notably the Archbishop of Canterbury George Abbot (1611–33). Persecution was fierce in the period 1610–22, when the king supported, and indeed demanded, rigorous implementation of the laws. For all that, certain stabilities in the position of the English Catholic community were becoming further consolidated under James when, although numbers tended to fluctuate upwards, the inescapable conclusion was that the community was fated to be a minority, characteristically made up of deeply committed individuals and families. In terms of international relations, the deaths of Philip II (d. 1598) and Elizabeth, followed by peace with Spain in 1604, meant that the Spanish crown need no longer be regarded as the instigator of plots involving English Catholics, but as a diplomatic lever operating pressure on the English monarchy to relax the penal laws. That role rose to prominence during negotiations for a marriage between James's son Henry and a Spanish princess and, when the focus of marriage bargaining switched from Spain to France, and when James's second son Charles succeeded him in 1625, soon to be married to an ostentatiously devout French Catholic princess, accompanied by the announcement of a suspension of the penal laws, the prospects for the English Catholic community seemed brighter than they had for several generations.

Early seventeenth-century experiments with the clerical structure of the Catholic community had the effect of facilitating its adjustment to the religious and political status quo in England. In 1623 the archpriest system gave way to an arrangement in which a vicar apostolic exercised quasi-episcopal powers and a chapter of secular priests had powers to elect future bishops. This could easily have been regarded as a bid to restore the pre-Reformation episcopal Catholic system and thus as implying a challenge to the evolved relations between lay Catholics, headed by the gentry, and the Church of England. The vigorous way in which the second vicar apostolic, Bishop Smith, whom John Bossy calls a 'doctrinaire hierocrat', exercised his authority provoked a reaction on the part of the recusant gentry who successfully pressured the crown to have him removed. Smith's departure for France in 1631 both revealed the reality of gentry predominance in the Catholic community and removed the threat of an episcopal renaissance which would challenge the Church of England, of which the monarch was supreme governor, with a parallel, or even a rival, episcopate. Instead, the reality of England as a missionary province with a small, if slightly expanding, Catholic population, received expression in the ascendancy of the Jesuits. Their numbers rose noticeably, from 18 in 1598 to 40 in 1606; by 1623 there were 123 Jesuits working in England and in 1639 193: numbers of seculars applied to join the Society of Jesus, and it was only appropriate in view of this growth that a separate English province of the Society was formed in 1623.[53]

It was not only the Jesuits who prospered in Charles I's reign. The seculars too acquired a more regularised organisation in the 1630s – in Essex, for example, whose small Catholic cells were served by seven priests, with lay funding producing a small income to provide for a 'rural dean' and with a special ministry devoted to poor Catholics in the county. In Lancashire, priests such as Ambrose Barlow acted virtually as parsons to the recusants in the 1620s and 1630s; a near-parochial system, which Dr Dottie terms 'an *ad hoc* or idiosyncratic organisation', existed in the county, funded by lay patronage and with responsibility shared between Benedictines, Jesuits and seculars. During Charles I's reign the English Catholic community might appear to have enjoyed a silver age. Fr McCoog writes, 'Between 1625 and 1640 only three Catholics were executed and ... few others suffered for their religion.' At court the Flemish Catholic artistic styles of Rubens and van Dyck were patronised by the aesthete Charles I and fashionable Catholicism attracted three ministers, the earl of Portland, Lord Cottington and Sir Francis Windebank. 'Indeed, many agreed that Catholics had not fared so well since the reign of Mary Tudor.'[54]

The rosiness of this picture must not be exaggerated. The crown itself had a direct pecuniary interest in the enforcement of the penal laws through the considerable proportion of its income accruing from the recusancy fines – even to the extent that large-scale conversions of Catholics to the Church of England were feared for the loss of crown income that would result: in other words, the crown acquired a stake in the survival of the English Catholic community as a religious minority in effect taxed to pay for its religious beliefs. A fiscalised penal system was regularised into the Compositions, or settlements with the crown in lieu of recusancy fines. Though not as heavy as the fines themselves, the Compositions were onerous and following Charles's break with Parliament in 1629 and his consequent search for other sources of income they rose from just over £6000 to £32 000. The Composition system provided English Catholics with a framework for survival in the years leading up to the civil war.[55]

Wales

The remoteness of Wales from the centres of power during the Tudor Reformations of the sixteenth century might well have fostered a resilient religious traditionalism there. There was in fact a strong attachment in the Principality both to Catholic ways and to the Tudors, assiduously propagandised as a Welsh family who had made good. The Edwardine Reformation, with its target in 1549 and 1552 of a Protestant liturgy in English, was not a success in Wales. Though the Welsh did not follow the Cornish in 1549 and rise up in revolt in defence of the Latin (or non-anglophone) Mass, one of the poets – those conservators and spokesmen of Welsh popular culture – may have spoken for many when he maintained that the Mass could not be rendered in English. At Mary's accession in 1553, the combination of support for the Tudors and for Catholicism in Wales was expressed in a dizzy acclamation of the queen as one placed by the Blessed Virgin on the throne so as to restore 'the privileges of the saints' and 'the old masses'. During Mary's reign Cardinal Pole took measures that might, given time, have made it possible to activate a vague traditionalism into a vital reformed Catholicism, harmonised with the Welsh language. Even before the Council of Trent had finished its business in 1563, Wales was exposed to a Tridentine programme, in ways that England was not. Pole installed Catholic reformists in key positions in Wales – a former Lady Margaret professor of divinity to a cathedral post in Bangor and, as 'the spearhead of his reform movement in Wales', his 'own dear friend and confidant', Thomas Goldwell as Bishop of St Asaph in 1556. Subsequently two younger men, 'unusually well-attuned to the needs of Welsh-speaking Wales', Morris Clynnog and Gruffydd Roberts, were made, respectively, Bishop-elect of Bangor and Archdeacon of Anglesey. As bishops Clynnog and Goldwell pursued a Tridentine reform programme, Goldwell concentrating on raising the priestly and educational standards of his diocesan clergy, as well as campaigning for the restitution of ecclesiastical lands.[56]

The poets celebrated these Tridentine reformers, thereby pointing to a strong potential link between Catholic renewal and Welsh speech and culture. Clynnog and Roberts were 'two of the most gifted Welsh prose authors of the sixteenth century' and a promising 'Counter-Reformation literature in Welsh' developed out of their inspiration. Yet what Roberts and Clynnog (who went on to become the clerical leader of Welsh Elizabethan expatriate recusancy and friend of the great

Tridentine reformer St Carlo Borromeo) made was only a beginning and, as it turned out, an abortive one, for the ten or fifteen years that were needed to introduce a full Counter-Reformation programme into Wales – including the provision of seminaries producing high-calibre priests, the establishment of the Jesuits, the building of new churches – were not forthcoming. With Elizabeth's accession Welsh loyalty to the Tudors, which had been easily twinned with Catholic faith under Mary, induced the Principality to succumb in large part to the Reformation, albeit with a small Catholic opposition led by men who had been raised up by Pole's protégés.[57]

Despite acceptance of the Reformation by Welsh people as an out-come of their 'unreserved and undiscriminating support for the house of Tudor', there emerged a resistant recusant core, especially identifi-able in North Wales – in Flintshire, Denbighshire and Caernarvonshire. Its continuing capacity for fusion with national culture and language, as well as an intense anglophobia, is on display in an anonymous, probably gentry-authored, poem written in the traditional bardic strict metre (*awdl*) and bringing eucharistic piety centred on the Real Presence in the Mass together with a clarion call to a crusade of national liberation:

> Rout them with sword, you true Welsh Britons,
> The hatred of Jesus by traitorous Saxons, unholy heathens,
> ... To arms! Now to the battle for the holy mysteries,
> The bread of grace which holds the holy form of God,
> His flesh and blood and wounds in mystic union,
> Which by the sacred power and utterance of priests
> Is brought from heaven to earth and sacrificed anew.[58]

Neither violently expressed Catholic patriotism, though, nor the existence of protective gentry refuges in Glamorgan, Carmarthenshire and North Wales (including the Denbighshire home of Richard Lloyd, where the old baptismal rites met new strands of Catholic literature in English and in Welsh) were enough to sustain a viable Elizabethan Welsh Counter-Reformation along the lines of the one that was estab-lished in Ireland; as Professor Glanmor Williams writes, 'the Counter-Reformation was a resounding failure as far as Wales was concerned', with only 808 open recusants (compared with over 212 000 church-goers) by 1603. True, there were assumptions that Wales remained Catholic – 'the province ... is a stronghold of the Catholics ... so Catholic that they long for nothing more than to see the Sacraments of Christ restored again in their country' – and in 1603 such beliefs were expressed in an estimate that one-third of the Welsh remained Roman-ists. However, those calculations failed to distinguish between imperfect Protestantisation and a positive, large-scale Catholic recusant commit-ment to a Counter-Reformation ethos, for not only did the 'Welsh Counter-Reformation', such as it was, fail to prevent the official estab-lishment of the Church of England in Wales, but it also failed to con-solidate a diffuse traditionalism into a popularly supported Tridentine programme underpinned by Welsh culture and language. On the con-trary, Welsh folk beliefs largely comprised a cult of luck, sympathetic magic and nature worship; they included an enduring reverence for holy wells, as at Holywell in Flintshire, were typified in a grove dedi-cated to St Beuno and acted as a barrier to Tridentine observance. Revered as a saintly thaumaturge until the eighteenth century, in a land in which cures were likely to mix 'ancient lore'with 'sheer black magic', the vengeful Beuno, to whom bullocks born with his mark were offered to bring good luck to their owners, would hardly pass muster in a Tridentine hagiography. As Glanmor Williams writes

> the medieval practices most obstinately clung to [in Wales] were not always the ones that commended themselves to thoughtful Catholics any more than to the Reformers. The relationship of these vestiges to Catholic dogma was ... very tenuous. They are far removed from the Council of Trent and the Counter Reformation.[59]

James's accession and the break with the beloved Tudors created a brief hiatus of uncertainty or even of Catholic opportunity in the Principality. The recusant Morgans of Llantarnam in Monmouthshire were accused of arming, and recusancy prosecutions were blocked by jurors in a group of parishes in Montgomeryshire; Wales being regarded as England's soft under-belly for a Spanish, or Spanish–Irish, Catholic invasion, there was talk of a Spanish landing at Milford Haven; 10 000 Catholics were rumoured to be on a standby for a rising along the Marches. For all that, an attempt in 1603 by the secular priest William Watson to test such alleged support in a bid to capture the king raised only a pathetic handful of Welsh recusant supporters. The gentry were far and away the dominant class in Stuart Wales and where they were Catholic they usually felt free to set up altars, shelter priests and foster Catholic worship. However, when it came to translating this local religious intransigence into political resistance, there was silence from

the Principality and 'no concrete evidence that Welsh Catholics were
privy to the Gunpowder Plot' – even though Wales was intended as a
refuge for the conspirators to fall back upon, and the coast of West Wales
exposed to Ireland was regarded as vulnerable.[60]

The areas of Stuart Welsh Catholicism's greatest strength lay in the
counties adjacent to England, in which recusant numbers went up from
99 in 1606 to 153 in 1624. In North Wales Flintshire and Denbighshire,
in South Wales Glamorgan and Monmouthshire – the latter the Catholics' 'most important Welsh stronghold' – were the major nuclei. Several
factors nourishéd Catholicism in south-east Wales. The area in fact
functioned as a reservoir for recusants over a wider region, that governed by the Council in the Marches. In that area

> certayne Jesuites and seminary priestes... doe keepe an intercourse
> and holde intelligence betwixt the recusants of Worcestershire, Here-
> fordshire, Monmouthshire and the recusants of these partes in South-
> wales, norishinge theyr discontentments and feedinge them with
> foragne and home-bredde hopes

–and also linking up to smaller recusant pockets in Pembrokeshire.
Monmouthshire was, on its smaller scale, the Lancashire of Wales.
Under James I it was reported that:

> ...the countie of Monmouth was wholy divided almost into factions
> by reason of the number of those who, being addicted and misled
> with Poperie, are so powerfull and they so daring to professe and
> show themselves, as that few causes arise in the shire that are not
> made a question betwixt the Protestant and the Recusant.[61]

Indeed, the link between territorial power and the sponsorship of
recusancy in south-east Wales was made clear in 1605 when some
Monmouthshire Protestant magistrates reported to the earl of Worcester that 'ther are more recusants in this sheere then in our harts and
conscience wee could wish': it was, however, the Catholic influence of
the Somerset earl of Worcester that was a foremost factor in encouraging the proliferation of recusancy in the county; the same point
applied to the gentleman Edward Morgan of Llantarnam, a major
inciter of Monmouthshire recusancy within his domains, where 'by
reason of his greate livinge, power and allegiance in the said county
[he was] accompted the chief pillar and only mainteyner of the papists

and recusants thereabouts'. Morgan, it was claimed, encouraged the doubling of the Monmouthshire Catholic population between the reign of Elizabeth and that of James, and was responsible for the way that Masses outnumbered Prayer Book services in Llantarnam and neighbouring parishes. Likewise in north-east Wales, the gentry power of the Mostyns of Talacre in Flintshire, with their collection of 'papisticall books' and marital links to those other regional recusant families, the Conways and the Pennants, fostered the survival of the old ways. However, the Mostyns' bookish piety failed to bring any marked Tridentine influence to the old medieval shrine at Holywell which lay within their sphere and where persisting rites remained pre-Tridentine in style: each August at the shrine popular festivity prevailed over the spirit of Counter-Reformation restraint, as with 'a companie of people dauncing and singinge of rimes about the altar in the said chappell . . . having pots and cups upon the said altar drinkinge and making merrie'.[61]

As the case of Edward Morgan, Llantarnam, shows, and as the instance of the Catholic, or crypto-Catholic, Sir John Conway, sheriff of Flint, confirms, the indispensable key to the survival or growth of Welsh Catholic communities was the entrenched power, patronage and 'allyance' (connections of kinship and patronage) yielded by co-religionist or broadly sympathetic gentry. Sometimes that recusant patronal power might even take on a piratical flavour of Welsh popular resistance to government: George Langley of Caerleon in Monmouthshire, an open recusant and a wealthy Bristol Channel smuggler, used some of his gains to help his fellow-Catholics at home and abroad. Perhaps Langley was making his own contribution, just as much as were the unruly revellers at Holywell, to upholding 'yr hen ffydd Cymru', 'the old faith of Wales', against 'y ffydd newydd y Saeson', the new, Protestant faith of the English.[62]

In south-west and north-west Wales there was not the same gentry support for Catholicism as obtained in the south-east and north-east – though in Gwynedd Sir William Maurice of Clennenau, a magistrate and a 'squire of some substance', was a suspected Catholic. In the southwest appreciable numbers of recusants began to appear in the 1620s and 1630s – 30 in 1622, and 19 at Carmarthen Sessions in 1637. However, on the whole these were more likely to be gentlemen's wives than gentlemen, and yeomen, husbandmen and widows preponderated. In 1627 it was reported 'for Pembrokeshire it hath not many recusants' – though Howell Lloyd speculates that the numbers returned represented a 'flotsam on a dark tide of papist feeling . . . the Catholic resistance in south-west Wales was obscure if considerable, and in the long term ineffective if tenacious'. South-west Wales's Catholics, a 'haphazard collection of unfortunates...backsliders...[the] simply ignorant', would have needed a steady supply of priests to maintain anything stronger than a residual and vaguely recalled 'popery', and that supply was declining steadily in the Principality, from sixteen under Elizabeth to four in 1603–4: 'Without the continuing commitment of young priests', writes Glanmor Williams, recusancy had to wither. Despite all the tenacious qualities of Welsh recusancy – its 'self-confidence, resourcefulness and timely pugnacity' – Catholicism in Stuart Wales could hardly sustain the hopes that might have been entertained for Pole's Tridentine experiment in the Principality.[63]

2

CATHOLICS IN SCOTLAND AND IRELAND, c.1558–c.1640

Scotland

We shall begin this chapter with a survey of the state of Catholicism in Scotland on the eve of the Reformation. We shall see that traditional religion possessed considerable potential for renewal, but that the Reformation, assisted by England, by the support of the nobility and by popular adhesion, dominated the scene in the years after 1559. We shall examine the factors that might have sustained a Scottish Catholic recovery but will also discount their lasting value for underpinning a strong endurance of the old faith.

There is no doubt that pre-Reformation Scotland had access to a rich Catholic religious life, of a kind that might have pointed towards strong conservative survivals following the adoption of the Reformation in 1559–60. In particular, the kingdom's towns had taken part in a vigorous liturgical life centred on the Mass. Services – with up to 30 priests in attendance in the main churches of Edinburgh, Aberdeen and Perth – were held for up to 12 hours daily in some collegiate burgh churches, reaching a high point with the celebration of sung Mass. The tenor of public devotional life was typically that of pre-Tridentine Catholicism at large. The general exclusion of most members of congregations from the Eucharist was compensated for by the passing around of the 'kirklaife', a blessed bread, amongst non-communicants; as elsewhere, the circulation of the peace symbol, the *pax*, before the priest's communion was designed to bring reconciliation into parochial communities.

Devotion to the saints was well integrated into urban and guild life: in
Perth, for example, the Glovers' Incorporation had its altar in the town's
church dedicated to St Bartholomew in 1534: as late as 1580 this 'idole'
was not destroyed but modified, as a guild emblem. There are also signs
of efforts to fuse traditional piety with Scots identity: in 1507 James IV
encouraged the creation of a distinctively Scottish hagiography, 'eftir
our awin Scottis sancts'; distancing Scots from English Catholicism,
James banned the import of copies of the English Sarum rite of the
Mass into the realm. It is true that the profusion of priests needed to
perform the elaborate liturgical routines described above – one person
in forty in orders in Aberdeen – their expensive financial maintenance
in a poor land and the opportunities for concubinage created by
priests's individualised housing fed anti-clericalism, thereby impeding
a popularly supported sixteenth-century Catholic recovery. The economic structures of the Scottish Church exacerbated the problem.
Eighty-six per cent of parish livings were appropriated, resulting, even
though the fees parishioners paid were high, in the recruitment of
poorly paid, badly motivated, ill-educated vicars, 'the impoverished
dregs of the clerical profession'.[1]

Efforts, however, were made to improve the clerical and educational
provisions of the Catholic Church in Scotland. Indeed, writes Dr Wormald, 'Scotland presents the extraordinary spectacle of what was almost
a "Counter-reformation" taking place before the Reformation itself',[2]
in a series of reforming councils held by Archbishop Hamilton of St
Andrews between 1549 and 1559. The influences behind this conciliar
reforming drive were Continental, including that of a provincial council
held in Cologne in 1543, heralding post-Reformation Scots Catholicism's strong German links, but above all they were those of Trent, for
the pre-Reformation Scots Church under Archbishop Hamilton had a
Tridentine programme: 'It was no small feat for Scotland to possess the
Tridentine decisions months after they were made,' Dr Winning wrote,
'and to put them into force years before any other country in Europe.'
The decrees of the first session of the Council of Trent were available to
the Scottish Church through the efforts of the conciliar theologian and
friend of Ignatius Loyola and of Cardinal Contarini, Robert Wauchope.
In 1549 the Scots provincial council denounced concubinage and the
involvement of priests in trade, but devoted its main attention to teaching – of the priesthood and, through them, of the laity. Cathedral
chapters were to have theologians attached to them, and vicars were
to preach on Sundays and feastdays. In the diocese of Aberdeen, an area

of noticeable Catholic survival after the Reformation, Bishop William Gordon, who was determined to 'give evidence of his will and ability to put in hand the reforms proposed by the Fathers of Trent', entrusted Canon John Watson with an extensive preaching brief within the city and the diocese, laying special emphasis on instructing congregations on the Mass and the Eucharist. Although the Mass was the main point of contact between priests and people, most people in this land of, as yet, high illiteracy were unable to follow a written text of the service. They were strongly attached to prayers, above all the Rosary, that were at best marginal to the action of the Mass, and may generally have had little grasp of its meaning, so that the main thrust of Watson's homiletics should be seen as part of a wider official didactic campaign on the significance of the Mass. Other aspects of that teaching programme included the order of the Scots provincial Council in 1552 that each rector or curate read out from Archbishop Hamilton's *Catechism* for half an hour before high Mass. Another Council, in 1559, on the very eve of the introduction of the Protestant Reformation, laid down that prayers for congregations to say at Mass be made available in Scots, while the elementary 'Two-penny faith' [creed] provided further instruction on the Mass. The Edinburgh Dominicans, despite their Scholastic outlook, provided an updated preaching that was, wrote Fr Ross, 'fundamentally Christocentric and little concerned with pardons, pilgrimages and prayers to saints....They turned to the Bible and early Christian teaching for their inspiration.'[3]

It would be easy to point to the deficiencies of all these educational efforts, whose reality was all too often that of ignoramuses attempting to teach illiterates. The Scottish Church was not alone in pre-Reformation Europe in concentrating resources to the intensive higher education of a tiny clerical elite, leaving the parish ministry largely untrained. Scottish bishops tended to have Tridentine goals without a Tridentine zeal, there was no Scottish Giberti or Borromeo and it was eloquent of the Scots Church's domination by aristrocratic patronage that, when the Diocese of Dunkeld fell vacant, the committed Tridentinist Wauchope was passed over in favour of the earl of Arran's brother. The Catholic influence of Mary Queen of Scots in the capital between 1561 and 1567 helped to nourish the Catholic presence that we can detect in Edinburgh into the early seventeenth century, and in the country as a whole, Dr Wormald writes, 'In 1560 the majority of the population was almost certainly Catholic.' However, as in Wales, not enough was done in Scotland under a Tridentine banner to activate this inert and passive

traditionalism into a firm popular Catholicism strong enough to overcome inbuilt anti-clericalism and to withstand the effects of the Knoxian
religious and political revolution of 1559–60; this represented a set of
vast changes whose results in making southern Scotland a model Calvinist society were steadily consolidated in the following decades.[4]

Amongst the European Reformations of the sixteenth century, the
Scottish variant represented an unusually complete break with the
Catholic past, signified in extensive material destruction, not just of
monastic but also of parochial fabric, eliminating so much of Scotland's
rich material apparatus for sustaining the old faith. The material
damage to the monasteries' fabric was, overall, as extensive as it was in
England, the difference being that the initiative in iconoclasm in Scotland was assumed by the crowd not the crown, revealing the strong
momentum of popular social grievance that gave Scots Protestantism so
much of its broad demotic base. (Monastic communities, though, were
another matter, and might, as we shall see, continue in existence.) More
damaging for any viable continuing prospects for Catholicism in Scotland after 1560 was the widespread damage done to parish and urban
churches. In Glasgow, for example, not only were the buildings of the
Black and Grey Friars attacked but the collegiate church of Our Lady
and St Anne was vandalised and St Mungo's Cathedral was so badly
damaged that a scheduled service could not be held in its interior, and in
1574 there was a risk that this 'greit monument will alluterlie fall doun
and dekey'. In Aberdeen, besides the spoliation of the Black and White
Friars, the chancel of St Machar's Cathedral was demolished; so was that
of Brechin, while Dunblane and St Andrews cathedrals were unroofed.
Extensive destruction took place over so much of the country – 'thair
hes bene diver paroche kirkis within this realme demolischit, cassin
doun and destroyit for the maist part...all kirkmennis goodis and
geir wer spoulyeit and reft frae thame in everie place quhair the samyne
culd be apprehendit' – and was followed by the depredations of sheer
neglect – 'bare walls and pillars al cled with dust, sweepings
and cobwebs, in steed of painting and tapestrie'. The effect was to
create, as it was all, surely, intended to, a sharp sense of revolutionary
discontinuity with the Catholic past, a year-zero effect, 'like to the
Ruines of Troy, Tyrus and Thebes, lumpes of wals and heapes of
stones', when

> Papists into Calvin's power
> Gaif up their strangest place.[5]

The sweeping physical destruction was accompanied by an equally drastic legislative break with tradition. A deliberate sense of discarding the past was built into the very terminology of abolition of the Reformation Acts of the Scottish Parliament in 1560 – 'Anent the Abolition of Idolatry and all acts contrar to the Confession of Faith published in this Parliament' and 'anent the abolition of the Mass'. In accordance with a dawning vision of a covenanted and Reformed people, celebrating or being present at the ancient rite was to incur a graded series of punishments from confiscation of property, through banishment, to death; the forms of punishment of priests were designed to identify them as the orchestrators of ancient idolatry rather than, as in England, the agents of treason.[6]

Expert opinion concerning the effect on Scots Catholics of persecution from 1560 varies. Dr Sanderson writes that 'there was little serious persecution in post-Reformation Scotland', while Fr Ross said that 'Scottish Catholics would envy the conditions obtaining in England, where it was possible to absent oneself from protestant worship by regular payment of a heavy fine.'[7] Indeed, repression in Scotland *was* less harsh than in England, and for a period avoidance of it was possible, either by temporary conformity or by studied ambiguity. The first of these devices was used, for example, by the priest John Wilson who submitted in the early years of the Reformation but who by 1564 was charged with 'saying mes and hearying tharof, and ministracion of sacramentis unadmittet and in privat housis'. The second strategy, avoidance, was certainly practicable for as long as Mary was reigning queen and the full machinery of repression was not operative, at a time when the Kirk itself seemed loth to disrupt the solidarity of congregations by applying excommunications to dissidents. The Catholic lawyer David Dishington used evasive tactics so as to exploit the Kirk's reluctance to excommunicate the recalcitrant: he postponed Kirk communion through 'a succession of legal shifts, temporary submissions and excuses of unavoidable absence at the time of communion'; proceedings did not even begin against him until 1568.[8]

This age of relative leniency came to an end with the fall of Mary Queen of Scots and the resumed political and religious 'revolution of 1567'; this accelerated the effects of the Reformation decisions that had been taken in 1559–60, creating a new alignment between a Reformed Kirk and a now fully Protestant state, strengthening the Kirk's confidence in the 'new drive to establish discipline' and dispelling inhibitions about applying excommunication as a blanket sanction which imposed

total social ostracism on recusants: 'evasion of the effects of excommunication became impossible as the framework of ecclesiastical authority
grew stronger,' so that eventually there was 'literally no rest or shelter
for the excommunicate'. Excommunication, then, in Scotland meant
exclusion from community as well as from communion. That being
the case, its effect was to isolate dissidents as *individuals*, so that in the
northern kingdom one loses that sense that one has, especially in Lancashire, of substantial local recusant social *groups*. Of course there were
Scottish recusant groupings but, because of the way the Kirk Sessions
operated, treating errant behaviour as an individual offence against
communal solidarity, Scotland increasingly showed up its Catholics dissidents in ones, twos and threes, proceeded against by the Kirk Sessions:
one of these individual dissidents might be a single priest seducing
people away from the parish church; or another, reconciled to Catholicism, who administered Catholic marriages and christenings and said
Mass in private houses for a penny per person; typical of the fragmenta-
tion of communal Catholicism into singularity and isolation were: the
'auld ladies' of Ardre and Culluthy with their servant; or Sir George
Read's servant; or a former chantry priest; or 'ane Papist unrecantit and
obstinet'.[9]

Increasingly, as persecution was stepped up, it was individual priests,
as purveyors of 'idolatry' that were spotlighted. But because the animus
against these priests was not, as least until later in the century, as it was in
England, that they were the organised, conspiratorial agents of a super-
power aiming to destroy the nation, the punishment of treason that
created in England an image of falsely accused religious martyrs was set
aside in Scotland in favour of degrading spectacles – 'dirisioun', discrediting priests as individual representatives of a superseded religious
regime. Anti-sacerdotal charivaris were designed to explode the super-
natural powers claimed for priests and to expose them, clad in their
vestments, bearing the vessels of the Mass, to public mockery and
degradation and, as was done in the religious riots of the French Wars
of Religion, to associate them with filth and pollution by throwing
rubbish and excrement at them in carefully structured rituals of popular carnival. In 1565 the structure of these 'rites of violence' was indicated when an Edinburgh priest was tied to the market cross in his
vestments and pelted with eggs. In Stirling in 1569 the preference on
the part of the authorities for 'dirisioun' over martyrdom was made
explicit in an action taken by the Regent Moray, with full popular
support, when

four priestes of Dumblane were condemnit to the death for saying of
mes againes the act of parliament; bot he [Moray] remittit thair lyves,
and causit thame to be bund to the mercat croce, with thair vestimentis and challices in dirisioun, quhair the people caist eggis and uther
villany at thair faces be the space of an hor, and thairefter thair
vestimentis and challices were brunt to ashes.[10]

A further intensification of persecution aimed against Catholic clergy
followed in 1572, with a priest hanged for saying Mass, and another in
Glasgow in 1574. In the 1570s, as presbyteries were established they
took on the task of enforcing credal conformity through the Kirk Sessions which, from 1572, required Calvinist confessions of faith from
parishioners, thereby squeezing out ambidexters and restricting the
scope of the Scottish equivalent of 'church papistry'. In 1573 the pressure on priests was stepped up once more when subscription to the
Confession of Faith was made a condition for holding benefices. Many
were now forced to decide one way or the other and opted for conformity so that, in Aberdeen, for instance, the 'amount of determined
recusancy was limited', resulting in only a few deprivations. Meanwhile,
the older generation of clerical intransigents, such as Alexander Anderson, vicar of Kinkell, who had earlier disputed with Knox, were dying
away in the 1570s and 1580s. For the laity, the official demand for
intellectual assent to Calvinism required the abjuration of 'all poynts
of papistry', backed by an order that all not only attend public worship
but also receive communion: thus the Kirk Sessions fought crypto-
Catholicism into a corner. The Mass, defending and attending it –
even abroad – were especially reprehensible: in Stirling in 1583 William
Lockhart, who admitted 'that the wordis that he has spokin in mentein-
ance of the mes was mair of ignorance nor uthirwayes', was ordered to
confess publicly in church on a series of Sundays 'that he hes offendit
God in geving of his corporall presens to the mes in France'. Clearly,
though, and even before the end of the 1560s, Lockhart's choice of
France, either permanently or temporarily, was attracting increasing
numbers of Scots recusants, for by 1569 the pope was said to be distributing 8000 francs to Irish and Scottish Catholics in that country.[11]
    On what sources of strength, then, could embattled Scots Catholicism
draw during these decades in which the Scots Reformation was being
consolidated? Within Scotland, supportive forces included: the Catholic
nobility; surviving clergy and the religious orders; urban lay adherents;
and a polemical counter-offensive to Calvinism. We shall see, though,

that all or most of these apparent assets that Catholic survival in post-Reformation Scotland apparently enjoyed proved to be at best only temporarily effective. From our study of this first period in the history of Scottish Catholicism as a minority creed, it becomes apparent that the Highlands, their Catholic potential developed by the religious orders including the Dominicans, provided the most likely regional redoubt for its survival.

In the first place, we need to note that it was the aristocratic and royal structures of ecclesiastical power and patronage, which had impeded the full reform of the Scottish Catholic Church before 1559, that, ironically, made possible the survival of a minority Catholicism under the aegis of a Catholic monarch in the years immediately after 1560. Thus the key to the survival of Catholic practices in the Diocese of Aberdeen was, alongside the lack of particularly capable local Protestant leaders, the influence of the earl of Huntly, who guarded Catholic artefacts in St Machar's, Aberdeen, in the Reformation tempest of 1559. In that diocese most clergy in place at the time of the Reformation do not appear on the lists of Reformed pastors thereafter; the Catholic bishop and close Huntly relative William Gordon still seems to have been saying Mass in 1565, and as late as 1587–8 it was reported that Jesuits went about freely in Aberdeen. Alongside Huntly's protection of Catholic valuables during the first shock of the Reformation, the laird of Balnagown in Easter Ross took under his wing liturgical objects from Tain parish church. In 1564, in open defiance of the 1560 Act of the Scottish Parliament abolishing papal jurisdiction, the laird of Luss, along Loch Lomond, was appealing to Rome in a marital case; his influence also prevented iconoclasm within his domain, where to this day the parish church remains 'a veritable museum of pre-Reformation Christian sculpture'. In Dumfries, it was Lord Herries and the Maxwells who sheltered Catholicism, which remained noticeable among the burgesses until at least 1601. Noble patronage may have had the further effect of preserving an old-style festal (but essentially non-Tridentine) Catholicism which, when contrasted with Calvinist strictures over the celebration of Christmas, had a popular allure: in Dumbarton the laird of Tintry won 'the hearts of the commons with banquetting at Yule'; in contrast, though, Lord Seton's Catholic home at Christmas 1581 was a mirror of Tridentine form, maintaining an edifying prolonged observance by the whole household; that household functioned as a church in miniature for whom priests 'celebrated [Mass] daily and preached ... [,]the greater part of the household which is numerous being present'.[12]

Support by local nobles for traditional rites is also evident, for example, in the provision by Kennedy lairds of armed support for the open celebration of Mass in Ayrshire in 1563; as late as 1588 Kennedy monks continued to encourage Catholic practices. In the north-east the earl of Errol put pressure on presbyteries to block prosecutions for recusancy and turned a blind eye to an accusation of violence done to a minister of the Kirk, all actions doubtless giving an example of aggressive defiance to the Catholic-inclined lower orders. Control of advowsons and the pervasive obligations of kinship also came together to impede Calvinisation and uphold Catholicism – as when, again as late as 1588, Bishop John Leslie used his right of appointment to the parsonage of Kinkin in Ross in favour of his Catholic kinsman Alexander Leslie. Other obstructive tactics included refusing to make financial provision for a presbytery's nominee to a living within a nobleman's gift, keeping benefices vacant over long periods and alienating Kirk property. In Ayrshire, where the Kennedys refused to fill livings, recusancy throve, as the General Assembly of the Kirk recognised in 1588.[13]

Bishops and priests played their parts in stiffening Catholic recalcitrance, led by Archbishop James Beaton of Glasgow who, in his person and office, provided an essential touchstone of continuity with Scotland's Catholic past: 'As the last survivor of the ancient hierarchy,' writes Fr McRoberts, 'he provided a "government in exile" for Scottish Catholics. He made sure that their cause was not overlooked by the civil and ecclesiastical powers on the Continent.' Wealthy, endowed with French benefices, Beaton subsidised scholarship, founding a library of over 600 works for the use of Scots in Paris, and helped émigré leaders, including the controversialist Ninian Winzet. It was in the field of education that the archbishop made his most important contribution to affirming the continuity of Scottish Catholicism's medieval past. Indeed, Beaton specifically intended his educational foundation, the Scots College, Rome, to house the regalia and muniments that expressed the Catholic Church's erstwhile position as the sole legally established form of religion in the medieval realm and its ancient intimate relationship with the crown: he intended the College to shelter all the papal bulls, royal charters and seals and even the mace that belonged to the Archbishop of Glasgow in his capacity as chancellor of the university – the artefacts of the ancient identity of Church and kingdom. 'The purpose of all this,' writes W.J. Anderson, 'was to ensure that the archbishopric could not function legally under any intruded prelate. Beaton had expected that the Calvinist regime would be transient and that he would, one day, bring back to the restored Catholic archbishopric these title deeds and regal symbols.'[14]

Beaton's leadership role was taken up by episcopal colleagues such as the deposed Archbishop of St Andrews, the scholar and diocesan reformer John Hamilton who, in 1563, was charged, with up to 50 priests and lay people, with saying or hearing Mass. Ordinary priests were the infantry of resistance to Calvinism and were, for example, rounded up for hearing Confessions in Paisley, Renfrew, Glasgow and other western districts. In the Dunkeld Diocese several priests continued saying Mass during the 1560s and as late as 1572, while in 1573 a relative of Bothwell, Walter Robertson, was prosecuted for conducting a funeral in the 'popish manner'. Michael Yellowless writes, 'For some time after 1560 there were strong traces of continuing devotion to Catholicism among the parish clergy and even amongst the few who had apparently conformed and accepted office in the reformed church'. In the remoter parishes, obviously, resistance to Protestantisation was easier to sustain, especially within those groups of three or four parishes in which each grouping was served by a single minister; indeed, in some districts two sets of clergy – pre-Reformation priests and Reformation pastors – functioned in parallel opposition.[15]

The regular orders, new and old, as well as the secular clergy also played an important role in succouring Catholic resistance. At St Andrews Catholicism clung on in the persons of two Dominicans at St Mary's College. In Perth the friar Thomas Aitken was charged in 1562 with 'contravening of the actis and ministratione of the sacraments in the papisticall maner'. The Jesuit John Hay was on the Scottish mission from 1579, was banished from Aberdeen in 1592 and in 1594 was in Edinburgh, concealed as a writing master at the grammar school and saying Mass in the capital as late as 1602. The Franciscan Robert Veitch, 'sumtyme gwarden of the gray freiris in Striviling [Stirling]', was said, as late as 1580 'constantly [to] go about the kingdom saying mass', and in 1583 was arraigned as an 'obdurate offendir'. Like the vicar of Dollar in 1573, prosecuted for not subscribing the Articles of Religion of the Kirk, and another priest summoned before the Privy Council in 1569 to clarify the doctrines he held, Veitch was a victim of a drive, which was perhaps more vigorous in Scotland than in England and Wales, against the religious doctrines – 'papisticall erruris' – as well as against the missionary activities or political views and actions of Catholic dissidents. The rigour of dogmatic inquisition in Scotland also made ambiguity and indifferentism difficult to sustain, and circumscribed the opportunities for even bland eirenicism or the expression of the opinion that there was no essential difference between the churches – as with the commissary of St Andrews who was censured in 1561 for saying, 'That he was nether ane Papist nor ane Calwynist, ... bot Jesus Christes man': 'that kynd of speking to say that he is nather Papist nor Protestane' was completely unacceptable in a polarised Scotland within a polarised Europe.[16]

As well as the Mendicants, ex-monks kept up the memory of the old ways – by their continuing presence in the places where they had lived their earlier lives as monks, by the occasional social prestige of an individual and by continuing patterns of benevolence. The Charterhouse in Perth had ten monks at the Reformation, a group of them subsequently continuing to reside outside the town, in community and evidently envisaging the restoration of their house. Only in 1567 did the 'Commendator of the Charterhouse', Adam Forman, depart, for France, closing down the operation of the Order of Chartreux in Scotland; even then, though, three former inmates stayed in the country, one of them James V's illegitimate son Adam Stewart. He and a confrère remained in Perth under an arrangement that, even at that late date, clearly envisaged the possible restoration of the Charterhouse; meanwhile, a bequest of £10 to the poor of Perth cannot have harmed the reputation of the old monks in the minds of the ordinary inhabitants of the burgh.[17]

At Paisley's Cluniac abbey a late spurt of construction in the period 1556–7 suggests the continuing vitality of the monastic ideal in Scotland. Subsequently, appointments continued to be made to the post of chaplain of St Ninian, to whom an altar was dedicated within the abbey. The survival of the Paisley monastic fabric must have softened the sense of a break with the Catholic and monastic past: in 1565 reference was still being made to the abbey's 'refectory', while the *magna aulis abbatis* – the abbott's great hall – was itemised in 1580. Here too monastic, or postmonastic, charity was still being targeted at the local poor – as when provision was made in 1562 for seven chalders (96 bushels altogether) of victuals 'for alms distributed weekly by the almoner'. Above all, the Paisley Cluniacs maintained a full repertoire of Catholic services following the Reformation; in 1563 Paisley monks and chaplains took part, with their abbot, Jerome Hamilton, in celebrating Masses and hearing confessions.[18]

Alongside the nobility, secular priests, friars and monks, urban groups, in some cases with aristocratic or royal encouragement,

sponsored the old religion. Aberdeen's Catholic circle looked to the
neighbouring earl of Huntly for assistance. In Inverness at the Reformation it was the bailies themselves who took custody of the chalices,
reliquaries, vestments and muniments belonging to the town's Dominicans. As late as 1591 Perth reputedly had 'papistical magistrates'. Town
schoolmasters, such as Ninian Winzet in Linlithgow in West Lothian,
might be as influential as burgh magistrates in preserving the old faith;
in Haddington in East Lothian it was the schoolmaster who organised a
parody of a Kirk baptism, christening a cat. In Glasgow, it was the guild
system that lent some support to tradition, with the deacon and master
of the Weavers' Incorporation carefully sealing up, obviously for safe-
keeping, a set of coloured horn pictures of the Crucifixion, the Madonna
and Passion scenes. Amongst the burghs, a significant Catholic presence
was maintained in the capital, 'much less of a reformed city than either
Dundee or St Andrews', where the ornaments of St Giles' were entrusted
to sympathetic citizens and where in 1562 the Protestant authorities
threatened with excommunication anyone associating with a 'great
favorer of Papystes', the provost of St Salvator's, William Cranston. We
should not, as John Knox tended to do, attribute the retention of the old
faith in Edinburgh entirely to the arrival there of Mary Queen of Scots in
1561: in July 1559 a possible indicator of mass opinion in the capital may
have been the rejections by Calvinists, on the grounds that 'in townis and
citeis the maist pairt of men has ever bene aganis God and his treuthe', of
a bid by Mary of Guise to put the religious issue to a vote. However, the
single most important factor in encouraging Catholicism in post-Reformation Edinburgh was undoubtedly the Queen, whose chapel within
Holyrood House functioned in the 1560s as 'nothing less than a catholic
parish kirk'; her presence in the city allowed Mary's co-religionists to
claim protection by virtue of a kind of kinship of faith with her, as the
priest John Scott did in 1564, when he invoked in his defence against
prosecution the fact that 'he was of the Queen's religioun'. Scotland's
most active Catholic controversialist of the period, Ninian Winzet,
upheld the queen's regalian rights against what he saw as a desire for
Swiss- or German-style independence on the part of Protestant urban
magistrates: 'thai are nocht principalis in a fre citie ... to mak lawis, but
sold be subdites to our Souerane lady'. It may be that it was as a result of
the queen's ambit of protection that Edinburgh gained its Catholic cell:
in 1565 the capital, where in October 1561 the council had issued a ban
on priests, friars and religious 'sawing their ungodlike opinions and
detestable workis', nevertheless retained 'a still strong catholic opinion,

prepared to assert itself on occasion', including riotous interference with the execution of a priest. In 1569 the priest Nichol Burne recalled, facing starvation in the city gaol, how he stretched out a purse from the Edinburgh Tolbooth window and received

> the reuth and compassion of Godlie and cheritable people, qhua bestouit thair almous on me maist liberalie, . . . for declaration of the erneast desyre quhilk thay had of the extirpation of thair seditious haeresie, and the imbracement of the treu Catholik religion agane.

A recusant cell was established in Edinburgh, centred at the beginning of the second decade of the seventeenth century on the Jesuit Patrick Anderson, who celebrated Mass for members of a 'little Catholic iceberg in Edinburgh'.[19]

It was an additional source of strength for post-Reformation Scottish Catholicism that it had able controversialists. In the early days of the Reformation verbal duels betweeen Catholics and Calvinists took place around the country, including a set-piece debate on the Mass held in the presence of members of the nobility. In 1585 the Jesuit James Gordon disputed justification and the Mass with James VI. In the field of literary exchanges, the Jesuit James Tyrie debated the nature of the true church with Knox and his followers in the 1560s and 70s. Having in 1558 published *Ane Compendious Tractive* on the subject of scriptural interpretation, in 1561 the learned and aristocratic Cluniac Abbot Kennedy returned to the field of controversy with *Ane Compendious Ressonyng*, a defence of the Mass as a sacrifice, not an idolatry, asserting Christ's presence within it. The Linlithgow schoolmaster Ninian Winzet – Knox's 'procurator for the papists' – had a long career as a Catholic disputant. In *The Buke of Four Scoir Thre Questiouns* (1562), as well as ridiculing Knox for his affected English 'Southeron' accent, he contrasted the moorings of Catholicism in the Fathers and the early councils with the novelty of Calvinism, while in 1560, with *The Last Blast of the Trompet of Godis Worde aganis the usurpit auctorite of Iohne Knox and his Calviniane Brether intrudit Precheouris*, he delivered a mordant *ad hominem* attack, and in *Flagellum Sectariorum* (The Scourge of the Sectarians, 1581) he returned to the central issues in contention, the Mass, the Real Presence, the priesthood, justification, invocation of the saints and religious vows. In his *Ane Admonition to the Antichristian Ministers in the Deformit Kirk of Scotland*, the priest and converted Calvinist Nichol Burne castigated the apostates to Calvinism who had left the people

without 'pastors and sacramentis, the saulis remeid'. Burne denounced
the campaign to degrade and abuse priests –

> the murther of spiritual magistrats and pastors, be felling thame in
> priuat streittis under silence of nicht, castin of rottin eggis and al kynd
> of filthe at thame in open mercat, be banisin, impresoning, and
> harling thame on sleddis.

Richard Maitland of Lethington expressed regret at the passing of a
festive – a 'mirrie' – Scotland full of rich and lordly 'houshaulderis'
dispensing 'hospitality':

> Quhair is the blyithnes that hes beine
> Baith in Burgh and landwart sene
> Amang lordis and ladyis schene
> daunsing, singing, game and play
> Bot now I wait not quhat thay weine
> all merines is worne away

Other contributors to the literary engagement were Archibald Hamilton, with *On the Confusion of the Calvinist Sect in Scotland* and John Hay,
SJ, in *Certaine Demandes concerning the Christian Religion and Discipline*.
Catholicism in Reformation Scotland did not seem to lack for able and
active defenders.[20]

Even so, many of the assets that might have seemed likely to accrue to
Scottish Catholicism, including advantages in the field of propaganda,
were ephemeral or illusory. This particularly applies in the political area
of royal and aristocratic protection. Even during the high point of
Mary's reign, in 1562, it was noted that a visit by the papal legate de
Gouda did not evoke the anticipated 'vital response' of the Catholic
clergy. In fact, during that reign – which, of course, came to an abrupt
end in 1567 – Rome itself failed to give steady and informed support to
Scots Catholics, for in truth 'great ignorance about Scottish affairs prevailed in Rome'. As for the nobility, its patronage could be fickle and
lukewarm: one nobleman was reported 'disposed to favour the Catholic
cause in the frigid manner which is customary here' and a group of
aristocratic Catholic sympathisers were reported to be ready to shelter
English priests on condition that this would not involve 'any expense'.
Nobles in key positions tended to adopt cautious attitudes of wait-
and-see. The atmosphere in the Aberdeen hinterland, where Huntly

patronage had earlier created the possibility of a Catholic redoubt, has been described as 'cool and rather indifferent to the reformed movement' – rather than zealous for reformed Catholicism.[21]

In our review of factors favourable to the survival of Catholicism in Scotland after 1560, we considered the pivotal position of Archbishop Beaton as leader of the clergy. Yet it is evident that Beaton himself encapsulated that preoccupation with survival *tout court*, with mere continuity and tradition, with the dream of what was in fact a dead *Scotia Catholica*, the nostalgic vision that in fact thwarted a vital Catholic revival in Scotland within the period of this chapter. And it was fully symbolic of the frustration of Beaton's backward-looking dream that in 1590 the Archbishop returned to the University of Glasgow the mace whose retention in Rome he had clearly seen as an icon of filiation from the past. When Beaton died in 1603 the accession of a Scots Calvinist to the English throne marked the sweeping triumph of Protestantism, the crushing defeat of Catholicism, in both of the two neighbour realms – and all the more conclusively in the northern kingdom.[22]

Catholic episcopal resistance to religious change was not always stalwart: even the conservative Bishop Gordon of Aberdeen in the event, 'like many of his colleagues vacillated between the old and the new, cautiously and patiently sitting on the fence'. Meanwhile, other factors ostensibly facilitating the retention of a Catholic presence in Scotland in the second half of the sixteenth century were of their nature ephemeral. Ageing and dying monks had no capacity to maintain monasticism, and it becomes apparent that as the decades went by, the fate of Scottish religious life epitomised so much of the future of Scots Catholicsm in retaining what existence it did *outside* of the realm. Thus Ninian Winzet, as we have seen, was a vigorous polemicist, but as his monastic career unfolded, his work was conducted from foreign bases: following study at Paris and Douai, he found favour with the Bavarian ruling house and in 1577 settled down as abbot of 'Ratisbon' [Regensburg], the centre of the cluster of ancient *Schottenklöster*, the Celtic abbeys in Germany which had been transferred from Irish to Scottish hands since 1515. John Hamilton, Winzet's nephew, was elected abbot of Erfurt in 1582. Such German monastic centres operated as nuclei of Scottish Catholic life in Germany, a life that was essentially contemplative and deeply scholarly, rather than activist and missionary. Out of the Germano–Scottish abbey of Würzburg, a research *studium* for recording the early work of the '*Scoti*' in Christianising Germany, came in 1610 the double publication entitled *Scotia*

Antiqua et Nova, which combined a Latin version of Winzet's 1562 *Certaine Tractates* with George Thomson's work of scholarly longing for the Catholic past, *De Antiquitate Christianae religionis apud Scotos*.[23]

As for the continued ability of the secular clergy to stiffen recusant resistance, they were, as we have seen, under intense pressure to conform: as Charles Haws has shown, the St Andrews Kirk Sessions focused attention on priests and, as Michael Graham observes 'special pledges' were demanded of Catholic clergy – as with the former canon of Holyrood Abbey, John Wilson who in 1560 had to repudiate his Catholicism and 'that lecherouss swyne the Byschop of Rome'. To press home the exacting terms in which priestly repudiations of Catholicism had to be made, eliminating any margin of equivocation, priests had to repudiate their own vows. Of the effect of these pressures upon continued lay attachment to Catholicism, Dr Graham writes,

> The importance of public recantation should not be overlooked. At least some of these clergy (e.g. those who had preached and publicly ministered the sacraments), would have had, by virtue of their office, a special relationship with God in the eyes of the faithful. Now they were required to declare in the presence of their former spiritual charges that it was all a fraud.[24]

We saw that a group of towns afforded support for Catholicism after the Scottish Reformation settlement. However, it was the burghs that were, like the priesthood, subjected to a campaign of repression and enforced conformity. This was achieved in part through waging an offensive against the support for Catholicism within urban popular culture, including observance of Christmas. Thus in 1574 the Regent Morton took the burgh council of Aberdeen to task for 'the superstitious keping of festivall days usit of befor in tyme of ignorance & papistrie'. In St Andrews, the suppression of Catholicism was the second most pressing task (after the prosecution of sexual misconduct) of the Kirk Sessions in the period 1559–81, though after that the problem, from the point of view of the authorities, was more or less solved. As for Edinburgh, in the 1570s determined measures were taken to erode the membership of the Catholic groupings that had been sheltered under Mary: in 1574, for example, the recusants James Marjoriebanks and Alexander Purves, who had remained excommunicated for six years, finally conformed, and were sentenced to public repentance. The anti-Catholic drive in the towns was assisted by the assumption on the part of the Kirk of responsibility for the surviving hospitals which had the care of 'Christ's poor' in such places as Aberdeen, Dunkeld and Edinburgh. This acceptance of civic philanthropic responsibility ensured that in Scotland no plausible case could be made that popery meant community and Protestantism anti-social individualism. Indeed, we should see the Scottish crusade against popery, especially in the last decades of the sixteenth century, as an increasingly conscious political struggle to create a Calvinist national community, defined in part by its anti-popery. The bonds of such a community were reinforced by awareness of enemies within succouring foes without, and 'The leading ministers', writes Dr Graham, 'saw themselves surrounded by backsliders within the nation, and threatened by the machinations of Spain and the revived papacy from without'. In 1588, the General Assembly of the Kirk ordered the presbytery of Edinburgh to crack down on papists, including noble courtiers; in 1592, a meeting of pastors in Edinburgh denounced the 'blodie decrie of the Counsall of Trent against all that trewlie profes the Relligioun of Chryst'. As Scotland acquired a national terror of Spain, Rome and Jesuits in the 1580s and 1590s, the sense of a beleagured nation resulted in the moves detected by the priest Nicol Burne to depict Catholicism as treason as well as heresy, 'transferring the caus from professione of religione to lese Majestie, and treassone as they vald haue callit it'. The vilification of Catholicism as sedition and treason, discrediting the Catholic religion by linking it with witchcraft, accompanied a drive to equate Calvinism with Scottish identity as a covenanted nation worshipping 'in ane Kirk' and responding to the presence of 'a contrare altar' with a determination 'with all speed to have rooted them [the recusants] out with destruction'.[25]

In these circumstances, dexterity in propaganda, which as we saw was a *potential* asset in Catholic hands, was presented with an uphill challenge. The Scottish Catholic contribution to verbal, as distinct from literary, dialectic was inadequate, for as the papal legate de Gouda reported in 1562: 'There are some catholic preachers of note, but they are few in number and seldom venture to attack controverted points, being indeed unequal to the task of handling them with effect.' Catholic polemic also generally lacked that populist gutsiness of the Calvinist offensive which was evident at the strategic point, the ballad, where argumentative religious literature met oral popular culture, and few, if any, printed Catholic controversial works could match the skill, deployed in a mixture of vernacular ribaldry and anti-Mendicant satire, found in the 1559 anti-clerical classic the *Beggars' Summons*. In the early years of the Scottish Reformation, popular ballads in favour of Mary, with her strong potential as a romantic and royalist rallying point, were rare and tended to focus on the political issue of allegiance rather than on the religious issue of faith. Nicol Burne's furious castigation of apostates in *Ane Admonition*, writes Brother Kenneth, 'would have pierced few skins in those days', and as for Maitland of Lethington's lament for lost 'merines', it was far from being specifically pro-Catholic or even anti-Calvinist, for he ridiculed 'popery and Calvinism alike with poetic indifference'. Abbot Kennedy was an able defender, for the more educated reader, and in updated Tridentine terms, of the central and, in Scotland, sharply controverted doctrines of the Mass, but his death in 1564, after a period of continuuous harassment for celebrating the rite, represented a serious loss to Catholic participation in doctrinal discourse in early Reformation Scotland. Nicol Winzet took Knox to task in his *Last Blast of the Trompet*, but in an *ad hominem* way that revealed his debating weakness, for in his German Benedictine retreat he semed incapable of realising that a great national sea-change was coming over Scotland, one even greater than the reformer who had inaugurated it, and that the Scots Reformation was a deeper, wider phenomenon than some passing fancy to be identified only with 'the minister of Calvin in Britain, John Knox, once of great fame'.[26]

Winzet's establishment on the Continent can be taken as typical, or even symbolic, of the inevitably increasing European orientation of Scots Catholicism from the later sixteenth century onwards. Indeed, even before the inception of the Scottish Reformation, the German orientation of post-Reformation Scottish Catholicism was anticipated in the sending of the Tridentinist reformer Robert Wauchope by Pope Paul III on a preaching mission into Lutheran Germany. Later in the century, Scottish Catholic internationalism is evident, for example, in the highly varied career of the Jesuit John Hay, who lectured in philosophy at the Society's college in Vilnius in Lithuania from 1572 to 1575, disputed in favour of Transubstantiation against a Lutheran spokesman in Strassburg, and taught at Bordeaux, Paris, Tournon, Lyon and Pont-à-Mousson seminary, the last-named institution of which he was rector at his death in 1608. Even more cosmopolitan was James Bonaventure Hepburn, the Catholic orientalist who travelled in the Turkish Empire and in Persia, joined the Order of Minims in Avignon in 1569 and went on to become librarian of the Vatican's collection of orientalia. Some years later, the 'pilgrimacious' layman William Lithgow was given an elaborate reception by the Franciscans in Jerusalem in 1612:

I was met and received by the Guardian and twelve friars upon the streets, each of them carrying in their hands a burning wax candle . . . . [S]inging all the way to their monastery *Te Deum laudamus*, they mightily rejoiced that a Christian had come from such a far country as Scotia to visit Jerusalem.[27]

In the years following 1560 Scottish Catholic education also re-grouped itself away from 'such a far country as Scotia', to find Continental locations. We shall consider whether or not these European bases could function well as launch-pads for missionary forays into the kingdom with particular reference to the Scots College, Rome. Loyola had set up the Collegium Germanicum in Rome to train priests for service in northern lands, and ten Scots students can be traced at it in the 1560s and 1570s. However, specifically dedicated institutions for the training of Scottish priests for Scotland, the Scots Colleges at Douai, Pont-à-Mousson and Rome, came relatively late in the day, and belong to the years following the establishment of Cardinal Allen's English seminary at Douai in 1568. The degree of missionary targeting on Scotland, in the case of the Roman college at least, was limited: according to Clement VIII's bull of foundation of the college of 1600, as the historian of the institution, Abbé McPherson, wrote,

there was no obligation laid on the students to embrace the clerical state, much less of returning missionaries to Scotland. Of the first eleven that entered the college four left it without receiving Holy Orders, two died, and the other five became Jesuits or of some other religious order. So none of these [eleven] and few in proportion to the rest that were received for a number of years returned clergy missionaries to their country.

Crippling discords soon struck the college from 1612, and in 1615 its administration was handed over to the Society of Jesus, a change of control that did not work to the college's advantage when the Jesuits' critic Maffeo Barberini assumed the papacy as Urban VIII in 1623 and neglected its requirements. Even so, with the Jesuit take-over, the college acquired a new, Ignatian sense of discipline, and its first Jesuit superior, James Anderson, gave an example of Jesuit activism by returning to Scotland, debating with ministers of the Kirk, getting arrested and being imprisoned for two years. Yet even under its new control, the

college did not thrive, least of all financially, for its rents were detained
by French tenants and some of its properties diverted. It is true that the
new constitutions of 1615 obliged the students to become ordained and
then go on to work in Scotland. However, the Jesuits and other
orders poached the college's best students and these often received
dispensations from the oath pledging them to return for work in their
homeland. Abbé McPherson gave an impression of lack of direction and
a general ineffectiveness in the life of the college, with a consequent
inability to rectify the then 'unhappy state of [the Catholic] religion in
Scotland'.[28]

Despite failure and collapse on so many of the fronts of the post-
Reformation Scottish Catholic enterprise – including the Protestantisation of the crown, the weakening of the Catholic nobility, the squeeze on
the Catholic priesthood and episcopate, the collapse of monasticism
within Scotland, the Europeanisation of the Scots Catholic tradition,
the lack of success of priestly education, the inadequacy of preaching
and of the Catholic polemical offensive – there was one area of survival
that was to emerge as the bastion of Catholic hopes between the seventeenth and the nineteenth centuries, the Gaelic north and west; we shall
evaluate in particular the important role of the regular orders in the
development of this Highland mission.

The Dominicans, along with the Capuchins, Franciscans and Jesuits,
conducted an energetic mission in Scotland. In 1623 Robert Calender,
OP, was working in Northumberland, a spiritual border reiver, using the
frontier to advantage in the escapades of his mission; in the same 1620s
James Murray (or Muir), OP, 'ex Gallia missus in Scotiam' [sent from
France into Scotland], was active in the field. Irish Dominican activity
in Scotland became increasingly significant, following the award of
faculties for an open mission in England, Ireland and Scotland to the
Irish Dominican Thomas Bath in 1613. Formal assignment of Scotland
to the Irish Dominicans was made by the chapter general of the order in
1629, and in 1634 the master general asked the provincial of the order
in Ireland for priests to serve in Scotland. In 1635 four Irish Dominicans were sent to work in the Gaelic Highlands, where Franciscans were
already active; there was a three-year grant-in-aid from the Roman
coordinating office of the Church's mission, Propaganda Fide. However,
it was fear of wasteful competition between the Mendicant preaching
orders that, in these zenith years of the Counter-Reformation, gave
Propaganda Fide, with its global strategy, reservations about committing
highly trained friars to unpromising territories, and in 1647 five Irish

Dominicans were refused faculties for Scotland on the grounds that four Franciscans were already at work there. A further difficulty, from within the Order of Preachers, arose in 1638 when it was reported that Irishmen sent abroad to study were reluctant to return to their own country, leave alone to go to Scotland, and above all its Highlands with their reputation for poverty and wildness.[29]

Yet it was Scotland's most rugged terrain in the Highlands and Islands that was to prove the most fertile mission field for the Dominicans and other orders – not because the area had remained firmly and consciously Catholic, but because it had not been won by the Kirk. A report to Propaganda in the early seventeenth century aptly summed up the as yet unrealised proselytising potential of a people deeply suspicious of religious change:

> these people are neither Catholic not heretical, since they detest Protestantism as a new religion and they listen to the preachers out of sheer necessity, straying in matters of faith out of ignorance caused by the lack of priests who would be able to instruct them on those issues.[30]

Yet the fact that there was considerable popular resistance in the Highlands and Islands to Calvinism as a 'new religion' was far from guaranteeing success to reformed, Tridentine Catholicism, as the Irish Franciscan Cornelius Ward found in 1625 when he was rebuked by an old island-woman for not distributing the *pax*, the old pacificatory and surrogate-eucharistic symbol. But that was not the worst that Ward had to put up with. Around Mull, for instance,

> with two attendants ... for five whole days [they travelled] over rough mountain slopes and through daunting loneliness of the forests.... Hunger and thirst became daily more pressing and, after the fatigues of each day, there was no place to lie down except on the bare ground at the mercy of the inclement night air.

And for priests the common risks of the unmade roads and unbridged roads of the Highlands – 'I was very nere drowned in the Water of Ylay –', recalled one priest in 1638 of his mission in Banffshire – were exacerbated by the burdens and the dangers incurred by their vestments and equipment: 'I see my ... masse vestments, swimming towards the river. I returned in once againe to the head and brought them out', the same priest recalled. True, there were ingenious devices designed to provide for a priesthood on the run; these included the miniature missals – the *Missale Parvum* – probably made in Antwerp, of which some copies still survive from the 1620s, along with low-cost basic chalices and foldable altars – though the possession of one of these gave away the Franciscan Edmund Calderwood. Obtaining wine for the celebration of Mass presented further problems to Cornelius Ward, in a wineless land where even wheaten bread, for Mass, was a luxury that had to be obtained, in 1636, from Edinburgh for Ward's West Highland mission.[31]

Such practical difficulties were compounded by the religious problem, from a Tridentine point of view, of ancient Celtic cultic survivals, including a seemingly ineradicable reverence for holy wells and popular devotions to saints such as Fillan who found no place in Tridentine hagiographies. Yet despite all these practical and spiritual difficulties, it begins to be possible to speak of an early seventeenth-century Catholic revival in the Highlands and Islands – in such areas as Harris, under the priesthood of Paul O'Neill and Patrick Brady, and under the protection of the McLeods. By 1615, under the shelter of the Macdonalds, with their links to Ulster, it could be said of Islay 'that the religioun that the cuntrie pepill has heir amongst them is Popishe'.[32]

As Scotland moved towards the political events of the seventeenth century that were to confirm the country's overwhelming Protestantism, the small Catholic remnant, with 13 secular priests reported at work in 1623, gained a measure of organisational stability. Following Archbishop Beaton's death, Scottish Catholics came under the authority first, of three successive archpriests and then of the English Vicar Apostolic, William Bishop until, in response to Scots complaints, Gregory XV suspended Bishop's authority in Scotland, having placed the country under Propaganda Fide, in whose charge Scottish Catholics were to remain until as late as 1908. Between 1623 and 1653 prefects of the missions oversaw the work of the seminary-trained priests who served the small communities until, in 1653, William Ballantyne was appointed prefect apostolic for Scotland.[33] Under such administrative arrangements the Scottish Catholic community was to face its next century of test and suffering. The martyrdom of John Ogilvie in 1615 was followed by a massive renewal of persecution in 1629–30 and then by the horrors of Britain's mid-century wars of religion.

Ireland

Topics to be considered in this section include: the survival of Catholicism in post-Reformation Ireland, with particular reference to the towns and to the crucial 'Old English', largely urban, element, which formed a key to the religious and political situation in Tudor Ireland; the survival and revival of institutional Catholicism, with special attention to the religious orders and to the restored, if unofficial, Catholic episcopate; and the emerging alignment between Irish identity and Catholicism.

The contrast between religious developments in Scotland and Ireland in the second half of the sixteenth century could hardly have been sharper: in Scotland a rapid and overwhelming popular acceptance of Protestantism and the elimination of Catholicism over most of the country; in Ireland, the precarious position of Protestantism as an alien implant along with a strong Catholic revival from the 1590s onwards. The common theme underlying these dissimilarities is the operation of political and social factors upon the popular adoption of one religious choice or another; feelings of community and proto-nationhood, of culture and identity influenced the retention of Catholicism by the majority of the Irish, while parallel factors conditioned the acceptance of Protestantism by the majority of Scots. However, within the triptych of group identities within Ireland – 'Old Irish', of Gaelic speech and culture, 'Old English', English-speaking and of a traditionally anglocentric political orientation, and new Tudor settlers – it was the 'Old English', a vital, albeit minority, element who did much to determine the outcomes of 'national' religious choice.

While Ireland was embraced more tightly in the English hold during the Tudor century – giving ever-increasingly tangible effect to Henry VIII's assumption of the title 'king of Ireland' in 1541 – a Catholic inspiration for anti-English resistance can be seen relatively early on, in papal backing by Paul III, who gave his support to the FitzGerald resistance against Henry VIII; the same pope in 1537 supported Manus O'Donnell, lord of Tirconnel, against the king. Active papal involvement in Ireland, so starkly in contrast with Rome's lack of interest in Scotland, took on an important pastoral, as well as diplomatic, dimension. In 1535 Pope Paul appointed his own nominee, Hugh O'Carolan, to the see of Clogher, inaugurating what Fr Jones calls a 'drastic and decisive' papal strategy of making parallel rival appointments to those of Henry VIII, as at Tuam, while at primatial Armagh Paul actually deposed Henry's man, replacing him with the reform-minded Robert

Wauchope. Thus, in that early period the papacy took a firm line towards Irish ecclesiastical affairs, in strong contrast with its hesitant policies in the rest of the British Isles, this decisiveness evoking a positive Catholic response within Ireland. It is true that an early Jesuit mission in 1542, by Fathers Brouet and Salmerón, was a failure, but from his appointment in 1555 Cardinal Pole's papal legateship extended to Ireland, where he gave his encouragement to Tridentine episcopal and parochial reform by delegating to Bishop Walsh of Meath powers to oversee his fellow-bishops, to regulate parish priests and to re-order Irish marriage law.[34]

Close papal involvement with Ireland continued into the pontificate of Pius IV who, in 1560, appointed the Jesuit David Wolfe to carry out extensive Irish church reform, with particular attention to encouraging bishops to teach their people and to developing the preaching skills of the lower clergy. This was a programme in which 'the norms of Trent were to be the guide' for Wolfe, and his partner Richard Creagh, appointed to Armagh in 1564 and given the bold goals – in a land under a Protestant government – of setting up Mass centres, appointing episcopal administrators and eliminating clerical concubinage and simony. These reformist targets, though, with their focused religious aims, gave the Wolfe – Creagh programme a politically neutral, or even politically acquiescent, cast, with an insistence on loyalty to the 'natural queen and crown of England whom the Lord God maintain now and for ever', and the excommunication, by Archbishop Creagh, of the rebel Shane O'Neill. Nevertheless, as the 1560s wore on towards the publication of the bull *Regnans in Excelsis*, the impossibility of holding in balance Catholic evangelism and loyalty to Elizabeth became increasingly apparent and a new political synthesis aimed at collaboration between Rome and Spain to dethrone Elizabeth and restore a fully Catholic Ireland. Thus in 1569 a new bishop of Cashel, and kinsman of the oppositionist Fitzgeralds, Maurice FitzGibbon, abandoned the Catholic Elizabethanism of Creagh and Wolfe, taking to Spain a manifesto, signed by four Catholic archbishops, eight bishops and 13 nobles, in which the the political grievances of the Gaelic chieftains were fused with a Catholic programe influenced by the thinking of the insurgent James FitzMaurice Fitzgerald. The manifesto declared that the overwhelming wish of the Irish people was

to remain firm, constant and unshakeable in the faith and unity of the Catholic Church; as also to persevere even to their last breath in their immemorial obedience and attachment to the Roman Pontiffs and the Apostolic See.

Philip II's designated role was to save this Catholic Ireland from 'the infection and ruin of the accursed and contagious heresy now raging in England', and he was invited to appoint a relative to the 'royal throne' of Ireland. Although a pro-Elizabethan minority continued to exist, and helped to bring about the downfall of the rebel Hugh O'Neill, earl of Tyrone, the militant Catholic option drew in ever wider elements from the range of the disgruntled in Ireland, including Anglo-Irish nobles such as the Butlers and the Fitzgeralds, full of resentment at their loss of lands and their political marginalisation, and at the introduction of new laws from England. The strategy of Bishop FitzGibbon – who expressed himself willing to fight in person in a Catholic crusade – was in fact sidelined in Philip II's diplomatic manoeuvres, but FitzGibbon's brand of militancy was reaffirmed by Rome, where in 1572 Gregory XIII even considered a plan for an invasion of Ireland, launched from the Papal States under the command of a Spanish or Italian admiral.[35]

Mediterranean perceptions of Ireland as England's soft under-belly were, of course, linked to an appreciation of the island's preponderant Catholicism. That this had become strongly etched by the reign of Elizabeth can be confirmed by looking at Ireland's towns, including Dublin which, with their commercial and political links with England, might have been expected to act as forward posts of Protestantisation. In particular the English Pale of Settlement around Dublin was home to a class of office-holders and gentry who were traditionally, as Professor Canny writes, 'more given to fawning after royal approval than were any other subjects of the English Crown'. Under Elizabeth, though, such people first manifested a quiet Catholic obstinacy and subsequently went on to function as advance stations not of Reformation but of Catholic renewal. In Dublin, evasive Catholic survivalism is evident in the St Anne's Guild, a confraternity which came through the Reformation institutionally intact and which, in the period 1592–1626 was taken over in post-Reformation Ireland's Catholic revival: by the early seventeenth century most members and all the officers of the Guild were recusants, typically being related to seminary priests. The Guild's history encapsulates the way that in Ireland as a whole government attempts to bring in Reformation created a hostile reaction which, in turn, facilitated a reassertion of Catholic identity: attacks on the Guild's privileges actually stimulated its re-emergence as a consciously Catholic institution, fortified by the defiance of a group of pious women. The process of re-Catholicisation is evident in the Guild's resolutions of 1597 and 1605 to restore a chapel dedicated to St Anne. In the course of time, the Guild's devotions became distinctively Tridentine. The post-Reformation evolution of the St Anne's Guild, Dublin, then – closely linked as its membership was to the personnel of the Dublin corporation, all the Guild masters down to 1630 being aldermen – epitomises the surviving, or rather reviving, Catholic commitment of Irish urban elites.[36]

As far as the Dublin corporation and the wider city elite of which it was representative was concerned, they do indeed exhibit a clear process of overt, and, indeed, defiant re-Catholicisation, from a position in which perhaps half a dozen corporation recusants could be identified at the beginning of Elizabeth's reign to a state of affairs in which it could be said, in 1564, 'The mayor, aldermen, merchants and inhabitants of Dublin are notorious papists.' A well-connected, intermarried and commercially adroit group, linked by marriage to the county gentry and very far from being by nature disloyal to the crown, the Dublin aldermanic circle moved from an earlier somewhat uncommitted attitude in the direction of a pronounced Catholic engagement, confirmed by the education they gave their children, which included the Catholic colleges on the Continent. Once again, government provocation had the effect of eliciting intransigence, as in 1603, when seven aldermen were punished for offences against the Act of Uniformity, or in 1604, when an elected mayor was deposed for not taking the Oath of Supremacy. The martyrdoms in Dublin in 1613 of Bishop Conor O'Devaney and the priest Patrick O'Loughram further hardened the Catholicism of so much of Dublin and its its ruling class. By 1613, when the freemen elected two known Catholics to parliament, the Irish capital's Catholic orientation had taken on the clear political form of a conservative opposition in a campaign 'to defend cherished liberties, including that of conscience'. The confident morale of Dublin Catholicism was further shown in the activities of skilled controversialists, such as Henry Fitzsimon, SJ, educated at Oxford and Douai, a lecturer at Louvain who arrived back in Dublin in 1598, or William Malone, also a Jesuit, who wrote in favour of allegiance to the crown as a guarantee of religous toleration for Catholics and who took part in a long series of debates with high-level Protestant spokesmen between about 1617 and 1641.[37]

In the west of Ireland, too, continuity, eventually emerging in a Catholic revival, found urban and corporate focus. As in Scotland, pre-Reformation Catholicism in Ireland showed great liturgical splendour in the towns, such as Galway, where the corporation expressed its Catholic piety up to the eve of the Elizabethan Reformation, for example sponsoring in 1557 a daily sung 'Mary Masse'. On such pre-Reformation foundations, Galway Catholicism traced a seemingly unbroken skein of Catholic continuity, proving highly resistant to Protestantisation for, as a reporter for the Lord Deputy observed, the 'godly' there dared 'scarcely show their faces', and Catholicism was securely, even triumphantly, re-established, 'the kingdom of Antichrist... erected, ... again'. This defiance was particularly evident in the western city's open maintenance of the Franciscans, who were certainly in place in their house, St Francis', in 1568, when the grant of this 'abbey' to the mayor and corporation in no way disturbed the friars' presence there: far from it – the Franciscans held their provincial chapter at St Francis' in 1572. The dominant territorial interest, that of the Burke earl of Clanrickard, fostered a Catholic atmosphere in Galway, evident in the presence of the mayor and some aldermen at a sermon given by a Franciscan from Ulster. From as early as 1573, the Galway Franciscans had re-introduced (if it had ever even been interrupted, that is) the medieval *modus operandi* of using the city as an urban base from which to missionise the countryside: by 1616 the Franciscan provincial Donagh Mooney reported that the friars were fanning out into the hinterland, from their large, well maintained and beautiful Galway city church, an institution to which wealthy citizens left donations. The overt presence of numerous Franciscans, reported walking the streets in groups of up to 20, and with a Franciscan school of philosophy in the city, formed a vivid illustration of the way in which Galway had quite simply and 'gradually resumed its entirely Catholic atmosphere'.[38]

Evidence of the continuing presence of other regulars in the west emerges from 1577 when a survey of supposedly dissolved houses revealed as many as ten of them to be occupied still by a named head 'and other friars'; at Clontuskert, County Galway, it can be assumed that the Augustinian Canons were established by 1585, serving neighbouring parishes; in 1633 new building work was being undertaken at Clontuskert. Numerous chalices in the Franciscan house in Kilconnel, County Galway, bear dates from the 1620s and 1630s; at Balintubber, County Mayo, where a dissolution *did* take place in 1562, the Austin Friars were back in possession by 1635.[39]

It was obviously very much in the interest of the crown under Elizabeth to introduce Protestantism rapidly so as to remove the religious base for political disaffection in Ireland. Thus, for instance, a proposal to introduce the Lancashire model of the Queen's Preachers into the island was couched specifically in terms of inculcating political subordination alongside Protestant doctrine – 'teaching the people sincerelye and directlie howe to feare god and obey their prynce'. The obverse of that equation was that, should Irish Catholicism remain ineradicable, efforts to enforce Protestantism, especially among key elements such as the 'Old English', who were threatened with displacement by new English settlers, might well prove damaging to political loyalty. Thus of the Old English gentry of County Dublin, Dr Walshe writes that they felt 'attracted to the Counter-Reformation as a means of forging a communal loyalty to act as a counterpose to the growing influence of…the New English'. The 'principal gentlemen' amongst this class on whom royal rule had traditionally rested were, it was reported to Elizabeth, sending their sons to 'Lovain, Doole [Douai], Rome and other places where your Majesty is rather hated than honoured in'. A separate Irish College in Douai was founded in 1594 and at St Anthony's, Louvain, in 1607, forming, with their dependencies in Lille, Tournai and Antwerp, 'the Irish centres of post-Tridentine Catholic learning'.[40]

This progressive alienation by the crown of a distinctive social and ethnic class, the Old English, can be studied by reviewing the history of families within it, such as the Stanihursts, culminating in Richard (1547–1618). The family typified the ancestrally royalist 'colonial' Old English and had served the crown since the fourteenth century. Three sixteenth-century generations of this family exemplify the gradual withdrawal from England of the goodwill of this grouping, whose Catholicism became the badge of their grievances. Richard Stanihurst's grandfather had maintained his family's traditions of close cooperation with the crown and benefited extensively from monastic confiscations in County Dublin and County Meath. In the second generation, James Stanihurst attempted the difficult blancing act of combining public service – as Speaker of the Irish Commons – with religious traditionalism. Having acted as host to Edmund Campion, he was to find that the two parts of his ambivalent political and religious formula could not hold together, and he failed to retrieve government favour, his death bringing to a terminus his family's traditions of state service. Influenced by Campion, Richard Stanihurst was more overtly Catholic than his father, taking in 1581 the option of exile from a land that his class no longer governed on behalf of the crown. His *De Rebus in Hibernia Gestis* (Historical Events in Ireland, Antwerp, 1584) formed a 'defence of the vanished power of the Old English', and it was indicative of the political estrangement from the crown of his stratum, whose religious conservatism drove them into sympathy with the Old, or Gaelic, Irish, that an ardent proponent of Counter-Reformation Catholicism such as Stanihurst was an equally enthusiastic political hispanophile.[41]

The background of a leader of the seventeenth-century Irish Counter-Reformation, Luke Wadding (1588–1657), was that of the old Anglo-Irish royalist urban elite, at the centre of an entrenched Waterford network of intermarried clans, a family who underwent a kind of collective re-Catholicisation. Wadding's own formation in bourgeois domestic piety included family recitation of the breviary, the psalms, the litanies and the office of the dead. Then, trained as a Franciscan, he gravitated away from England, towards Spain and became a protégé of Philip III. But in this case it was a whole kindred that was becoming fervent and at the same time moving out of an English orbit and towards a Habsburg world, for of the half-dozen Wadding cousins who entered the Society of Jesus, one became chancellor of the University of Prague and another a missionary in Mexico.[42]

A progression over three generations similar to that of the Stanihursts is evident in the Barnwalls of the County Dublin Pale. Sir Patrick Barnwall, a king's serjeant, 'played an active part in reformation politics', but his grandson, also Patrick, was one of the early leaders of the Irish Counter-Reformation and also part of a recognisable opposition to crown policies. James I's accession and the failure of Irish resistance in the Nine Years' War (1594–1603) resulted in the suppression of the Barnwalls' class of Catholic lawyers – 'for the greatest numbre of them', it was reported, 'are Iryshe, arrogant papysts that wyll neyther com to church, nor take the oath of obedyence'.[43]

Understandably from the government's point of view, the Catholic legal profession was singled out for investigation and discrimination. In 1560 the Oath of Supremacy denying the pope was reintroduced for judges and other law officers, even though for some time suitably qualified Protestants were not forthcoming to fill positions. In England itself the Act of Parliament requiring the oaths was not as yet enforced stringently enough to exclude recalcitrant Irish students from the Inns of Court; they were, however, increasingly subject to interrogation and, as the atmosphere heated up in the tense 1580s, the suspicion arose that

being all of the Roman religion (as the rest in Ireland)...they never came to our churches...but having got a smack of the grounds of our law...returned to practise the law in Ireland.

As late as 1604, a complaint was made 'that chief and principal places of justice in that realm are supplied by such of the Irish as are open recusants or dissembling hypocrites'. Conformity, however, was enforced much more strictly thereafter, and John Everard, forced to resign in 1607, was the last Catholic Irish judge in this period; after 1613 all Irish judges were professing Protestants, shortfalls in personnel being made up through the import of English barristers. Then, from 1627, the non-statutory 'instructions and graces' offered Catholics in the legal profession security of a sort, but one that was essentially precarious. 'Lawyers,' as Dr. Kenny writes, 'may have got what they wanted', but more widely and over a longer term the key process taking place in Ireland between the reigns of Elizabeth and Charles I was of the exclusion of Catholic elements, including those that might, in other circumstances, have been sought out by the crown for service and loyalty: instead, a 'sense of betrayal exacerbated ill-feeling in Ireland and came to a head in the rebellion of 1641'.[44]

As for the 'Old Irish', Dr Morgan has shown how the Tudor state's attempts to impose control and uniformity alienated Gaelic elites which sheltered those 'counter-reformers' who in turn went on to create a 'refortified catholicism' from which the crown could not subsequently win over the majority of the Irish.[45]

Indeed, the evidence for a vigorous Catholic renewal in the Gaelic heartland, Ulster, during the period when Protestantism was supposed to be introduced into Ireland is impressive, the Jesuits in the 1560s following in the footsteps of the Observant Franciscans. Raymond O'Gallagher, Bishop of Derry, one of the three Irish bishops at Trent, was said to be maintaining his episcopal jurisdiction across Ulster, ordaining priests, confirming children, opening churches. Also present at Trent and appointed to the northern diocese of Raphoe was the Gaelic scholar Donald McGonigle; the succession of the Dominican Niall O'Boyle to O'Gallagher in Derry bespeaks the strength of the regulars in Ulster, where 20 monasteries and friaries were said to be in operation in 1594: indeed a *new* Franciscan friary opened in Lisgoole in Ulster in 1583. Ulster, indeed, was beginning to emerge as a model missionary province of the Tridentine Church: contacts between it and the Holy See were close and Ulster benefices were keenly sought at Rome; the Gregorian calendar was promptly adopted in the province; pre-Tridentine defects were vigorously attacked, including clerical concubinage, which was condemned by the insurgent Hugh O'Neill, earl of Tyrone, who was also active in the appointment of reformist bishops.

There is, of course, no necessary link at all between 'Gaelic' culture and sub-Tridentine standards: the 'Gael' O'Neill's prayerful habits and cult of the sacraments – 'his daily and devout hearing of holy mass... He frequently confesses and receives the eucharist, is assiduous in prayer' – seem very similar to the domestic devotional routines that the urban 'Old English' young Luke Wadding knew. With such leaders of Gaeldom, it is not surprising that the prospects for Catholic survival and recovery in Gaelic Ulster were promising: 'the catholic church was maintaining itelf institutionally and strengthening itself ideologically', the state Church losing the struggle for the allegiance of Gaelic speakers.[46]

Ultimately, if not inevitably, Irish Gaeldom was lost to the crown and Protestantism, and ultimately, too, the Catholic Old English were to be just as irrevocably lost, throwing in their lot, as Catholics, with the Old Irish in the rebellion of 1641. However, neither the political alienation of the Old English, nor their eventual ideological alignment with the Old Irish was unavoidable. It is true that various commentators, in particular Spanish observers seeking to play up Irish disaffection from the English crown, as well as Protestant onlookers attempting to associate Catholicism with treason, laid considerable stress on Catholic Ireland's subversiveness: for example, a report from Galway to the Lord Deputy in 1577 linked 'defiances against professors of God's word' to 'a foul stink of rebellion breeding in the town', and, more widely, it was reported that 'popery...hath alienated the hearts of that people from...loyalty ...towards their sovereign'. Spanish propaganda also took for granted a necessary progression amongst the Irish from acceptance of Catholicism to rejection of the English crown and recognition of Spain's claims: in 1601, for example, Don Juan de Aquila justified his landing in Ireland with the assertion that its purpose was to guarantee that the 'Irish may freely profess the Catholic faith'. Irish sources made the same link between the profession of Catholicism and resistance to the crown; thus, in 1635, Hugh O'Donnell, earl of Tyrconnell, recalled the struggle against the crown 'which my father and uncles carried on *for the Catholic cause*' (emphasis mine). The Galway adventurer James Blake in 1602 made the conceptual connection between Catholicism and rebellion even more explicit:

The Inhabitants of Galway are...all Catholics and most eager to shake off the heavy yoke and tyranny of England and at the same time anxious to live as Catholics with the free exercise of our holy religion.

Conversely, in 1612 it was only through the deliberate omission of the subject of the 'State Ecclesiasticall' that the Solicitor-General John Davies could maintain his claim that

> the clock of the ciuil Gouernment is now well set, and all the wheeles thereof doe moue in order; The strings of this Irish Harpe, which the Ciuill magistrate doth finger, are all in tune...and make a good Harmony in this Commonweale.[47]

Indeed, if the problems of 'the State Ecclesiasticall' could have been solved, then Davis's vision of an ordered Ireland might have been realisable, and in the early seventeenth century there were prospects of an accommodation to give the Irish Catholic community some political freedom as well as the opportunity for religious growth. A partial retention of influence in Catholic hands allowed for the protection of the faith, as in County Meath where, in 1622, it was reported that a 'Romish bishop', his surrogates and the priests under his authority were living in gentry homes, saying Mass openly and confidently expecting the return of church benefices to them. In County Limerick in the 1620s two-thirds of the justices were recusants. A recovery of Catholic confidence was evident in towns, including Dublin where, when the Protestant archbishop and the mayor went to demolish the Franciscan chapel and arrest the friars, a mob forced their release. In Galway in 1609 and 1611 mayors were debarred from office for refusal to take the Oath of Supremacy, but by 1628 the practice of co-opting mayors by the Protestant aldermen was replaced by election on the part of the freemen, who were overwhelmingly Catholic. Although in 1633 the government ordered the taking of the oath, leading to the deposition of the mayor and sheriffs of Galway, in 1635 the 'grave simple honest' Catholic Patrick French FitzGeorge was elected mayor, overcoming Protestant objections with his perfectly credible claim 'that he was as good a subject to his Majesty as they were'.[48]

This loyalism probably represented a response to the overtures by Charles I to Irish Catholics, as reported to Rome in 1624 in these glowing terms:

> that the king of England, in order to gain the good will of the Irish and through fear of Spain, has declared that the Irish are free to practise whatever religion they wish, and that the Catholics are not to be molested; it is said that he has revoked all the penal laws against the

Catholics, and has decreed that the Irish nobles may become members of the council of state and be admitted to the leading posts in the
country which were formerly denied to them

Leaving aside that kind of over-statement, a thawing of the penal atmosphere undeniably took place under Charles I and was the precondition
for an extraordinary acceleration in Catholic activity in Ireland during
his reign. By 1627, an Irish Catholic episcopal system was working with
such efficiency that the chapter and clergy of Armagh could write to the
Vatican Secretary of State concerning a new archbishop, to be appointed
by the Pope, the Infanta of Spain putting forward three names. By
1630, four Catholic archbishops of Ireland were all in residence and
the country was 'once more placed under the authority of a properly
constituted native hierarchy'. Five years later Roman satisfaction was
expressed with a situation in which 17 or 18 bishops or vicars apostolic
could be enumerated. Below this well developed diocesan administration was a full parochial system in areas such as Waterford diocese in
1639, with 45 parishes, 59 secular priests and 45 regulars. Lay numbers
fully warranted these clerical provisions, especially in the towns, including Dundalk, Drogheda, Wexford, Waterford – the last-named of which
was reported mostly Catholic in 1635 – and Dublin, where a baroque
Jesuit chapel was built; indeed the Derry Company, entrusted with
Protestant plantation in Ulster, itself built six Catholic chapels on its
lands before 1631.[49]

While the statistical picture of Catholicism in Ireland in the 1630s thus
looks broadly healthy, the qualitative view is murkier. Indeed, problems
arose over the very success of this Catholic recovery in the years before
the Catholic rebellion of 1641 and in particular over the difficulty of
defining Ireland's status as a Catholic land with a Protestant government. If it *were* the case that Catholicism was basically secure in the
island, then a well developed episcopal structure, possessing a high
degree of authority, of a kind we shall study more closely in Chapter
4, was in order. If, on the other hand, the kingdom ought more accu-
rately to have been regarded as a mission field in which it needed to be
appreciated that, however, numerous the Catholics were, they lived
under the permanent shadow of persecution, then it might have been
more appropriate to bracket Ireland with other mission fields and
confer more freedom of action on the religious order, Catholicism's
commandos, with their flexible manoeuverability within an unesta-
blished Church. The way in which that flexibility provided appropriate

responses to Irish Catholicism's situation as a penalised majority faith, or what Fr Flynn calls 'the exigencies of the Irish pastoral situation', can be conveyed in a review of the faculties granted by the Roman Congregation of the Holy Office to the Vicar of the Irish congregation of the Dominicans, Ross MacGeoghegan in August 1617. These special faculties included:

(1) matrimonial dispensations, dispensation of clerics from offences and of penitents from canonical penances, along with liberal provisions for granting plenary indulgences;
(2) permission to read heretical books so as to counter their contents and to publish works without observing Trent's censorship rules;
(3) permission to conduct very basic, unceremonious administration of the Sacraments and reservation of the Host, as well as to substitute the Rosary for the Office, and to celebrate Mass outdoors, underground, or in the early hours, or in the afternoon, or in front of Protestants and excommunicates.

These unusual privileges, which allowed the Dominican friars massive discretion in ecclesiastical matters and which were transferable, throughout the British Isles, 'to secular priests', represented an adaptation of rules and regulations to what remained fundamentally an emergency situation for the Church in Ireland but they also posed an actual or potential challenge to normal episcopal, canonical jurisdictions. When, in 1626, Propaganda Fide required the Irish archbishops to bring about peace between regulars and seculars in Ireland, it was not taking full account of the antagonism between these two wings of the clergy, aroused by the seculars' suspicion about the political impact on the Church at large of the regulars' freelance activities; such suspicions were revealed in the resolutions of a synod of secular priests in the province of Munster in 1634 to the effect that:

> Any doubtful or contentious privileges which might be claimed by the religious are to be jealously watched over by their respective superiors; their assemblies, too, and chapters, are to be held with secrecy ...not to alarm the government.

The resentment of the seculars, marshalled by the bishops, was probably compounded by the exceptional popular esteem that the regulars, and above all the Franciscans, enjoyed. For example, it was said to be 'almost impossible to find a lay person in Ireland who would wish to die without having been clothed in some religious habit' – a survival of a late medieval devotional cult which, with its flavour of 'mechanical', or even Pelagian, forms of popular piety, may not have accorded fully with Tridentine norms or with the anxiety of Catholic bishops to repel Protestant mockery of Catholic 'superstition'. Rivalry between bishops and regulars, which was a recurrent feature of Irish ecclesiastical politics until the victory of the episcopate in the nineteenth century, seems to have been intense during the Irish Catholic episcopal revival in the first half of the seventeenth century when, in 1609, there was a complaint that friars were invading the episcopal prerogative of admistering the Sacrament of Confirmation; in 1632 the Irish bishops wrote to Propaganda to complain about the exaggerated claims made for his order by the Franciscan provincial. In view of the remarkable popularity of the friars, not least as a result of their responsiveness to some characteristically Irish forms of piety, especially obituary rituals which reaffirmed kinship, it is all the more indicative of the strength and assurance of the Irish episcopate by the 1630s that, in the face of rivalry from the Mendicants, the bishops could complain of the way in which the Franciscans' funereal rites invaded the precedence of 'parish priests' under the bishops' jurisdiction: these were expressions redolent of confidence in canonical Catholic institutions that could not conceivably have been employed anywhere else in the two islands, not even in the more heavily recusant parts of Lancashire, at that point in time.[50]

Yet the presence and activities of regulars were far from necessarily inimical to an episcopal regime: the Cistercians returned to Ireland after 1613 with no evident damage to episcopal structures. At the same time, though, the bishop were faced with another concern, the state of their own 'diocesan' clergy. Thus, for example, Bishop Patrick Comerford of Waterford voiced typically Tridentinist complaints at an over-provision of under-motivated secular priests, leftovers from a late medieval reformist's nightmare of drones in priests' orders:

Our country is soe furnished with clergie men that ere it be longe we are like to have one against every house, so many in a poor beggarlie country that the laytie begins to frowne on us especially considering that most of the clergie are idle contentinge themselves to say mass in the morning and until midnight, playing [cards] or drinking or vagabonding.[51]

If all was not well on that front, and if Rome heard that Catholicism in Ireland was in a 'sorry state', yet Comerford's remarks show that conscious Tridentine goals for the priesthood were set and, indeed, considerable progress was made in achieving the targets that the Council of Trent had set for the Church. For example, ecclesiastical legislation passed in Drogheda and Kilkenny in 1614 aimed to make baptism a Sacrament of the Church rather than a ritual of the kin; in the 1630s Tridentine marital regulations were more strictly enforced; conferences of priests and a system of episcopal visitations were put in place. Preaching and the religious education of the laity were expensive undertakings in this 'beggarlie' land, though a surprising amount was achieved. For example, Alexander Lynch, who trained at the Irish College, Salamanca, from 1602 onwards, left the Society of Jesus on grounds of ill health and took over the running of a school in Galway, eventually making it a magnet for Catholic youth throughout Ireland and an alternative attraction to Trinity College, Dublin (1592); the Galway school was revived by the Jesuit Dr John Lynch in the 1630s.[52]

Yet such institutions as the Galway school were rare, and the major challenge facing Catholic educators was that of instilling a basic knowledge of Christian doctrine in their people, especially those of Irish speech. Works by the Jesuit-influenced secular priest Geoffrey Keating, *Eochair-Sgiath an Aifrinn* (An Explanatory Defence of the Mass) and *Trí Bhior Ghaoithe an Bháis* (The Three Shafts of Death) set out in Irish comprehensive explanations of the Real Presence, Confession and Purgatory. Related to the work of the Louvain-based Franciscans who produced Tridentine catechisms in Irish in the early seventeenth century, Keating's *Eochair-Sgiath* enjoyed a lasting popularity evident in its frequent transcription down to the mid-nineteenth century, suggesting that Keating was found useful by priests as a sermon source, while the transmission of its anecdotes into Connacht folk stories shows how his work was able to bridge Catholic faith and Irish vernacular culture, albeit through the intermediation of priests' sermons based on his books. At the same time, though, and in a society of such widespread illiteracy in both of the island's languages, iconographic representations continued to serve as didactic statements of such doctrines as the Trinity.[53]

Between the late sixteenth and early seventeenth centuries close connections had been made between Catholic faith and Irishness, not least among exiles, who are usually keen to assert their nationhood. Thus the Irish troops serving with the Spanish armies in the Netherlands acquired a distinct Counter-Reformation devotional identity, joining confraternities, saying the Angelus twice daily, abandoning bad language, observing fasts and acquiring copies of the catechism published in Irish at Louvain 'for the instruction of Irish soldiers in the doctrine of Trent'. An identification had been put in place between 'Counter-Reformation Catholicism and a growing sense of national consciousness'. Insofar as that process had also taken place within the island of Ireland, it was to produce explosive consequences in the middle decades of the seventeenth century, following the continued growth that the Catholic Church underwent during Wentworth's government between 1632 and 1640.[54]

3

CATHOLICS IN ENGLAND AND WALES, c. 1640–c.1740

England

The outbreak of the civil war initiated one of the most serious crises for Catholics in the British Isles in the whole of their post-Reformation history. The relative favour shown by Charles I to the English Catholics and their grateful response, as shown in the 'Contributions' of 1639, revived 'popery'as a live issue from 1640 onwards; fears of a 'popish plot', whipped up by the Irish rebellion of 1641 served as a coda to the mounting tension between the crown and the Long Parliament. The latter's role as the sounding board of the nation's Protestantism induced it to demand savage action against priests, with the result that eleven of these were executed in the period 1641–2. The historian Archbishop Mathew noted two points about these victims – their seniority of years (two of them were well past seventy), and the fact that 'They had lived quietly and laboriously without concealment...[A]ll were well known to the authorities who had suddenly descended upon them.'[1] In other words, for Catholics the period around the outbreak of the civil war was one of catastrophe because it brought renewed suffering on a community, and above all on its priests, that had in the preceding decades been building up a *comparatively* stable presence in England and Wales. Executions of priests apart, the sharp contrast between relative security for the recusants before 1640 and danger thereafter while tension increased as war approached can be illustrated in the misfortunes of the Spanish Embassy chapel in London which, before

1640, had provided a rich liturgical life for London recusants. However, at the time of Strafford's trial in 1641 'a great many Apprentices and loose people [,] discontented because mass was said in the Ambassador's House', threatened to pull it down and kill ambassador Cárdenas. Anti-Catholic pressure also came from the Commons, which demanded a ban on foreign embassy staff employing English priests 'under pretence of being their servants or otherwise'. The Catholic issue fuelled the mood of distrust leading up to the outbreak of civil war, a mood evident in the Militia Ordinance of January 1642 which summoned the county militias as a precaution against 'the bloody counsels of papists'. Following the outbreak of civil war in August, further executions of priests took place, and that of the Franciscan Thomas Bullater in Chichester in October 1642 reflected a mood of apocalyptic dread when 'many who were there present cryed out, that his bloud would fall upon their heads, and divers protestants also still say, that they feare the vengeance of God will lye heavy uppon this citty for the shedding of this, and other innocent blood'.[2]

Political tension may have encouraged the flourishing of a contemplative rather than activist Catholicism. Of course, in the period down to the outbreak of civil war, Catholic worship had, even in the easiest of times, to be discreet: perhaps the most significant phrase in recollections about Mass said in a Yorkshire household in the 1620s is the one that reads 'On the Sundays we locked the doors'. In such circumstances, devout reading came into its own as a religious sustenance. Amidst the political tension in the pre-civil war period, the convert Benedictine Dom Augustine Baker died in 1641. His collection of treatises published in 1657, but for the most part composed during his chaplaincy to the Benedictine nuns at Cambrai between 1624 and 1633, take us into a world of interiorist spirituality more reminiscent of the medieval mystics whom he admired than of a politically committed post-Reformation recusant community. Baker envisaged a recipient of his meditations as a female 'secular person [,] not obliged really and personally to withdraw herself from worldly conversation' but by choice 'carefully avoiding all anxiety of mind, care of multiplying riches . . . [,] vain conversations, complimental visits, feastings etc.' However, the real extent of Baker's detachment from the busy world is evident in his advice on disengagement from the duties of the mision to England itself:

Some will perhaps have a mind to take the [Benedictine] habit for that end and intent principally of going afterward into England. What miserable distractions would such a resolution cause during all the time of their abode in the convent!

The whole militant strategy, involving aggressive controversy as well as political engagement, which we associate with some Elizabethan priests, was thus abandoned by Baker, who expected more results from exemplary 'humility, modesty, and edifying conversation, but especially by the practice and teaching of internal prayer' than from the efforts of 'the most acute and cunning controvertists'. Baker's rejection of confrontation in England would probably not have characterised even the majority of his co-religionists. Even so, when the civil war came Protestant fears of the Catholics as a solid military phalanx in support of Charles I were to be shown as exaggerated – partly, no doubt, because what benefits the recusants had received from the king they paid for in the Compositions.[3]

That said, the political values of that conservative class, the recusant aristocracy, were instinctively royalist. Henry Gorse, the Jesuit chaplain to Henry Gage, who fell on the king's side near Oxford in 1645, captured the combination in this veteran mercenary of the Thirty Years War of Catholic patriotism and personal fealty to the king: Gage 'could not be won to do anything against his natural sovereign or inconsistent with the interest and honour of his nation'. A romantic saga of Catholic royalism comes from Wiltshire, where Lord Arundell commanded the force he had raised for the king while his son enlisted and his wife, with but 25 men, defended Wardour Castle against 1000 Parliamentarian troops. In Lancashire Catholic royalist militancy was even more prominent, and, writes Mr Hilton, the 'Lancashire Catholic gentry entered the war with enthusiasm and out of all proportion to their numbers': 65.5 per cent of active royalist families were Catholic, compared with 28.6 per cent of the county gentry's total being of the faith; the Catholics served bravely as well as numerously: 71 per cent of Lancashire royalist gentry killed in the civil war were Catholics. A lead was given here by Richard Viscount Molyneux, who in 1642 led against Manchester the infantry regiment he had raised. The Catholic Molyneux treated his county as a recruiting ground for the king, fought at Edgehill, Bristol and Gloucester and took part in the decisive regional engagements at Bolton and Liverpool, surviving as a royalist conspirator until his death in 1654. Like Henry Gage and his fellow-Lancastrian Richard Gerard of Bryn, Sir Thomas Tyldesley of Myerscough was a Thirty Years War professional; from the begining of the English conflict he was active in regional battles at Manchester, Whalley, Bolton and Liverpool, and in the national theatre, at Edgehill and Marston Moor. Like Molyneux, Tyldesley was an unreconciled cavalier, falling at Wigan in 1651.[4]

The spectacular military careers of the likes of Molyneux and Tyldesley drew particular, indeed, perhaps, disproportionate, attention to the role of Catholics in the civil wars in Lancashire. It was a gift to Parliamentarian propagandists that they could depict Lord Derby's royalist force as 'the Catholic army', and that they could emphasise both the dangers of a foreign Catholic invasion via the county as well as the extreme vulnerability of Protestant Manchester, 'having...multitudes of papists near unto it, and being reputed a religious and rich town...- much envied and often threatened by the Popish and malignant party'. When Derby led the recusant squires in a march on Lancaster in 1643, it was reported that 'the papists [were] rising wholly with him'.[5]

Yet, propaganda notwithstanding, there must be doubts about the real number of Catholics in arms for the king, even in England's most Catholic county. A cool-headed Parliamentarian analysis worked out something that many Catholics below the level of the top gentry and the nobility had themselves, evidently, concluded: that neutralism was the best and safest option and that lower-class recusants 'had a good ground to have been neuter in this war'. The poorer, and hence more vulnerable to recrimination, people were, the more likely they were to take the neutralist option for 'upon the meaner sort' the consequences of involvement could lie heavy. Therefore, while, at 39 per cent, the proportion of Catholics in the Lancashire royalist officer corps is undoubtedly impressive, only 21 per cent of other ranks were recusants, and that figure itself must allow for the application of various forms of pressure, from outright impressment to subtler forms of influence. In a critique of Keith Lindley's view that in none of his surveyed counties 'did the Catholics form anything more than a minority of the royalist party', P.R. Newman cites Northumberland, where 39.5 per cent of the 43 royalist commanders were Catholics, and Lancashire, where 59.7 per ent of the total were, again, recusants. However, Dr Newman's figures come from unrepresentative shires with relatively strong Catholic populations and traditions of recusant militancy, and they concern the gentry and nobility, not the entire Catholic community, which was, of course, numerically dominated by classes below the level of the gentry. If we move outside the northern shires, we find confirmation of the view that 'the majority of Catholics...remained neutral'. In Worcestershire the

Catholic Yate family of Harvington were so determinedly non-partisan that they diffidently let Charles II pass by their gates, unwelcomed by them, after the Battle of Worcester in 1651. In that county a distinction can be drawn within the Catholic rural upper class itself between a militarily active elite within the gentry and a broad base of politically and militarily disengaged poorer squires. The contrast in Worcester-shire between intense Catholic activism at the time of the Gunpowder Plot or in parliamentary elections during the first decade of the century and the detachment of many recusants in the civil wars may indicate a longer-term pattern in the direction of diffidence and opportunism: for example, the Yate family's Catholicism can be described as religious rather than political.[6]

Whether or not English Catholics were as enthusiastically involved militarily on the king's side as propaganda, or ideological stereotyping, might have depicted them as being, they had no easy time during the civil war in areas controlled by Parliament, or in the nation at large during the war's aftermath. The penalty for high treason still attached to priests ordained abroad, while the Mass remained illegal, and six priests were executed between 1643 and 1645, and four in 1646 alone. Measures to shore up Parliament's security and bolster its finances led to new raids on papists' estates, and pressure was brought to bear on them over the doctrines of Purgatory, Transubstantiation, the Real Presence and good works. Other legislation levied double taxation on former Catholic combatants, who were classed as war criminals – 'Papists . . . and such notorious Delinquents as have taken up Arms against Parliament'. In the London area the residence of recusants was severely restricted and in the city itself in 1643 the number of foreign embassy chapels where Mass was permitted was cut by half; in the following year a Commons committee of investigation was sent to investigate Catholic activities within the Spanish Embassy and in 1647 there was a real possibility of a violent attack on the premises. However, Parliament's need for Spanish cooperation to avert royalist conspiracy in the Span-ish-controlled Southern Netherlands paved the way for agreement between Spain and Parliament over the Catholic issue so that when, in 1645, Edmund Lushing was arrested at Dover, the Committee of For-eign Affairs ordered his release on the petition of Ambassador Cárdenas and on the grounds that Lushing was the ambassador's servant. Cárde-nas, the English Catholics' most effective foreign protector, indeed 'encountered almost a benevolent attitude' from Parliament. Something that normally only those English Catholics who travelled abroad would witness, the public singing of the *Te Deum*, took place at the Spanish Embassy in 1653; although the less stable years before the Restoration afforded less protection for English Catholics, the embassy chapels continued to make available a full range of the Tridentine Catholic rite.[7]

During the 1640s and 1650s, in fact, real possibilities opened up for an accommodation between the English Catholic community and the government in power. No new recusancy laws were passed and individual Catholics could be included in the terms of the 1652 Act of General Pardon, Indemnity and Oblivion. There were guarantees, under what was now in some ways a secular state, against enforced church attendance, and the opportunities, albeit restricted, for Catholic toleration are reflected by the fact that what is reputed to be England's oldest recusant register dates from Cromwell's regime, in 1657.[8]

English Catholic political thought showed itself capable of responding to the openings for toleration, in the form of a scheme put forward by the secular priest Henry Holden to procure favour for Catholics 'in exchange for some affirmation of allegiance to the new regime'. In return for an oath of allegiance to Parliament, the English Catholics would be allowed to establish 'six or eight bishops more or less', taking their titles from ancient English sees, though without (of course) their revenues. This restored episcopate, enjoying extensive independence from Rome, would, it was envisaged, deliver the allegiance of England's Catholics to its republican regime. A more theoretical accompaniment to Holden's plan was the 1655 work, *The Grounds of Obedience and Government* by Holden's mentor, Thomas White (alias Blacklo) described by Professor Bossy 'the one first-class intellect produced by the English secular clergy during the seventeenth century' and by Fr Bradley as 'a reformer of unusual power and individuality'. White's model of the recognition of the reciprocated self-interest between government and governed was captured in his dictum 'the immediate motive which the subject is to propose before his eyes in his obedience, is the good of the Commonwealth; that is, the very same motive the Magistrate ought to have in administering'. The model was of a secular state and was attacked at the time as being 'cut out of Mr. Hobbes' Leviathan', which was to say that it was derived from the secularist, amoral doctrines of political absolutism that Thomas Hobbes put forward in the *Leviathan*, published in 1651. Whether or not Holden's work was in fact indebted to Hobbes, it did provided a cogent theoretical base for the kind of plan devised by Holden for adjustment on the part of the English Catholics to living under a republic devoid of divine-right legitimation, one whose claim to authority could only be the Hobbesian utilitarian argument of *de facto*.[9]

Such options were removed from view with the end of the Republic. The year 1660 saw the restoration of an Anglican king widely suspected of having Catholic sympathies and resolved on a policy of religious toleration, set out in his pre-Restoration Declaration of Breda of April 1660. Two years later, Charles II explicitly included, in a declaration in favour of liberty of conscience for non-Anglicans

> Roman Catholics subjects of this kingdom having deserved well from our royal father of blessed memory, and from us, and even from the Protestant religion itself, in adhering to us with their lives and fortunes for the maintenance of our Crown.

Though forced by Anglican–Cavalier intransigence in 1662 to give up his plans for toleration of Catholics and Protestant Nonconformists, Charles resumed his attempt to gain toleration in 1672 with a fresh Indulgence setting out to include Catholics in an 'exemption from the execution of the penal laws, and [allow] the exercise of their worship in their private houses only'. Again these moves had to be withdrawn in the face of orchestrated opposition but evidence given in them of royal favour may have been a factor in the upswing of Catholic numbers, certainly in Lancashire, in the 1670s, despite the Privy Council's insistence in 1673 that the penal laws must be enforced: this county, Catholic England's heartland, shows an unmistakable expansion: from 5216 recusants in 1667–8 to 5782 in 1678–9 to 6206 in 1682. Fears of a popish resurgence in reaction to Charles II's second Declaration of Indulgence found expression in the first Test Act, (1673), which, by winkling Catholics out of the civil and military services as a consequence of demanding an abjuration of Transubstantiation, forced the resignation from the post of Lord High Admiral of the king's Catholic brother and heir presumptive, James duke of York; the resignation, though, also made it public knowledge, in a realm whose most widely shared feature of political culture was anti-popery, that the next king in line of succession was a professed Catholic. The dangerously high hopes nourished by some recusants, amounting to plans for a Catholic restoration, can be seen in the letters sent in 1674–5 by York's secretary Edward Coleman to Louis XIV's confessor and to the papal internuncio in Brussels planning the re-conversion of England 'which has for a long time been oppressed and miserably harassed with heresy and schism'. Thus in the years before allegations in 1678 of a 'Popish Plot' to reverse the English Reformation, militant Catholic hopes do seem to have been riding high: William Leslie, of an Aberdeenshire recusant family and ordained at the Scots College, Rome in 1647, wrote in 1677 of his vision of a Catholic 'Britain' under Charles II, flourishing

> not only in Catholic faith, in religion, piety and doctrine, far above all the other kingdoms in the whole world, as it did when we had that happiness in Catholic times to our immortal renown, fame and glory throughout the whole world,... united and joined together under our own prince.

Showing something of the same kind of optimism, a Yorkshire Catholic farmer made a will providing funds against the day 'that the Catholic religion come in'.[10]

Confidence in some recusant quarters was to run into a surge of anti-Catholicism when the Popish Plot allegations of 1678 led on to a parliamentary campaign between 1679 and 1681 to exclude Catholic York from the succession, in a crisis during which 24 Catholics, including 17 priests, were executed. The renewal of persecution created in the mind of the Lancashire recusant squire William Blundell an attitude of sectarian defensiveness: like Quakers and other Nonconformists, carefully recording the sufferings of their persecutors, he noted 'horrid judgments upon sequestrators, committee men and farmers of Catholic estates'. The English Jesuits suffered with particular sharpness, being identified in Protestant public opinion with the most violent excesses of 'popery', backed by France and Spain. Nine members of the Society were executed and 12 perished in gaol; a French Jesuit wrote that 'The name of Jesuit is hated above all else'. However, it is significant that the Jesuits, earmarked as the *political* arm of Catholicism, were targeted for attack during the Popish Plot crisis. By the 1670s 'popery' had become a blanket term of abuse for all that was politically objectionable from the viewpoint of the patriotic constitutionalist Protestant ideology of the Country tradition and the emergent Whig party. In a work that is often seen as the classic statement of Country–Whig anti-popery, Andrew Marvell's *An Account of the Growth of Popery and Arbitrary Government in England* (1677), the author did indeed indulge in standard popery-bashing: Catholicism was 'such a thing as cannot, but for want of a word to express it, be called a Religion'. He went on to attack

The Idolatry... of adoring and praying to Saints and Angels, of worshipping Pictures, Images and Reliques, Incredible Miracles and
plapable [*sic*] Fables to promote that veneration. The whole Liturgy
and Worship of the Blessed Virgin... Vestments, Consecrations,
Exorcismes, Whisperings, Sprinklings, Censings, and Phantasticalls
Rites.

However, once he had delivered himself of this routinised attack, Marvell, to whose sceptical Protestant humanism the 'ceremonyes of Juglers
and Conjurers' in Catholicism presented no intellectal threat or seduc-
tion, got on with his main task, the subject of the great bulk of his tract,
the alleged absolutism of Charles II's government within England in the
1670s. Marvell's historical recall of the political crimes of Catholicism
ground to a halt with the implausible tale of Romanist responsibility for
the Fire of London in 1666; though Catholic France represented a
terrifying international security threat, English popery in itself, whether
or not it was believed to be inspired in the direction of treason by Rome
was, it appears, perceived by Protestant publicists as less of a domestic
threat than it had been a hundred years earlier; indeed, we might even
see the Popish Plot in 1678 as a last attempt to re-invent popery as
sedition.[11]

John Bunyan also took international Catholicism less than seriously
as any longer a threat to Protestant England: in *The Holy City* of 1665 he
wrote of the 'shaking, tottering, staggering kingdom of Rome' and in
the first part of *The Pilgrim's Progress*, published earlier in the year that
the Popish Plot was alleged, he ridiculed the giant Pope, once a formidable threat in his 'younger dayes', but now 'grown so crazy and stiff in
his joynts, that he can do little more then sit in his Caves mouth,
grinning at Pilgrims as they go by, and biting his nails, because he
cannot come at them'. As a result of the Plot, political popery – but
not religious Catholicism – was briefly revived in the late 1670s and
early 1680s as the key issue in politics. However, as the political crisis
came to be resolved, the religious attack stalled. Indeed, with the final
clerical execution, that of Oliver Plunket in 1681, the bloody period of
the long penal age from the Reformation to the nineteenth century was
over. And a recovery in the fortunes of the recusants synchronised with
the pick-up in the crown's fortunes following the defeat in 1681 of the
Whig party which had promoted the 'Exclusion' of York from 1679.
Following that defeat, York returned into government in 1682 and the
results of a consequent renewal of favour to the recusants can be seen in

a drop in recusancy fines, from about £5500 in 1681 to £2000 in 1683–4 and to a mere £384 in 1684–5. In Middlesex, whereas at the height of the Exclusion Crisis, in 1679, 70 per cent of those convicted for absence from church were Catholics, after 1681 the figure was only 6 per cent, the onus of persecution shifting heavily towards Nonconformist absentees. Similarly, figures of arrested priests now tailed off – in Lancaster Castle prison in 1683 there were only two amongst the 80 inmates, while the eight lay recusant prisoners had more comfortable quarters in the town.[12]

Needless to say, the greater confidence that English Catholics were able to show in the last years of Charles II's reign was intensified when York succeeded his brother, as James II, in 1685. There was, for one thing, an extraordinary explosion of the Catholic press, covering such issues as the relationship between Scripture and tradition, the defence of Transubstantiation, and the validity or otherwise of Anglican orders. The king himself gave an example in his Whitehall chapel of liturgical spendour which was emulated in the provinces with such establishments as Birmingham's Franciscan Chapel, given a magnificent stone-laying ceremony in 1687 and opened the following year by the Vicar Apostolic Giffard as a resplendent edifice, 95 feet long and 33 wide, with pillars and a painting of the Risen Lord with Mary Magdalen. Also in the Midlands, but set up earlier, in 1684–5, the Fowler family's chapel near Baswick in Staffordshire was furnished with wonderfully rich ornamentation – pictures of Jesus and Mary, a *pietà*, St Monica, a Deposition, St Thomas Becket, St Dominic, St Thomas Aquinas, St Peter, St Mary Magdalen (the latter two saints emblematic of the Sacrament of Penance) and other saints, along with 'one triangular frame for Tenebrae', a cope and even a mitre: a range of vestments in all the liturgical colours making complete provisions for a full liturgical cycle. Even more spectacular, for its impact on non-Catholics as well as Catholics, was the recognition of Bishop Leyburn's episcopal authority as Vicar Apostolic in 1685 and the massive response, in the shape of Catholics seeking Confirmation, to his episcopal tour in 1687. In the north-east, in Swinburne in Northumberland 123 came forward for Confirmation, in Newcastle-upon-Tyne (which was to have a Catholic mayor in the last year of James II's reign) 360; in the Midlands, 422 were confirmed in Stafford and 499 in Edgbaston, while in the North-West, in tiny hamlets around Lancaster, the Vicar Apostolic confirmed 223 and 87. The recognition paid at that point in the reign to Catholic notables as a compliment to the king was shown in Lancaster in 1687 when the Anglican Bishop of Chester, Thomas Cartwright, attended Mass, in company with the Catholic judge Sir Richard Allibone. While such incidents undoubtedly both reflected and expanded Catholic collective self-assurance, Leyburn's vicariate also manifested the increasingly mature organisation of the seventeenth-century English Catholic community, as noted by Michael Greenslade.[13]

That evolving organisational articulation was also on display amongst the secular clergy below the episcopal level, for example in the Association for Staffordshire Clergy set up in 1686, as a benefit fund and a clergy fellowship designed to provide a future supply of priests and a provision of books. As one would expect from secular priests, episcopalian loyalty ('to give all obedience to our Lord Bishop whom God shall place over us') was twinned with suspicion of the regulars, reflected in a resolution 'in the sacraments to make use of our [secular] brethren and not to recommend our penitents to [regulars]'. Focused on England – on 'our own duties and our country's good' – rather than on Rome, the Staffordshire scheme envisaged the permanence of a kind of parochial and deanery structure and the model of the residential and territorial cure of souls envisaged by Trent: '[resolved] That a common prove [pastoral message] be appointed in the county and that once a month it be read to our flocks... that every penitent may know his own pastor and call for him when need require.' This drive to set up a parish-style ministry, with identified and settled congregations served by priests in regular residence and answerable to a structure of command, was shored up by a directive to priests 'not to depart any considerable distance out of the county without notice first given to the superior of it'. The professional ethos of the priesthood in the Staffordshire plan was set by the rules of the Counter-Reformation as implemented by sixteenth-century reforming bishops such as Cardinal Gabriele Paleotti of Bologna in their emulation of the diocesan reform model promulgated by Carlo Borromeo in Milan. Keynotes of the Staffordshire system were regularity of sacerdotal practice – for example,'not to say more than two masses in one day', and a sense of clerical *esprit de corps* evident in a ruling, designed 'to promote God's honour and the clergy's good', against the poaching of clients for weddings. The Borromean approach was particularly to the fore in rules for the Sacrament of Confession, in which close and sensitive pastoral care of penitents, each well known to the confessor, was expected, alongside use of the rite for purposes of instruction and moral improvement, as well as those of absolution:

To retain absolution from habitual and customary mortal sins without reasons of [i.e. 'unless there were grounds for expecting'] amendment. And this to be done with a paternal love and with great prudence, that so no fear of despair may be given....To advise...about doubtful cases and guiding of consciences.

Alongside these proto-parochial arrangements for priestly ministry in the Confessional, the Staffordshire plan demanded liturgical propriety of the highest Tridentine standard, so 'That all with one uniformity do perform the ceremonies of the church in all our functions'. The Staffordshire Association presaged a parochial, rather than missionary, Catholic Church in England.[14]

Alongside the development of the secular clergy in the direction of a diocesan priesthood, considerable progress was made in the evolution of the religious orders. James was particularly attached to the Jesuits and in 1681, thanks to his intervention, Henry Nevill petitioned to be allowed to return to England so as to contest in the Court of Exchequer sums held for the Society of Jesus. With James king, the Society expanded in such towns as Preston and Wigan, while the Franciscans established a resident mission in Warwick and the new Franciscan chapel in Birmingham received £180 worth of timber from the king himelf, plus gifts from Charles II's Portuguese Catholic widow, the dowager Queen Catherine and from other leading Catholics.[15]

The attacks on the Birmingham chapel before the end of 1688 – it was violated by Lord Delamere's troops in October and burned down by the mob in the following month – could be taken as an apt symbol of the sudden downturn in the fortunes of English Catholics with the abrupt departure of James II before the year was out: from zenith, or even hubris, to nadir in a matter of months. In the north, in Ulverston in Lancashire 'north of the Sands', where the house of the Jesuit chaplain Clement Smith 'was beset by a mob of nearly 300 men', the priest, for a while under James securely established, reverted to refugee status:

He passed the night in a little hut. At day-break he betook himself to the woods...For three months he was compelled to lie so closely hidden that he was unable even to pace about his room.

The Catholic gentry also faced a dramatic switch from power to persecution. The political ascendancy that they enjoyed in such towns as Wigan was followed by the renewal of persecution in and after the

Revolution, piling on new handicaps – exclusion from the legal profession and from inheriting or buying land, prohibitions of keepng arms or serviceable horses, disfranchisement, all, surely, forcing English Catholicism's focus ever more firmly on the Continent.[16]

The images can certainly be assembled of an English Catholicism with a European orientation after 1688 – intensifying its profile in Protestant eyes as exotic, alien, at once alluring and repellent: 'that faintly cosmopolitan character which marked the richest recusant circles in the period between [James II's] flight to St Germain and Emancipation,' as Archbishop Mathew termed it. Typical of the trend, the Worcestershire recusant Sir John Yate of Harvington escaped to St Germain and died young in Paris; Lady Mary Yate, whose mother, Abigail Yate, had been educated at the Benedictine convent in Cambrai, showed the influence of French piety in her collections of French sermons and French religious meditations; £1000 of her money went to fund a divinity chair at Douai, in French territory.[17]

The Yate family were far from alone in the orientation of their devotional life towards France. Paris was a prime Continental centre in providing a full liturgical life for expatriate recusants. The Convent of Our Lady of Syon in the French capital provided a particularly rich routine – the whole office, from matins to compline, on first-class feasts, frequently the office of Our Lady, High Masses, and requiems sung by an internationally renowned choir. At the English Poor Clares in Rouen, the rites of French baroque Catholicism, opulent and aristocratic, were on display, for example at the ceremony to mark a canonisation in 1712 which witnessed processions with banners 'followed by a hundred young maids representing various saints [who] carried in their hands crosses, palms, wheels, towns, churches, baskets of fruit...; also a Judith who held the head of Holofernes by the hair'. Sermons on that occasion were preached by an archdeacon, a bishop, an abbot and representatives of five religious orders; a 90-minute *Te Deum* was sung by a choir of 50. Nowhere in Britain, certainly not outside the embassy chapels, could one have seen the magnificence of Tridentine ceremonial on that scale; nor anywhere in England could the regular life be witnessed as the earl of Perth saw it at the Carmelite house at Hoogstraten in Brabant, in

a family of saints; everywhere in their houses you see a clearly sweet poverty, you hear no discourse but of God, you can see cheerfulness and content in every face...; and certainly it is God's spirit that conducts them in that sweet peace and joy that reigns among them.

It was also in one of those Continental convents, that of Our Lady of Syon in Paris, that the cult of James II was cultivated as a martyr and as the initiator in his realms of a Catholic renaissance destroyed by usurpers who went on to pile further agonies on the recusants – including the double land tax that endangered the financial base of entries into the conventual life:

> Holy King James, of blessed and glorious memory...was by the perfidious, undutiful and unnatural baseness and his son-in-law and nephew [William III]...dethroned and driven out of the kingdom; that detestable Prince joining with the treacherous defection of the Protestant subjects of England, and a malevolent party which were the dregs of Cromwells Vipers blood.

The prioress of the Paris house, Ann Tyldesley, of the Lancashire recusant Tyldesleys, secured a relic of James and had it exposed in the convent chapel, while *De profundis* was recited daily for the soul of the deceased king.[18]

Perhaps to mourn James overmuch was inappropriate for English Catholics – or, at least, it was to make too much of what he had achieved for his co-religionists or to deplore too stridently a contraction in their position consequent on his fall. For it is clear that a longer-term and unspectacular improvement in conditions for Catholics, especially in the provinces and in the steady evolution of their ecclesiastical structures and provisions, datable at least to the Restoration, remained largely in place following the immediate crisis of 1688–9, so that the damage, again, in the longer term, done to the prospects of the community by James's self-dethronement were less than castastrophic. We saw that James's reign witnessed the emergence of a quasi-diocesan priestly organisation in Staffordshire, but the extent to which it operated independent of short-term political factors is revealed by the Association's expansion in or after 1695, forming a kind of province which took in Derbyshire, Shropshire, Warwickshire and Worcestershire – *Institutio Clericorum Seculorum in Communi Viventium* (The Organisation of Secular Priests Living in Common, a term implying a chapter structure).[19]

The English Province of the Society of Jesus also experienced stabilisation in membership, organisation and security over the course of the seventeenth century. Apostasy had posed an acute problem for the Society, for renegades tended to know too much about its workings, but better administration of the English mission resulted in a 33 per cent decrease in apostasy from the Society in the period between the sixteenth and seventeenth centuries. The Jesuits also achieved considerable progress in the field of education, for example in Nottinghamshire, where, under the protection of the Pierrepoints of Holme Pierrepoint, 'a settled College of Jesuits and a Library of Books belonging to them and worth about a Thousand pounds', can be dated to, perhaps, the late 1660s.[20]

The recusant gentry also were assuming a greater degree of audacity, at least in more purely religious terms. The Yate family of Harvington in Worcestershire showed how politically induced misfortunes – their home was pillaged by Roundheads in 1647 and Sir John Yate had his estate sequestered for recusancy in 1651 – could be accompanied by a steady improvement in conditions for religious observance. The family sheltered the priest Humphrey Lutley until his death in 1653 and, even before the Restoration, Sir John Yate's widow boldly erected a monument to him as one who had remained '*in Sanctae Romanae Ecclesiae communione*' (in communion with the Holy Roman Church). In the post-Restoration decades the family continued to combine politicial inoffensiveness with quiet piety and the patronal protection of a little recusant community consisting of 28 (regarded by the Anglican vicar as harmless) out of Harvington's 447 parishioners in 1676. Although the Revolution temporarily disrupted the Yate family's effectiveness as patrons of recusancy within their territory, they speedily resumed a function of religious leadership from their base at Harvington. An inventory of 1696 described their chapel there, which was furnished in splendid high baroque taste: 'One carnation Indian satin vestment and Antependium laced with silk lace.' There was a library that grew eventually to 1728 volumes and an air of a pious magnificence that culminated, under Lady Mary Yate, 'the matriarch of Stuart recusancy in Worcestershire', with the endowment of Harvington as a secular mission funded with capital of £1000 to produce a priest's stipend of £25 a year; this went along with almshouses and an apprenticeship scheme which did not exclude Protestants. In Lancashire Thomas Tyldesley of Myserscough showed how a Catholic life of leisure, without the pains or pleasures of public service, could be lived – for, as the marquis of Halifax said of the recusant gentry, 'The laws have made them men of pleasure, by excluding them from public business.' Tyldesley did his rounds of touring and sightseeing, hunting, shooting and fishing, drinking and gardening, sociability, charity and undemanding piety:

to prayrs [Mass] and home to dinr. Afterwards wentt to fowling . . . and
to see Ashtons gardens . . . Alday in town [Lancaster],a bussy in
improving ye Dame garden . . . Spent with Bro Dalton, Cos. Rigby
and others at the King's Arms 1s 6d. . . . I went a-duck hunting with
3 gentlemen. Took 3 young ducks and a cute . . . . We spent 2s each,
being invited to a pig feast.

Tyldesley went to Confession from time to time ('went to X'); heard
vespers ('evening song') and sermons ('Dr Hawarden preached glor-
iously'); kept Lent and the days of fast and abstinence, not uncomplain-
ingly ('much out of order with abstaining from meat . . . Tom Carus and
his wife stayed till the Brook Lenten neeke [they broke Lent's neck –
ended the fast]); detested apostate Catholics ('Tom Carus Renegade');
expressed pious gratitude ('Blessed be the holy and undivided Trinity
for ever more, for the merciful preserving and bringing me to the age of
55 years'); enjoyed a wide circle of friends, Catholic and Protestant, and,
though he died just a few months short of having his loyalty tested in
1715, maintained a stout Jacobitism which extended to rebuking a
priest who refrained from praying for 'our Master': 'I had occasion to
chide Mr Jo Swarbrick for disloyalty.'[21]
     Tyldesley's contemporary fellow Lancashire squire, Nicholas Blundell
of Little Crosby, was in a postion to arrange for an event as resplendent
as an obituary Mass concelebrated by five priests and may have had
Benediction of the Blessed Sacrament at home: all this in contrast with
the necessarily quieter devotional styles of Nicholas Blundell's grandfather, William,whose religious life was typified in the 1660s by his
forming a small family sodality of the Rosary. Nicholas Blundell was
charitable, to the poor at large and to Catholic causes; he observed times
and seasons scrupulously and made a fuss, in the traditional manner, of
Shrove Tuesday; he was on close terms with clerics, his brother having
become a Jesuit (and his mother and sisters nuns); he went on pilgrimages to Holywell but was eirenic enough to serve as churchwarden
in Sefton parish church, whose services he could not, of course, in
conscience attend. Yet the whiff of Jacobitism led to the search of
Blundell's house and his own prudent exile in Flanders in the aftermath
of the 15, for, as Dr Walker wrote,

after the Revolution almost all the Roman Catholics espoused the
Jacobite cause, and in South-west Lancashire and the Fylde, where
Roman Catholics were especially numerous, the strength of the Stuart

cause was potentially so great that many anxious references were made to the dangers of a Roman Catholic and Jacobite rising.

Plotting was under way from the very time of the Revolution onwards and mounted by 1693, coming to a head in the planned Lancashire rising of 1694 whose Catholic leaders, from the families of Molyneux, Tyldesley, Standish, Gerard, Poole and Towneley, were tried in Manchester. Jacobite conspiracy was abetted by groups of Irish Catholics in villages of south-west Lancashire, but at the centre of Jacobite insurgency were the grievances of the indigenous recusant gentry – for, as Walker wrote, when the privations of such families are taken into account, 'one is forced to the conclusion that insurrection was practically inevitable'. The identification of Catholicism with the Jacobite threat polarised the political atmosphere in Lancashire, and above all in those parts of the county where Catholicism was most strongly entrenched, Nonconformists demanding strict application of the penal laws.[22]

The Low Church and Whig Anglican Lancashire-based cleric, Preston's Samuel Peploe voiced the fears of many over the dangers of popery, in a region where 'The best Estates in the country are in the hands of Papists. . . . and the Romish party is of late very upish'. That observation was made in 1714, when the Hanoverian Succession confirmed the power-base of the anti-Catholic Whig party whom the Catholic writer Thomas Ward chose to vilify, with a verse political satire, in an approximation to the ironic style of Dryden and written from a decidedly High-Tory viewpoint, drawing attention to the exceses of the Whigs, led by Shaftesbury in the period 1670–81:

> They vote at first the Tolerating
> Dissenters, and *Associating*
> All *Sects* and *Schisms* in the Land.
> This you may guess a Loyal Band.

Arguably, the adoption of that kind of High-Tory, anti-toleration, anti-Nonconformist rhetoric ill behoved a spokeman for Catholicism in early eighteenth-century England. Yet Catholic leaders continued to adopt ultra-Tory and Jacobite strategies rather than seek accommodation to the status quo enshrined in the Revolution Settlement, the Toleration Act and the Hanoverian Succession. Thus, when the Jacobites marched into England's most Catholic county and reached Preston in November 1715 the identification of Catholic and Jacobite was deeply rooted in reportage:

> Here they [the Pretender's army] were also joined by a great many Gentlemen with their tenants, servants and attendants, and some of very good figure in the county; but still all Papists.

On parade were the gentry chieftains of Lancashire Catholicism – Townelly, Shuttleworth, Anderton, Hesketh, Leyburn, Standish, Dalton, Tyldesley. Walker argues that this link between the Stuart cause and Lancashire Catholicism caused disastrous divisions within the Jacobite ranks, through alienating Scots Presbyterians and putting off Anglican Jacobite Tories. On the more purely religious front, extensive damage was done to Catholic centres such as the pilgrimage chapel at Fernyhalgh in Lancashire. At the same time, the recusant community lost key lay leaders – including the earl of Derwentwater, as a result of his activist Jacobitism, and the Lancashire Catholic gentry Jacobites executed in Preston. In the place of this aristocratic leadership, though, a new Catholic elite was emerging, one less laden with heroic and tragic dynastic loyalties. To take an instance, it is true that the rich coal fields of the Jacobite Lord Widdrington in the North-east were forfeited, as punishment for involvement in the '15. However, Widdrington's Catholic agents, Albert Silvertop and Joseph Dunn, worked hard to salvage for him what they could. Silvertop, in particular, the professional steward and colliery manger respected by Protestants for his solid business ability, can be taken as an archetype of 'the professional hard-headed businessman who was taking over from the old gentry'.[23]

The English Catholic community survived the '15 successfully because of low levels of active involvement in it by the majority of recusants outside the ranks of the northern gentry. Indeed, what Dr Walker wrote of English Catholics and the '45 – 'They took practically no part' in it – can equally well be applied to the great mass of recusants in 1715. While, as Dr Blackwood shows, it is true that 148 out of Lancashire gentry were Jacobites in the '15 – either rebels or non-jurors – only 762 (27 per cent) of the 2858 of Lancashire Catholics below gentry rank can be classed as Jacobites, and of those the overwhelming majority were Jacobites in opinion only, against only 157 who were Jacobites in arms. Evidently, variant patterns of Catholic activism and inactivity established during the civil wars, when the militants came from the gentry and the neutrals from the commons, had become fixed. And if Jacobite insurgency within Lancashire was concentrated heavily on the gentry, beyond the north, as Dr Haydon writes, 'Most gentry families outside Lancashire, Yorkshire, Cumberland and Northumberland would never have taken up arms against George I.'[24]

Catholic abstention on a large scale from belligerent Stuart support in the '15 may help explain the government's subsequent extraordinary leniency, when even the activists Edward Tyldesley and Richard Towneley were acquitted of Jacobite treason. For, instead of punishing the Cathoic community with a mass of new penal legislation, as had been the case after 1689, the government following 1715 concentrated on *controlling* the recusants. A new oath stressed peaceful demeanour under the Protestant Succession; it was not concerned with inner religious convictions and refrained from calling on Catholics to repudiate the *principle* of papal dispensations from oaths:

> I, AB, do promise to live peaceably and quietly under his Majesty, King George, and the present Government, and that I will not disturb the peace and tranquility of this realm...and.. .will not make use of any papal dispensation from the said oath I have taken.

What was in effect the de-politicisation of the English Catholic community as the price it paid for 'the tolerance of the Hanoverian monarchs' formed the context for Professor Bossy's 'three quarters of a century of modest growth' for the recusant body. That growth is evident particularly in the towns, including established recusant urban centres such as Preston, for whose Georgian Catholic life the diehard anti-Catholic Peploe provides us with a detailed picture:

> We have 5. or 6. Houses in this Town where the Papists meet,...: In these Houses they have Chappels deck'd with all the Popish Trinkets. They go as Publickly to their meeting as we go to Church, and on Sabbath Days they go by our Bells. One Knight is the only Priest that lives in the Town, who sometime agoe came from Ireland. There are others that come in to officiate every Sunday and Holy Day. In the country part of this parish, which is made up of 12: large Townships, there are several Preists who live among them...Since I came to Preston I have observed that a Popish Bishop one Layborn, has kept his regular Visitations, and there is not a month passes, but I am credibly inform'd, there is a great number of Popish Priests who meet in this Town, on Market Days, to consult together. There are

several good Estates in this our Parish which we are Satisfy'd serve to Superstitious Uses, but as things are we cannot tell how to come at or discover 'em.[25]

Peploe described there the expanding self-assurance of a well-established urban Catholic community which, even if it had no fixed place for Mass, and assembled in private houses, yet provided elaborately for its worship, and had a resident town 'parish priest', assisted by curates from villages in the countryside, which was itself well supplied with clergy in residence. The Vicar Apostolic Leyburn maintained a full episcopal routine, and a kind of 'chapter' met by regular appointment in Preston. Peploe went on to enumerate up to 700 Catholics within the borough, their numbers, clearly, encouraging them to behave in an ostentatious and, indeed, defiant, manner which included holding a splendid funeral in which they used the cross in the parish churchyard as a marker. One of the priests even had the 'Hardiness' to treat Peploe as if he were a ministerial colleague belonging to another persuasion and in that way discussed with the vicar the pastoral case of a young man dissatisfied with the Roman Church: 'I tell you [all] this', Peploe explained to his correspondent, 'to lett you see the Height Popery is at with us' – though he was also quick to point out how handicapped the Church of England was in its battle with popery by its own institutional rigidities: 'I have but one chappel [of ease] in this great Parish, and that but slenderly provided for.'[26]

The picture the vicar of Preston gave of the solid entrenchment of Catholicism in early eighteenth-century Preston may be compared, on the wider canvas of Lancashire, with the scenario revealed by the research of Dr Blackwood, who counts 3000 Catholics in the county in 1715, their areas of highest concentration being, in diminishing order, the hundreds of West Derby (around Liverpoool), Amounderness (around Preston), Leyland (south of Preston), Blackburn (in the east), Salford (Manchester) and Lonsdale (in the north and across Morecambe Bay). The patterns evident there were by the eighteenth century extremely well established, concentrating the pockets of Catholicism, as had been the case since the Reformation, in south and west Lancashire, the Ribble Valley and the Fylde, and the hinterlands of Preston, Wigan and Liverpool. Equally well established was the tradition of gentry dominance, for 5.6 per cent of the recusants were of the gentry, compared with 1.6 per cent of the overall Lancashire population. Patronal patterns were also anchored in tradition. In a typical arrangement a township might have at least one resident Catholic gentry household to provide leadership to a clientage of non-gentry recusants. In fact, Claughton-on-Brock, north of Preston, had no fewer than seven Catholic gentry, and Brockholes, in the same district, four, with 56 other Catholics. A further legacy of the patterns built up during the seventeenth century, when the Catholic social elite increasingly put their sons into the priesthood, was the extension of gentry patronage over the small rural communities through the provision of priests from Catholic squires' families. The Brockholes family of Claughton-on-Brock can be taken as an archetype of Lancashire gentry Catholicism, royalist and Jacobite. Of the six children of John Brockholes, the eldest died of his wounds from the Battle of Preston in 1715, but three became priests; of these, Roger, born in 1682, was trained at the English College, Rome and, ordained in 1708, settled down to a long priestly service within his family's sphere at Claughton, dying there in 1742. Elsewhere in the north-west the vital need for a network of household chapels to sustain a mission was evident in the career of the 'diligent and laborious missionary', Thomas Roydon, who between 1699 and 1718 rode the 'Westmorland Circuit', linking Mass-centres at which vestments were inscribed with the Circuit's initials. Robert Stephenson of Dodding Green north of Kendal set aside £1000 for the support of a priest to serve a cluster of neighbouring Mass-centres. Stephenson's generosity culminated in the transfer of Dodding Green itself to Roydon, who settled there in 1718, using it as a base for his circuit as far afield as Brough and Appleby in Westmorland. A further example of the expanding scope of northern gentry Catholic philanthropy is the establishment in 1725 by the Lancashire gentleman John Shireburne of six almshouses at Ribchester in the Ribble Valley for a school teacher and 'poor old single women or widows professing the Roman Catholic religion'; carefully restored, the lovely almshouses are still in use today, eloquent testimony to an extraordinary sense of confidence in a stable future for an eighteenth-century Lancashire Catholic community of considerable size. Within the wider north-west, the Isle of Man was opened up as missionary territory in the 1720s, though the Irish or Scottish friar 'Allesio Dondale', who reported to Propaganda Fide enthusiastically on his progress on the island in 1727, revealing survivals of pre-Reformation patterns of observance: 'They fast in Lent and keep the vigils and the days of abstinence, and . . . retain many of our ceremonies . . . , conducting processions on Our Lady's feast day. They bless the fruits of the field.'[27]

Dr Blackwood indicates that styles and patterns within a north-western Catholicism that was, traditionally, rural and gentry-led, socially, financially and, to a degree, sacerdotally, were changing even in the early eighteenth century, and all the more rapidly with the massive social changes that hit Lancashire from the second half of the eighteenth century onwards. For one thing, an autonomous artisan Catholicism was springing up, for example among the weavers of Walton-le-Dale near Preston, with their two resident priests. Brindle, with 55 recusants, Little Plumpton with 67 and Samlesbury with 95 provide further instances of non-seigneurial recusancy in Preston's hinterland. The social spectrum of this 'plebeian' Catholicism was varied and becoming more so. The proportion of yeomen, though still only 15 per cent of the total, was rising, while the largest single group was made up of farmers and husbandmen, with labourers and servants a lesser element. The continuing rural location and occupational orientation of the community, and its profile as a social 'alliance between the gentry an the lower orders' represented links with the past, but pointing to the future was the emergence of urban professionals, in the medical profession.[28]

Outside Lancashire there is evidence of growth, of social diversification, of urbanisation and of stabilisation in conditions within the eighteenth-century English Catholic community. In this period for which Professor Bossy estimates a 30 per cent increase in Catholic numbers, the rate of conversions was brisk and even the unexcitable Vicar Apostolic Bonaventure Giffard commented on the 'daily increasing number of persons coming into the church', while another priest remarked on 'the incredible success we have had in bringing proselytes of all ranks into our communion'. This conversionary expansion, Dr Duffy reports, was taking place, not in the old rural centres but in the towns, where Catholicism had an appeal within an expanding middle class. In Birmingham the Franciscan Randolph, abandoning a dream of a time when it would please 'God to convert this nation', re-grouped his congregation in secluded Edgbaston, which remained its base for another hunded years. In just the few years between 1693 and 1696 getting on for 57 converts were recorded around Birmingham. The urban congregation was becoming increasingly independent of and physically distanced from the gentry-supervised recusant nuclei of rural Warwickshire and Staffordshire. Catholic schooling began at Osmotherly in the 1680s but shifted its focus into Birmingham between 1716 and 1720. In Walsall, where the Purcell family provided funds for a priest to say Mass 'for all the poor Catholicks . . . in the neighborhood . . .', as well as trusts for apprenticeships and schooling, Catholicism also throve, amidst a dispersed maze of Anglican chapels of ease whose confusing territorial attachments provided ready-made excuses for absenteeism – in favour of attendance at Mass-centres; in that politically and socially polarised industrialising area, in which Walsall borough, and especially its entrepreneurial elite, was tarred with Whiggish Presbyterianism, Catholics enjoyed the reputation, highly acceptable to the local High Tory lower-class populace, of unswerving Stuart royalism, fed by golden memories of aiding Charles II after Worcester. With industry, population was filling up the former woodlands and there was no reason that the Catholic element should not keep up with overall demographic increase in the area.[29]

Within the Midlands the Jesuits were also making strides, and by 1718 were able to mount an audacious publicity offensive from Holbeck in Nottinghamshire to which the fathers offered 'the free liberty of the People of the Neighbourhood of the place to come at any time to their prayers and devotions'.[30]

Catholicism in London showed particularly clear signs of stabilisation, growth and the establishment of a regular schedule of services in known locations. The Catholic middle class of the metropolis were the patrons of the provision of worship: in 1737 London's zealously anti-Catholic Anglican Bishop Gibson received a report that 'Mr. Yates in Southampton Street has Mass said in his house every day, as also has Mrs. Conquest in the same street. Mr. Talbot in Bloomsbury Square – his house swarms with priests'. Preaching was to the fore in the repertoire of this West-End Romanism: 'Mrs. Ems in Eagle Street has preaching in her house. At the "Hand and Pen" in Little Queen Street, they have constant preaching in their house.' Some of London's vast number of public houses offered Catholic sermons; indeed, the future leader of the community, Richard Challoner, served an apprenticeship in hostelry homiletics: 'At the "Sign of the Ship, called the Royal Ann"...between Holborn and Lincoln's Inn Fields, one Chaloner, who lives with a lady in Queen Square, preaches on Sundays to Men only and on Thursdays to Women only.' Emphasis on sermons was almost certainly linked to the rate of conversions, which in London was brisk, Catholic female employers being noted for influencing servants: one of these, a linen-draper, first encouraged the conversion of a boy and then proceeded to finance his studies for the priesthood at St Omers. Within this metropolitan Catholicism, which had so many of the social features of the Nonconformity from which converts such as the devotional writer John

Gother had come, and which seemingly loved preaching as much as the Dissenters did, the cyclical pattern was based on weeks rather than seasons, with Sunday or weekday sermons separately for men and women and a perceptible stress on the Sabbath rather than the feastday. The Mass, though, was central, and a vernacular literature to read alongside the celebration of the liturgy and to follow the scriptural readings was Gother's special contribution to English Catholicism in the first half of the eighteenth century and beyond. Indeed, Gother made a kind of breakthrough in fostering a degree of congregational participation in the sacrifice offered by the priest. Publishing figures indicate clearly that his publications in the popularisation of the order of Mass and of the lectionary secured an eager readership: *Instructions and devotions for hearing mass* was reprinted in 1705, 1712, 1721, 1725, 1729, 1730, 1740, 1753 and 1767. The readings of the proper of the Mass were rendered in *The collect, epistles and gospels that are read throughout the whole year, . . .* ; alongside this, with *Instructions and devotions for the afflicted and sick, . . .* and above all with *Instructions for confession and communion and confirmation*, reprinted 15 times, in its variants, between its first appearing in in 1702 and 1796 (and added to *Instructions and devotions for hearing mass*), Gother made a major contribution to the emergence of a literate and liturgically and devotionally instructed Catholic community. In London, this kind of Catholic society received expression in the emergence of a sodality life, with at least one London group staying on after Mass.˙ In industrious London, the emphasis in mores fell on orderly patterns which lent themselves to bourgeois diligence and an appreciation, as Professor Bossy says, of 'regularity, rationality and work'. Gother's *Instructions for particular states and conditions of life*, first published in 1689 and reprinted, for example in 1718, upheld a strong work ethic, perhaps transposed from Gother's own Calvinist background but ingeniously converting the Calvinist concept of the calling into a conceit of a religious order of the Church, the order of 'laborious and working Christians', committed to what we might term 'inner-worldly asceticism':

> a Kind of religious Order, in which God himself has instituted their Rule: He has expressly commanded that they shall eat their Bread in the Sweat of their Brows; and if, in Submission to this Command, they undertake their Work, it is certain that their daily lives will be as much an Act of Religion and Obedience, as what those do,who live in a Cloyster, and observe the Rules of their Founder.[31]

Lots of 'laborious and working' Catholics were to be found, far away from the periwig-makers, apothecaries and linen-drapers of Blooms-bury, among the 'miserably poor and ragged' Irish who heard Mass in Shoreditch in 1735 'in a private Mass-house in a little ale-house... where near an hundred people were got together in a garret'. Even in this congregation 'some few were well dressed' and in a position both to own and read Mass-books, but this Irish community was especially vulnerable to raids. Indeed, exposure to such risks remained a feature of the lives of even the highest ranking of English Catholics in the first half of the eighteenth century, and Jacobite scares were, of course, likely to exacerbate the danger. The Duke of Norfolk himself was arrested in Bath at the time of the High Anglican Jacobite Atterbury Plot in 1722 and in 1745 Bishop Yorke, coadjutor to the western Vicar Apostolic, had to flee the Somerset town when a forged letter was disclosed in which he was thanked for assisting the Stuart cause. However, and despite spas-modic Jacobite panics, the western spa provided examples of the accept-ability of a fashionable and aristocratic Catholicism within eighteenth-century English society. Catholics came to Bath, on the whole, for con-viviality rather than conspiracy; the corporation, whose members were heavily involved in the catering trade, accommodated their religious requirements, and the town provided a marriage mart for a nationwide recusant gentry and nobility whose marital choices were restricted in their regions by religious strictures. Through the operation of the Bath marriage market, in 1709 the daughter of the 'red lettered' [Catholic] Sir Nicholas Sherburne, 'of the North' and worth £3000 p.a., married the Duke of Norfolk, who 'lives great both in table and equipage'. Bath Catholicism added literary to social distinction with a visit by the Catho-lic poet Alexander Pope, acclaimed by the Abbey bells. Early Hanover-ian Bath became acquainted with the stylishness of the wealthiest members of a class that was, of necessity, leisured. The Bath community's leading lights were the Norfolks, Arundells, Fitzherberts, and Jerning-hams, and it was supported spiritually by the Benedictines, whose house was conveniently placed between the baths and the Pump Room. Gen-erous gifts were made from Bath to English Catholic religious institu-tions on the Continent, though for the sake of concealment one of the best known of the colleges became a person, 'Mr. Dowaie'.[32]

Concealment and discretion were the preconditions of what Arch-bishop Mathew termed a 'general slight lessening of hostility' towards Catholics in England in the first half of the eighteenth century. When the War of the Austrian Succession broke out in 1740, Britain's Austrian

Catholic ally against France, the devout Maria Theresa, became a 'national heroine', while in fashionable society Catholic celebrities such as the Irish actress Miss Ambrose were idolised. Significant shifts took place in institutionalised anti-popery. The Society for the Propagation of the Gospel set about stemming Catholicism, closing loopholes in the penal laws and drafting bills to prevent proselytising. It is significant, though, that a voluntary society had to assume these tasks that belonged properly to Parliament itself and to the magistracy and constabulary. It is also noteworthy that the SPG pledged itself to counter Catholicism 'without Persecution and violence', and, indeed, that eventually, even its anti-popish zeal waned.[33]

Dr Haydon concludes that, on the national level, 'the period between the Atterbury plot and the Forty-five...turned out to be one in which English Catholics' difficulties lessened'. Much of the progress made or mooted depended on distancing Catholics from Jacobite involvement. Although a promising scheme for an acceptable Oath of Allegiance had to be abandoned, the negotiations leading up to it, along with opposition from within Parliament to a new tax on Catholics proposed in 1723, showed that statesmen and parliamentarians were coming round to realising the essential tolerability of a non-Jacobite Catholicism. Dr Duffy confirms that pragmatism was coming to characterise the political thinking of an increasing number of English Catholics, all the more so the further they were away from the centres of pious and sentimental Jacobitism on the Continent. Sir Robert Throckmorton led a group of fellow recusants in the direction of receiving the Oath of Allegiance, if only as a way of avoiding the double land tax. Even before the '15, the Duke of Norfolk was campaigning for a statement of Hanoverian allegiance that would make possible the conferment on the recusants of the benefits the Nonconformists received under the Toleration Act. The elderly Vicar Apostolic Giffard prevaricated over the plan for an accommodation, which failed, but, following the rising, efforts continued 'to establish the Englishness of English catholic hearts', and from 1716 plans for a new relationship between the Catholic community and the crown were resumed by two members of eminent Catholic landed families, the Vicar Apostolic of the Midland District, John Talbot Stonor, and the priest Thomas Strickland. At one point the Vatican itself endorsed Catholic 'fidelity and intire Obedience to the present Government'. A major obstacle to such schemes was the virtual inevitability of Parliament's refusing to repeal the existing anti-Catholic legislation. The withdrawal of the Duke of Norfolk and his associates from the

Stonor–Strickland plan damaged it, as did Rome's ultimate adhesion to the Stuarts.[34]

In a longer term, a number of political factors worked in favour of relaxation for the conditions for Catholics. Under George I, who was formed, as Archbishop Mathew showed, in the sceptical atmosphere of the Electress Sophia's court, where political and dynastic interests were preferred above precise religious considerations, the royal family was on friendly terms with the Catholic Norfolks. The long Walpolean peace with France allowed the French to bring gentle diplomatic pressure to bear to ameliorate the position of the recusants. In the provinces, Dr Haydon notes, 'life for the Catholic population gradually became more relaxed', as local authorities responded to the government's more benign attitudes that were motivated by the need to placate the French. In fact, even the cooling of Anglo–French relations following 1731 did little to reverse what was an extensive relative tolerance in practice – shown, for example, in the flow of pilgrims to Holywell, in the open work of priests in Gloucestershire and in the indulgence extended to Catholic gentry in Yorkshire in return for their not opposing ministerial candidates in elections. High Anglican Jacobites saw recusants as ideological kindred spirits, and in Warwickshire the Tory-dominated grand jury took exception to indictments of papists. There was also growing Anglican clerical forbearance, especially among those High-fliers who hated the Toleration Act for permitting the growth of those they regarded as their real foes, the Nonconformists.[35]

To set against these favourable factors we must realise how deeply entrenched popular anti-popery was in Georgian England. As the easing in conditions encouraged conversions to, or open profession of, Catholicism, these raised once more the spectre of 'the Growth of Popery' which gave a 'general & just alarm' to Dissenters such as Philip Doddridge, the influential Independent minister of Northampton, and to the Nonconformists who held a series of London lectures on the subject in 1735. At about that point in the mid-1730s, the numerical strength that London recusancy had been accruing from Irish immigration resulted in anti-Catholic riots. Persecution of Protestants in France and Austria and the alleged cruelty of the Spanish towards Captain Jenkins in 1731 gave renewed nourishment to the anti-popery long sheltered in the national psyche. In the year, 1738, that Captain Jenkins' case came before Parliament, fuelling demands for war against Spain, French actors were attacked in London, 'almost everybody having the greatest abhorrence of papists coming over to a Protestant country to pick Protestant pockets'. Indeed, the Sardinian Embassy chapel itself was violated by a mob who 'not only ridiculed the divine service then performing...but struck several persons who were at their devotions'.[36]

However, such actions were extra-legal, and indeed illegal, and although Bishop Gibson in London encouraged anti-Catholic offensives, the law was becoming slow to act, often leaving the initiative, as we have seen, to the voluntary SPG. When London magistrates acted on 'Complaint' to enforce Elizabethan legislation against the possession of liturgical objects, having little idea of the significance of the items they were supposed to seize (the constables found 'a Surplice, a Toga'), they refrained from examining the couple charged with possession of the goods, simply tendered the new declaration of allegiance,' which they both took, and dismissed the pair, though detaining the mysterious 'Relicks' 'made use of in the Romish Superstition'. In an age of reason, Catholicism had become an arcane cult rather than a threat to national survival. Attendance at Mass itself was coming to be regarded as at best a misdemeanour, of approximately the gravity of, say, 'disorderly smoaking and tippling in time of divine service', and when constables came upon the group of poor Irish at Mass in Shoreditch, they took the names of the terrified worshippers and let them go as if they were drinkers at an after-hours club – the mildness of British practice in these matters being contrasted with Continental Catholic severity.[37]

Thus, in the years before the question of English Catholicism's political tolerability was once more raised acutely in a Jacobite rising, considerable progress had already been made in the construction of a *modus vivendi* between the recusant community and the Protestant state.

Wales

Between the seventeenth and eighteenth centuries Welsh Catholicism went into a steeper decline and after the Restoration 'entered its sunset years...largely unmilitant in character, a "sleepy, dust-laden", unreflecting allegiance to an old faith', owing 'little to Jesuit evangelism and...far removed from the crusading passions of the Counter-Reformation'. There was no catastrophic collapse, only a concentration of the faith into the south-east corner of the Principality – a situation not of 'a few Catholics thinly spead over thirteen counties, but [of] large areas from which Catholic traditions had utterly vanished, alongside one small district [part of Monmouthshire] where Catholic practices never ceased to be as familiar as anywhere in England'. The defection from the Welsh recusant community of landed magnates, and especially of the Somerset family, earls of Worcester and later dukes of Beaufort, did not destroy recusancy in its south-eastern redoubt. However, the formula by means of which Welsh Catholicism had clung on to life since the Reformation – dependence on small gentry, concentration on largely rural and agricultural locations and resistance to change across a broad front – was not one designed for adaptation to the massive transformation of Welsh society through the arrivals of Methodism and of industrialisation in the later eighteenth and early nineteenth centuries.[38]

In 1642 around 17 priests were needed to provide for Monmouthshire Catholics, while 19 Jesuits were at work in Wales as a whole. Abergavenny in Monmouthshire was, perhaps, Wales's most Catholic town: where 100 people would hear Sunday Mass and only 40 attend the parish church; where in the early part of the seventeenth century a Catholic taught at the grammar school; where a town recorder was related to priests and a vicar came of Catholic stock; where the Gunther family offered protection and Thomas Gunther sheltered the priest and martyr Philip Evans in 1678. The town still had 71 recusants in 1706 and 66 in 1719, and the area betwen Abergavenny and Monmouth remained the heartland of Welsh Catholicism. The pilgrimage centre at Skirrid in Monmouthshire focused a devotion with distinctly pre-Tridentine sounding resonances, even though it received a papal endorsement in 1676: the mountain there was reputed to have been split when Christ died. Monmouth itself also had a strong and growing Catholic presence and, for the county as a whole, it was believed, with considerable exaggeration, that half the population were recusants: a more realistic figure would be closer to 20 per cent, though in 1676 that was only a few dozen short of the total of Nonconformists in the county and, as Dr Jenkins has written, in around that year 'the public administration of the shire seems to have been honeycombed with Papists and Papist partisans'. Thus Catholicism was, inevitably and especially in the elections for the Exclusion parliaments between 1679 and 1681, an acute political issue in the county. Even though in Monmouthshire the 'quietly-practised, inoffensive Catholicism ... of ... neighbours and relations' was normally indulged, the national political crises of the Popish Plot and the Revolution adversely affected the county's Catholicism: Jenkins suggests that numbers fell from about 800 to around 208 in the 1690s, while following a disastrous raid on their base at Cwm the Jesuits' establishment declined from about 20 to four or five in 1690. However, the period following the Revolution was one of only temporary crisis for Monmouthshire Catholics, and by 1706 their numbers were back to 715, subsequently holding fairly steady at 610 in 1719: in the latter year, in two neighbouring groups of parishes recusants amounted to as many as 8 and 4.5 per cent of the overall population. As late as 1773 Monmouthshire still contained 475 recusants and the Jesuits' numbers recovered to 12 in that latter year. Gentry protection survived, too; for example, the Powell family at Perthîr provided a base for the Western Vicariate Apostolic set up in 1688, and residence for Bishop Prichard until 1750.[39]

In the Monmouthshire Catholic gentry's pecking order, below the middle ranks – the echelon from which James II hoped to recruit a Catholic political class – were the urban notables and lesser squires, traditionally clients of the Worcesters; these headed the households which provided Mass-centres and harboured such priests as the Popish Plot martyrs John Lloyd, Philip Evans and David Lewis; the squires in this social stratum, with their annual incomes in the range of £10–17, could be considered gentry only by the standards of Wales's, or of Monmouthshire's, 'backward, undeveloped and poor agricultural society'; however, families such as the Joneses of Llanarth, the Milbournes of Clytha and the Gunthers of Abergavenny enjoyed, regardless of their relative poverty, inherited respect in the little communities in which they resided: they gave the lead to their tenants, influenced notaries and retailers and, largely excluded from public office, devoted attention to the needs of the Catholic community. For as long as Monmouthshire retained, as it did for most of the eighteenth century, its traditional profile of a rural and closed society, the lesser gentry provided a source of strength and helped the recusant community to survive the defections and extinctions of the greater Catholic dynasties, the Worcesters, the Abergavennys, and the Morgans of Llantarnam.[40]

Below gentry level, smaller freeholders and craftsmen formed a social base for the Monmouthsire recusant community: in the Skenfrith hundred the 300 Catholics included, besides 28 (minor) gentry, six farmers, 36 labourers, three innkeepers and skilled trades and service workers; there was an incipient professional element, represented by the Beauforts' Catholic agent, Edward Mornington. Dr Guy has detected an attitude of underlying dissidence amongst these strata, irritated as they were by tithes. Monmouthshire Catholicism was also quite autonomous in its organisation, tending towards 'congregational' structures, having survived without a bishop for 60 years before the establishment of a Vicariate Apostolic. Of necessity, the community's worship was simple and, although they conformed for purposes of marriages, they were 'Papists', yet very far from italianate, hardly ever, for example, going on pilgrimages to Rome. Nor were they necessarily invisible in eighteenth-century politics in the county, and the religious issue flared up with the election as town clerk of Monmouth of the Beaufort protégé and suspected Catholic Halfpenny; in the county town, though, where the Catholic chapel was 'as publicly resorted to as the established church', Halfpenny survived in his office, with the backing of the burgesses; indeed, Thomas Belchier, from a Catholic family,was four times mayor of Monmouth.[41]

The Welsh language remained strong in Monmouthshire, including the more Catholic east of the county, in the seventeenth and eighteenth centuries and, indeed, may, as in neighbouring Glamorgan, have undergone a territorial recovery: in fact, English was so poorly understood by some that Anglican prayers in it were regarded as charms. Catholicism could still be well integrated with Welsh language and culture, as was the case with the Popish Plot victim, the Abergavenny-born Jesuit David Lewis. Known as *'tad y tlodion'* (father of the poor), Lewis preached in both Welsh and English. In his devotional work, *Allwydd neu Agoriad Paradwys i'r Cymry* (*Key or Opening of Heaven to the Welsh*,1670), John Hughes (1615–86) also showed how Catholic piety and Welsh literature could be combined. Yet over the course of time, Catholic religious provisions did not keep up with the persistent strength of the Welsh language in Monmouthshshire, and the Welsh writings of the Benedictine William Pugh – his translation of the Jesus Psalter and his catechism, *Crynodeb o'r Athrawiaeth Gristnogawl* (*Précis of Christian Teaching*) – circulated only in manuscript. Dr Guy concludes that 'Welsh-speaking Catholics...were spiritually starved to death....The Church in Monmouthshire failed its people'. Though the language kept its hold, the old Monmouthshire entrenched rural recusancy was increasingly under threat from the commercial, demographic and cultural lure of Bristol.[42]

Elsewhere in Wales, the Catholic story is one of long-term attrition, numbers in the four Anglican dioceses tumbling from 1062 in 1676 to 750 in the 1770s. Yet the gentry supplied priests, including the Vicar Apostolic Matthew Prichard, along with other priests from such families as the Turbervilles and the Scudamores; in the north, the Mostyns, guardians of the shrine at Holywell where James II prayed for a son in 1687, gave three nuns, and a priest who served in Wigan. The Glamorgan Catholic gentry could be politically activist: in the height of the Tory Reaction Richard Carne of south Glamorgan 'discovered' a Welsh variant of the radical Whig 1683 Whig Rye House Plot and three Carne brothers 'served as enthusiastic Catholic justices under James II'. The Carnes' crypto-Catholic allies, the Stradlings, adopted a strong Tory line: Sir Thomas Stradling purged Cardiff's Whig corporation during the Tory Reaction of the earlier 1680s. Both Sir Thomas Stradling and Richard Carne went on to develop royalist military careers, though in the eighteenth century the Carnes, along with their Glamorgan neighbours the Turbervilles, conformed to the Established Church. Incidents such as the arrest of priests at Holywell in 1716 showed the vulnerability of the Welsh recusants. Indeed, in the course of the eighteenth century Catholicism increasingly lost the battle for Welsh hearts and minds. Charles's Edwards's adaptation of the *Book of Martyrs* in Welsh injected fear of popery into the national psyche, a syndrome that was given even stronger currency in Thomas Jones's best-selling prophetical almanacs and also in the flurry of anti-Catholic literature at the time of the '15, when the Welsh writer Jeremy Owen asked 'Is it possible for us to forget all their [the Papists'] massacres...in which they have slain thousands...?' Further millenarian prophecies promising the downfall of the papacy helped to ensure, even before the arrival of Methodism, that the destruction of '*yr hen ffydd*', the old faith of Wales, was well on its way to accomplishment.[43]

4

CATHOLICS IN SCOTLAND AND IRELAND, c.1640–c.1745

Scotland

The situation for Catholics in Scotland between the mid-seventeenth and the mid-eighteenth centuries was bleak, though perhaps not entirely so: established communities continued to exist in Banffshire and Aberdeenshire and there was continuity – indeed, as we shall see, remarkable growth – in the Highland mission; a few Scots abroad were converted from time to time, attracted, perhaps, by the glamour of Continental Catholicism on display in Paris or Rome; some were per- suaded that, although the first, Knoxian, Reformation might have been a necessity, the second, Presbyterian and Covenanting variant was not.

Before the late 1620s, Scots Catholicism was, relatively speaking, sidelined as an issue in the nation's politics, though John Ogilvie was hanged in Glasgow in 1615 for alleged treason. In 1625 James VI alleviated the penal measures against recusants in celebration of Prince Charles's marriage, and Scottish anti-popish nerves were sensitised, in an anticipation, perhaps, of the trouble that would brew between Charles as king and his Scottish subjects over religion. However, once he was king, Charles's attitude to Catholics was, initially at least, severe and therefore agreeable to Scots generally. New and sweeping powers of investigation of priests and lay Catholics were introduced in 1627 and in 1628 a regional campaign began, swooping on the entrenched Roman- ism of the Huntly domains in Aberdeenshire. 'The objective', writes Maurice Lee, 'was to drive priests, especially Jesuits, and Catholic laity

out of the country.' However, the fall from royal favour in 1633 of the
'bitter persecutor of the Catholics', the earl of Menteith, opened up an
era of tolerance, symbolised by the favour in which the papal emissary at
Charles's court, George Con, a Scot, was held. Subsequently, the
attempted imposition of Anglican ritualism on Scotland by Charles I
and Laud with the new prayer book in 1637 involved 'popery' in the
national detestation of ritualism and evoked George Gillsepie's *Dispute
Against the English Popish Ceremonies* in that year, expressing the Scottish
belief that English Arminianism and popery were 'essentially compati-
ble'. Therefore, the National Covenant of 1638 in defence of Scottish
Calvinism arose from the 'vitriolic anti-catholicism of the Scots'. Dread
of popery, and in particular fear for the safety of the 50 000 or so
Scottish Protestants who had emigrated to Ulster since 1603, was
further inflamed by the Irish Rebellion of 1641: 10 000 Scottish troops
were to be poured into Ulster from April 1642 to suppress the Catholic
rising. The conversion of opposition to Charles on both sides of the
Tweed into an alliance against him between the Scots and the English
Parliament was enormously facilitated by shared anti-popish grievances,
such as the presence of papists in Charles's army, and helped produce
Parliament's aceptance of the Solemn League and Covenant in 1643.
Following the Scots' re-engagment to the Stewart monarchy in the
person of Charles II in 1649 Cromwell's regime in Scotland established
in 1651 saw no diminution of anti-Catholic action; in 1656 the death
penalty was proclaimed for any priest found in Scotland from the Sunday after the issue of the decree, and JPs were ordered to take securities
from lay Catholics. After all these disturbances, the Restoration in 1660
ushered in a reign in which much of the political attention within the
religious sphere was taken up in the crown's campaign to restore epis-
copacy and its linked contest with radical Covenanters.[1]

On James VII's accession in 1685, Scottish Catholic hopes, even for a
national reconversion, ran high in some quarters, though it was James
himself who at that juncture counselled caution and the need for activists to 'do their business quietly and calmly at the beginning otherwise
they may undoe all'. However, by October 1686 James had ordered all
Scots priests abroad to return home; a conference to plan the re-establishment of Catholicism, including the appointment of a bishop, was
held in April 1687 and by the time the future Vicar Apostolic Thomas
Nicholson arrived in November to occupy that role, the operation of
the penal laws was suspended and James had committed himself to
toleration, though guaranteeing the rights of the Kirk. With the Lord

Chancellor, Perth, a Catholic, the practice of the faith was openly displayed in the capital: a Catholic press was set up, and a Jesuit school
established in Holyrood House; sung Mass was celebrated in November
and December 1687. However, 'there were few places more bitter
against catholiques' than Edinburgh, where the 'Jesuits schools made a
great deal of talking amongst the people and incensed them extreamly'.
James's fall revealed the full extent of Scotland's anti-popery, when in
the month of the king's departure, December 1688, rioters sacked the
Chapel Royal and the king's own chapel and, as Nicholson reported,
'One of [the rioters] went in front with a great crucifix, surrounded by a
crowd of children and women carrying lighted torches and shouting for
joy.' It is true that, as Dr Doran says, James's maintenance of a 'lower
profile' would have prevented anti-popery from reaching 'the
hysterical peaks it did', but it remains the case that anti-Catholicism,
lodged deep in popular culture, needed little activation. The Lowlands
manifested in fact a seemingly ineradicable anti-Catholicism, where, in
'whyggish' Galloway the Benedictine James Bruce found 'the commons...much averse from poperie', while 'at Glasgow there was...a
great noyse when Father Leslie opened up a kynd of private chapel
there'.[2]

    However, if the south was overwhelmingly Protestant, the situation
north of the Highland line, producing now both a 'Protestant *Gaidhealtachd*' (Gaelic-speaking zone) and a 'Catholic *Gaidhealtachd*', provided a
more promising range of opportunities for a Catholic mission. By the
mid-seventeenth century, although the *Gaidhealtachd* had fewer – three
or four – priests than the Lowlands, with 15, it sheltered many more
Catholic lay people – about 12 000, compared with the south's 2000 or
so – and around 85 per cent of Scotland's recusants were living in the
Gaelic zone. When Bishop Nicholson toured the north-west in 1700, he
found about a dozen priests at work. In 1712 the Vicar Apostolic Bishop
Gordon set up a minor seminary in the western mainland north of
Ardnamurchan and Moidart. The disappearance of this institution following the '15 (it was subsequently re-founded in Banffshire) should be
seen as part of the crisis for north-western Catholicism in the aftermath
of the rising, as it was squeezed by a drive both to modernise and to
Protestantise the Highlands – or, as the secretary for the Scottish Society
for Promoting Christian Knowledge put it, to eradicate the inhabitants'
'Ignorance, their Inclination to follow the Customs, Fashions and
Superstitions of their Forefathers.' The attempt to encourage a move
on the part of those 'who can speak only Gaelick towards English' in

itself fostered emigration to centres of work for servants. Propaganda Fide responded to this campaign of de-culturation with the establishment in 1727 of a new Vicariate Apostolic expressly for the *Gaidhealtachd*, its first Vicar Apostolic, Hugh Macdonald, being consecrated in 1731. A period indicating some promise, with, once more, about 12 priests serving well-defined areas within the Highlands and Islands, was to end in the disastrous involvement of several priests in the '45, with 'catastrophic' consequences for Highland Catholics.[3]

The religious orders remained the arrowheads of the mission to the Highlands, though in reviewing the contrasting fortunes of two of them, the Dominicans and the Jesuits, we may be able to assess factors making for defeat or victory in the mission at large. Around the middle of the seventeenth century progress was clearly evident in the Dominicans' missionary offensive. Three notable scholars were converted to Catholicism and, becoming Dominicans, were central to what Fr Ross called 'the most sustained and systematic effort until modern times to involve the Order [of Preachers] in Scottish life'. These were William Bannatyne, first prefect of the Dominican Scottish mission, John Walker, third prefect apostolic and a notable controversialist, and Patrick Primrose, vicar general of the Scottish Dominicans. In 1650 Primrose won 'faculties' (documented authorisation) from Propaganda Fide to act at large in Scotland, Ireland and England, and in November was appointed vicar-general of the Scottish province of his order. The Dominican master general responded to what seemed encouraging prospects by approaching heads of Dominican houses on the Continent to accept Scottish novices, and it may have been the extension of such educational opportunities beyond Scotland that actually thwarted the Dominican mission's success within the country. James Cunningham of Coldoch, Stirlingshire, '*modestus et pius adolescens* (a virtuous and God-fearing young man)', was professed a Dominican and earmarked for Scotland in 1652, but in 1656 was listed as a student at Nantes and following 1658 was assigned to the Order's house at Rennes. Patrick Primrose's protégé, Edward White of Buchan, 'of a sharpe piercing witt', was professed a Dominican and ready to begin work in Scotland in 1659 but was talent-spotted by Fr Philip Howard for an English Dominican house in Flanders. There is even the possibility that the most zealous Dominicans were discouraged from embarking on the Scottish mission, with all its perils: in 1652 the master general de Marinis wrote to the recently professed (and, probably, Gaelic-speaking) Vincentius Marianus Scotus, who had pleaded, even at the risk of martyrdom, to be allowed to join

Primrose in Scotland, pointing out how even noble and experienced men had sunk in Scotland's dangerous shoals and counselling further study: Fr Vincentius was posted to the Dominican friary near Dunkirk. Perhaps it was a reflection of his zeal that this friar *did* eventually come to Scotland, even though by 1677 he had become preacher general to the English province of the Order; likewise, the Gaelic-speaker Alexander Lumsden, registered as being in Scotland in 1671, subsequently appears in England, in prison in the height of the Exclusion Crisis in 1679, and died in England in 1700. In these ways the Dominicans' involvement with Scotland was undermined by the pull of the Continent and of England, eradicating a Scots structure for the Order, so that, by 1700, Fr Ross wrote, 'any Scots Dominicans in Britain were members of the English or Irish Provinces'.[4]

It is true that individual Dominicans could be well anchored in the affections and suport of lairds and people within Scotland. Thus, for example, the virtually free-lance friar, George Fanning, who had 'not received a sixpence from the Sacred Congregation [of Propaganda] for the past eight years', might 'have perished...were it not that he lived with the Laird of Barra'; the people of Arisaig, amongst whom he had worked for 15 years, were reported heartbroken by his death in 1678. Patrick Primrose, whose life as a Dominican epitomised the pulls between Scotland, the Continent and the Court in London – that of James II – also gave an example of practical labour, 'an eloquent man and full of zeal', in the unpromising territory of the Lothians.[5]

Yet it was the Jesuits rather than the Dominicans who provide us with the most remarkable example of priestly commitment to an astonishingly successful mission to the people, within Scotland. Within the territory of their mission on Upper Deeside in western Aberdeenshire, Braemar in 1800 had a Catholic majority, while in neighbouring parishes the recusants amounted to a third of the population. The Deeside mission gives us a fascinating insight into the possibilities for establishing – largely from scratch – a substantial Catholic presence in Scotland's Gaelic north from the later seventeenth century onwards.[6]

The statistical success of the Deeside Jesuit mission is unmistakable and confirmed in Kirk records. Its story begins in 1671 when Lewis Farquarson, who had been in training for the ministry of the Kirk, and who had been converted by reading Catholic controversial works, approached the – initially timorous – Jesuit Forsyth with his disclosures of massive popular resentment at official religious provisions which, costing dear in a poor land, gave nothing in return. This analysis opened up the prospect for a ground-breaking Jesuit campaign, not one seeking to keep the faith alive amongst a few ancestral Romanists but opening up what would be in effect a new church. Success was phenomenal, and the earliest Jesuit reports confirmed that this was indeed a new mission territory,

> in places where the Catholic religion has scarcely been heard of before, since the introduction of heresy, and into which one of our fathers has for the first time penetrated, as if laying the foundation of a new church.

For that reason any instruction that took place would have to come from the basics up, in 'the principal points of the Catholic Faith and motives of credibility'.[7]

Kirk sources agreed that the Jesuits were working virgin territory, that before Forsyth's arrival 'there was hardly a papist to be found in all the country', but that the Established Church's failure to provide pastoral care – 'parishes were very wide and populous, under the care of but two Ministers' – fostered the Jesuits' work amongst people who were 'grossly ignorant (for it is in such dark waters that they love to fish)', so that Forsyth found 'his conquests very easy amongst an Ignorant people naturally given to Superstition, . . . whereby several hundreds were perverted in a few years'. Both Jesuit and Kirk sources were agreed on the phenomenal growth in both numbers and confidence amongst the Deeside Catholics by the early eighteenth century, sustained by an increasing number of priests: 'they are become so impudent,' it was reported to the General Assembly in 1706, and 'upwards of 200 persons were in on[e] day confirmed . . . [In] Braemar and Glengairn . . . popery is much prevailing[,] both which parishes will be entirely popish if not speedily prevented.' A report in the same year by the Vicar Apostolic Nicholson gave the same impression, though from exactly the opposite point of view: 'zealous and pious' Jesuits were sustaining a Catholic community of about 500 in Braemar. Just a few years later, in 1714, Catholics in Braemar could be described by their opponents as 'barefaced', while Forsyth's successor, James Strachan, noted, 'the Catholics are becoming more and more confirmed and strengthened in their faith'. And whereas Nicholson was under the impression that the Braemar Catholics had ancestrally 'continued firm and constant in the Cath: Relig:', Strachan, on the ground, knew full well that his success came from proselytising among new converts: 'I have brought more than three hundred grown-up people to the faith.' Between 1703 and 1736 776 baptisms are recorded in the Braemar district Jesuit register, and a 1714 report by the Kirk confirmed that growth rate. Not only were these conversions in themselves impressive, but they were also stable, and, indeed, expanded through natural family increase, giving the Braemar district 900 Catholics, including children, by 1764.[8]

How may we explain this extraordinary efflorescence of Highland Catholicism in the eighteenth century and what does the situation in Upper Deeside tell us about the possibilities for Catholic growth in Gaelic Scotland in that period? In accounting for the progress of the Jesuits in the Braemar district, we may, as we saw, discount the influence of an indigenous surviving Romanist tradition in this area where the Reformation came early and where Catholicism was quite dead a hundred years after the introduction of Protestantism; we may also disregard any impact of the surviving Catholicism of eastern Aberdeenshire, for the part of the country in question, a difficult 50 miles west of the English-speaking county city, was deep in the rugged Grampians and overwhelmingly Gaelic-speaking. In fact, though, it was those apparently hostile factors – the 'steep and sterile mountainous' and rugged terrain of 'steep and pathless' hills and the Gaelic speech and culture of the area – that gave the Jesuits their best opportunities to exploit. We may indeed surmise that features of Highland Gaelic culture, including the strength of kin ties, helped the fathers in their work – as, for example, in 1706, when 200 people, doubtless encouraged by kin emulation, presented themselves for confirmation when Bishop Nicholson visited. Apart, though, from the advantages they derived from encouragements between kinspeople to foster Catholic practice, the Jesuits on Upper Deeside exploited educational, cultural, economic, linguistic, and even topographical, opportunities that the Kirk had overlooked or even disparaged in the period when it eradicated Catholicism without successfully implanting Calvinism. Indeed, there were ironies in the imposition on Braemar by the Kirk of a latinate academicism so often associated with the Jesuits themselves. Thus, though the minister of Braemar and Crathie, Adam Ferguson, was 'very well skilled in the Irish [Gaelic] language' that prevailed in his joint parishes, the Presbytery was hardly exploiting this linguistic ability when it set him, just prior to his ordination in 1700, the task of a public oral extrapolation of the proposition '*Num papa Romanus sit Anti-Christus*' ('Whether or no the Pope of Rome is the Antichrist'), a scholastic exercise requiring aptitudes entirely appropriate in the lecture halls of St Andrews, but, surely, entirely irrelevant in the fastnesses of the Grampians. Worse, the Kirk's tendency to intellectualise faith fostered an assumption that the Deesiders were 'ignorant...naturally given to Superstition...grossly ignorant...an Ignorant prejudiced superstitious people', on the whole dismissed as fit fodder for the Jesuit fathers.[9]

In contrast, the Jesuits such as Forsyth (Douai and Malines), Seton (professor of humanities and philosophy at Douai) and Strachan (Aberdeen, prefect of Douai), who were all clearly far from dunces, tended to assume, not that they had to 'teach' everything to an 'ignorant' people, but that they had to learn from them, and above all their language. Thus, for example, Hugh Strachan, whose 'knowledge of the Erse [Gaelic] language' has been particularly emphasised as the key to his missionary success, insisted on the need for missionaries to learn to 'read, write, preach and catechise in the vernacular'. However, even beyond the acquisition of Gaelic in the more limited sense of language-learning, the Jesuits on Deeside out-manoeuvred the ministers in adjusting to some of the deeper, and not always fully articulated, requirements of Gaelic popular culture and piety. Fr Seton, for instance, by deploying 'such skills as I had acquired in the medical art', operated as a priest-healer. Fr Strachan's 'social work' included the reconciliation of disputes – 'I have...brought about a happy solution of quarrels and misunderstandings... between...friends and neighbours...I have procured...restitution of goods or of good name' – and the provision of the conditions for 'happy death', assisting 'very many in their last struggle to their great consolation'. In addition to these provisions, the Jesuits on Deeside exhibited a hardihood in coping with the region's landscape that seems to have found a response within its popular culture: in 1702 Seton, for example, literally made a virtue of the necessity of his 'constant journeys by day and night over steep and pathless hills', while Strachan, working on the assumption that if the Highlanders would not come to the Kirk, then the Jesuits must take their mission to the mountains, made that harsh terrain his own: 'the region I dwell in is steep and sterile, mountainous and rugged'. In sharing that bleak landscape, the Jesuits shared its poverty. Men on the run, the Braemar fathers drank to the lees the penury of their people. Seton, of a well-to-do advocate's family, recalled, 'my food was barley bread, my drink cold water, my bed the hard ground or a litle chaff or straw', and Strachan, a baronet's son, described the vegetarian and non-alcoholic regime he shared with the Deesiders. Robert Seton, though, gave these rigours a higher meaning, one grounded in

Ignatian asceticism: 'Before lying down at night he spent about half an hour on his knees in prayer with arms *alla croce* [in the shape of the Cross]; rose early in the morning to his prayers, even during the severe winter cold.' This meagre fare of the Braemar missionaries also chimed in with Jesuit norms for diet, as set out in the *Spiritual Exercises*, in Loyola's recommendation that 'abstinence in the matter of foods,... may be observed... in habituating oneself to eat coarse foods'. Jesuit first principles and missionary constraints here came together.[10]

There were several reasons for the success of the Jesuit mission on Uppper Deeside, including the support of a convert laird, Farquarson of Auchindryne. However, high on the list of factors making for the fathers' achievement was their successful adaptation to regional popular culture, including their recognition of the need to win over youth, for Seton made it his particular business to reach out to 'rough villagers and boys to inspire them with devotion and love to Our Lady'. Far from imposing on their adherents a discipline of 'acculturation' to their values, the Jesuits on Deeside adjusted their mission to the attitudes and assumptions of the lay people they successfully targeted for conversion, in a process in which a cohort of seminary-educated clerics adapted themselves to the demands that popular piety made of the priest – strenuous commitment, heroic adventure and courage, the performance of a social undertaking, with an emphasis on peace-making, a tireless, indeed ubiquitous, presence within communities, eminent sanctity, austerity and poverty of life. These exigent criteria being met, the continuing erosion of Scots Catholicism in the eighteenth century need not have been a foregone conclusion.

Indeed, elsewhere in the Highlands opportunities presented themselves for a popular Catholic mission, albeit less spectacularly successful than the Braemar model. The Benedictine James Bruce claimed that conversion was not so much a matter of persuasion as of building on Catholic beliefs already largely accepted, for 'In the Highlands the people are generally well disposed and stands more in neid of instructione then of any pressing arguments or reasons to convince them'. The very absence 'for many years' of either Catholic priests or ministers of the Kirk had created a fertile virgin soil, if it were possible to provide 'labourers in place for the harvest is very great', particularly in the Western Isles 'lying neir unto the Lewes and belonging unto them'. The opportunities presented in the western archipelago, in which Irish priests proceeded to recover individual islands for Catholicism and where Irish Recollects, Augustinians and Dominicans were at work in the early eighteenth century reminds us that the Deeside venture (with a kind of offshoot at Strathglass, north of Loch Ness) was not the only success story in priestly missionary activity in eighteenth century northern Scotland.[11]

It is in the context of opportunities for a Catholic renaissance in Highland and Gaelic Scotland that we should review the remarkable career of the earlier eighteenth-century Benedictine missionary priest Gregor McGregor. McGregor's father, Callum, of Dalfad, north of Balmoral, was a man of strongly etched personality who showed how a powerful laird could influence religious configurations within his area of influence, having dramaticaly signalled his conversion to Catholicism amidst the stimulating atmosphere of a Highland wedding, in 1701 when

> before a great many people, after he had first rideculed the protestant religion he next went to his knees and in a loud voice uttered a great deal of horrid blasphemie, pretending to personate ministers in their prayers, and then fell a preaching, to the great astonishment of beholders.

A Jacobite opposed to the Presbytery and linked to the Farquarsons of Auchindryne, the protectors of the Upper Deeside mission, Callum McGregor not surprisingly headed a 1704 list of 'Apostates, Popish Priests, Papists and their Children'; indeed, he had built 'a chapel for them, [and] erected a very high crucifix on a little hill near to his house, to be adored by all their neighbourhood'. McGregor also built a house for the Jesuit Fr Strachan where 'They keep publick Mass... in and about the said place almost every lordsday.' In the early eighteenth century the Gaelic speech and the link to lairdship that were Gregor McGregor's inheritance were formidable assets to his mission, though the stormy temperament that he also inherited from his father was a less useful characteristic from the point of view of negotiating the political currents of Jacobitism and the theological rapids of the dissident doctrinal movement, Jansenism. Gregor McGregor had arrived by 1720 to minister to a population 'generally all Popish, extending above the number of seven hundred persons', in Glengarry in Invernesshire, inland from Knoydart, north-east of Morar and Arisaig. There, the Macdonell head of 'the only Popish clan in the kingdom' was a prominent Jacobite after 1688. However, neither before nor even after 1715 did Jacobite associations particularly damage Catholicism's prospects in these north-western districts. Before the '15 the western mainland above Mull and the Ardnamurchan peninsula was well supplied with priests: at Lochaber, for instance, in 1714, it was reported 'the priests swarme like Locusts'. In the immediate aftermath of the rising, it was to be expected that priests would become prime targets: for example, when royal troops recaptured Invergarry Castle, taken for the Pretender in 1716, priests were 'forced to night in the hills in very cold weather, . . . and some seek to leave'; throughout western districts priests were said in 1716 to be 'in the most miserable condition they have ever been in'. Even so, the vigour of Catholicism in the north-western mainland remained impressive and was revealed in lay support for fugitive priests: in 1720 the Presbytery's report on the parish which included the Braes of Lochaber revealed 'there are above ffour hundred persons perverted'; the priest Peter McDonald showed enough confidence to minister within four miles of the garrison at Fort William 'and publickly Invited the people of that Town to hear and joyn him'. And Gregor McGregor took care of 700 souls in his seven-year-long mission in the Glengarry country, a tour of duty during which numbers increased three-fold.[12]

Not surprisingly in the circumstances of the 'dangerous growth of popery in some places . . . especially in Ardnamurchan, Sheuart and Mull', a growth achieved largely through the efforts of the priest Colin Campbell, the Kirk responded energetically, calling freely on the civil authorities for assistance, as in 1726 when troops were sent in to arrest priests. In parochial reorganisations the vast units assembled as a result of the earlier merger of about 50 pre-Reformation parishes were made more manageable through sub-division; payments were disbursed to Presbyterian itinerants out of a royal fund of £1000. A Catholic source revealed that now a 'constant war is waged against the faithful', and McGregor grew dispirited in 1724 under the impression that 'Our trading [the coded Scottish priests' term for ministry] was never in a lower condition than it is at present'. In the context of a vigorous Presbyterian counter-offensive, theological divisions within the Catholic community over Jansenism were all the more damaging because they were exacerbated by personal rancour. Where, in its beleaguered condition, the Highland Catholic Church needed more priests of the stamp of Vicar Apostolic Nicholson, 'slow to speak and slow to anger', in fact the western Highland mission has been seen as dominated by the 'deeply flawed character' of the 'perfectly ungovernable', 'troublesome and factious' McGregor (who had held the unenviable Scots seminarian double record of expulsions, first from the Scots College, Rome, and subsequently from Würzburg). Even in the best of times, clerical rivalries, and in particular those between Jesuits and the seculars – who 'suspected every Jesuit move or policy as placing the interests of the order before those of Scotland's Catholics' – damaged Scots Catholicism both at home, and at Rome – where the consequences of lassitude and failure, including the complete drying up of entries into the Scots College in 1704, were blamed on the Jesuits. As an avid foe and prosecutor of Jansenism, McGregor, with his 'passionate temper', may have sharpened the tensions present in an already divided Church, fuelling the 'atmosphere of mistrust which surrounded the Scottish mission' in the first half of the eighteenth century. However, the division in the Scottish Church over Jansenism, went far deeper than interpersonal discords; or rather we might say that the Gael Gregor McGregor was able to focus the anti-Jansenism of Gaelic-speaking priests serving the Highlands and Islands, a theological antipathy arguably reflecting a deep cultural division in approaches to Catholicism between the two Scotlands.[13]

Dr Roberts, indeed, describes McGregor as 'a significant and representative figure', expressing

> the general complaint of Gaelic-speaking priests. Helped by a wave of Jacobite fervour, the Highland and Irish missioners achieved a remarkable increase in Catholic numbers during the first quarter of the eighteenth century; in return they got increased labour, increased persecution, but no increase in their very meagre means of subsistence.

The issue of Jansenism, Roberts argues, focused the antagonism, social, cultural and educational, between, on the one hand, the Lowland-based 'scholar-chaplains' in noble houses (for example, at Gordon Castle and Traquair) who opposed the anti-Jansenist papal bull *Unigenitus* and the Highland Gaelic-speaking 'itinerant holy men familiar in the region since Columba' – peripatetic charismatics, we might add, in the style of the Braemar Jesuits, who subscribed, one assumes, to their order's anti-Jansenist soteriology. To the theological and social cleavage we should add the presence of opposed devotional tendencies, the north and west looking to Ireland and its Dominicans' encouragment of the Rosary, along with a fondness for medals and indulgences, the Lowlands more diffident towards those features of popular piety, influenced by the austerity of the Jansenist Port-Royal tradition, and perhaps, even more, by the 'restrained and even dour' practices of the Calvinist south. However, the divisions that came to a head when McGregor pressed heresy charges against the Scottish Jansenists in 1731 had more to do with the opposing forms of Catholicism that arose in Europe in the later Counter-Reformation period than with his reputedly stormy temperament or even with Highland–Lowland discords. That said, the Jansenism whose Augustinian severities chimed in with Lowland Calvinism confronted a northern popular Catholicism that was in some ways 'medieval', or even pre-medieval, in its accents, and which found focus in an attachment to the vicarious sanctity of ascetic and heroic holy men of the stamp of the Jesuits on Upper Deeside.[14]

The profound nature of the theological divide meant that when McGregor's anti-Jansenist crusade was taken up by Colin Campbell from 1731, prevailing on the Vicar Apostolic Bishop Gordon to demand a subscription to *Unigenitus* from Scottish priests and calling for a purge of the allegedly Jansenist-tainted Scots College, Paris, which was portrayed as the main source of the movement within Scotland, his campaign precipitated 'discord and division among the Catholic clergy in Scotland on a scale not seen since the Reformation'. Between 1736 and 1740 Propaganda Fide conducted three investigations into the 'great jars' over Jansenism in Scotland, and the issue rumbled on until the mid-1750s. Professor McMillan argues that Scottish Jansenism was much more than a figment dreamed up by Colin Campbell. The country's traditional cultural link with France fostered the influence of the Parisian Scots College which, in turn, served 'to diffuse *port-royaliste* and Gallican notions through the Scottish mission'. With an intellectual champion as impressive as the anti-Jesuit Thomas Innes, the 'major intellectual influence' at the College in the first half of the eighteenth century, a man rooted in the heritage of Port-Royal, an opponent of *Unigenitus* and enrolled in the Jansenist *Nouvelles écclésiastiques* as a 'friend of the truth', Franco-Scottish Jansenism, so firmly entrenched in the Scots Catholic clerical elite, had to be taken seriously, for it marked a division between 'Romans' (anti-Jansenists), and 'Parisians' (pro-Jansenists), between, on the one hand, Jesuits and, on the other, seculars and Benedictines and, as we have seen, between north and south.[15]

Popular Catholicism was strongly anchored in the Rosary, a devotion that strongly linked post-Reformation Scottish Catholicism with its antecedents in the later middle ages when, as Mgr McRoberts writes, the Rosary enjoyed enormous popularity in Scotland by adoption from the

Low Countries, of which the kingdom was a 'cultural extension': Stewart monarchs, urban clerics and bourgeois all kept their splendid sets of 'ane pair of beidis'. The martyr John Ogilvie added his prestige to the post-Reformation Scots Catholic cult of the Rosary, when at his execution in 1615 he 'flung his rosary from the scaffold as a last souvenir for the Catholics who were near him'; in the course of the seventeenth century in Scotland, the Rosary, rather than the Mass, with its complex accoutrements, may have come to be recognised by its foes as the visible expression of Catholic profession: thus, for example, in Aberdeen the Kirk Sessions in 1657 instigated a search for 'the Papists beids'. In the north-west the Rosary, light, portable, inexpensive and concealable, was particularly suitable for an itinerant mission: the Irish Dominicans, members of the order that was the custodian, if not the inventor of the Rosarian tradition, were permitted by Pius VI the use of the Rosary in lieu of the breviary when the latter was too dangerous to carry, and in 1625 the Franciscan missionary Cornelius Ward was asking Propaganda Fide for Rosaries for his western territory. There, as in Upper Deeside, where Fr Seton encouraged the Rosary's recital among 'the ignorant and rough villagers and boys to inspire them with devotion and love to Our Lady', the Rosary was well suited to a community with an overwhelmingly oral and pre-literate culture. That said, and though the Rosary united Scots Catholics, Highland and Lowland, noble and plebeian, in a common devotion, there were divergent ways of approaching the devotion as between literates and non-literates. Thus, whereas in Gaelic and predominantly non-literate zones and social strata, the beads provided the foci of social gathering for oral prayer even (or rather especially) when a priest was not available, for the literate the Rosary might be part of a regime of pious reading and reflection, emphasising 'method'. It was this book-centred aspect of Rosarian piety that came to the attention of the Aberdeen Kirk Sessions in 1657 when it proscribed 'books of poperie, . . . namelie one called the Rosarie'. An approach to the Rosary underpinned by reading was taken up by the marquis of Huntly's wife, Elizabeth Howard who, following her marriage in 1676, set up a confraternity on the model of the one described in Fr. Howard's *The Method of Saying the Rosary . . . as it is said in her Majesties* [Catherine of Braganza's] *Chappell of St James*. Such literature flourished briefly under James VII, when the king's printer included in a devotional manual a section on 'The Method of saying the Rosary of our Blessed Lady.'[16]

Over much of Scotland the Rosary compensated for the infrequency of visits by priests. During those periodic appearances, though, priests exercised canonical functions, and especially matrimonial jurisdiction, in particular in regularising 'irregular' marriages, either those contracted in the presence of a minister of the Kirk or those not formally or sacramentally contracted at all. In the latter cases priest were seen, and saw themselves, as retrospectively legitimising and setting to rights 'handfast' marriages, informally contracted by the couples involved. Thus an Irish Vincentian wrote of the situation in Eigg, Islay and Canna in 1651, 'The greater part of the inhabitants were living in concubinage [irregular marriages], but we have remedied this by joining in matrimony those who were willing and separating the others'; we could compare the Deeside Jesuit Fr Seton's recollection of bestowing 'legitimate marriage' on couples 'who had lived together, some of them for years, in an unlawful union'.[17]

Marriage was a vital factor in the social history of Scottish Catholicism within this period. Contracted with non-Catholics, it both impeded tendencies towards sectarian introversion within the community and at the same time permitted some expansion of numbers, by encouraging the upbringing of the children of mixed marriages as Catholics, for in cases of 'papists and protestants marrieing with one another and Imploying the priests to celebrate them. . . . Commonly either the Protestant party is perverted or at least the children brought up popish.' Evidence for the role of mixed marriage in increasing Catholic numbers comes from Deeside, where, from 1703, Fr Seton's register recorded a bias in mixed-couple marriages in favour of the Catholic baptisms of children, in such a way that, where the father was a Catholic, Catholic baptism was taken for granted, and, where the mother was, strong pressure could be exerted in the same direction. Such trends were further fostered along the Upper Dee where the scarcity of parish kirks even encouraged Catholic priests to conduct the baptisms of the children of entirely non-Catholic marriages. In the Enzie, in the Gordon country of the north-east, however, there was a slightly different effect, according to which children tended to take on the father's religion, whichever that was, giving Catholic families Protestant relatives and thereby facilitating (normally) practical tolerance among the kins brought together by wedlock.[18]

Attention has recently been directed at the important role of women in Catholic survival in Scotland. For example, in the mid-eighteenth century Lady Rothiemay, Lady Frendraught, Lady Aboyne and Lady Murray exercised noble patronage, of a kind from which the priest Gilbert Blackhall benefited. Blackhall's recollections provide vivid insights into the details of the liturgical and devotional, and especially the Lenten, cycle that he provided for Lady Aboyne's household:

> I made exhortations every Sunday, Tuisday and Fridday upon the Passion of our Saviour, which did please her and her domesticks, ... I failed very seldome to say messe to her and for her every day, and preached to her and her household and neighbours and tenants, who were Catholicks, every Sunneday and holiday, and once every month she did confesse, and receive forby all the great feasts of the year.

Lady Aboyne, to whom Blackhall gave absolution at her death in 1642, deeply appreciated her priest's ready presence and 'punctualities': 'oft tymes she said, now I may say with truth that I have a preist, because aither he is within my house or I know where to find him whenever I need him'. There could, surely, be no clearer example of the patronal chaplaincy relationship of priestly subordination to the requirements of a noble sponsor.[19]

The passively exercised power of recusant noblewomen encouraged Catholic recalcitrance. Lady Frendraught adopted a strategy of procrastinating immobility – 'Promises to hear the word, ... Is willing to hear the word in any kirk but Abercherdour [Aberchirder, in Banffshire] ... promises to give up the detestable wayes of poperie or popish idolarie'. In contrast, her neighhbour, Lady Kinnairdy, having conformed once and regretted it, was more overtly obstinate,

> declaring hirself to be none of our church, and she would neither hear herselfe nor [permit?] her daugher to heare; ... shee [said she] had reason to repent all hir lyfe time for suscryving the Nationall Covenant.

Lady Kinnairdy was 'remaining stil obstinat' in 1654, just as Lady Rothiemay was was still 'popishlie disposed' in 1653. The persistence of Catholic women from further down the social scale, including the recusant 'goodwives' of Auchanachy and Cairnborrow, reflected the resistance of the Catholic noblewomen of the north-east. After 1660 that obduracy continued to be manifested by Lady Marie Gordon and her daughter Marie Gray, both excommunicted by the Kirk in 1668. Female Catholic fortitude figured prominently in Jesuit reports, with women outnumbering men 14 to 2 in the lists of persistent recusants sent, for example, in 1663–4. With the window of freedom opening under James VII, plans were mooted for a convent school in Aberdeen. Subsequently, though, an intensification of the kind of upper-class domestic piety described by Gilbert Blackhall attracted accusations from within the Catholic community of Jansenist perfectionism; these included charges made by the Deeside Jesuits Hugh Strachan, John Innes and Robert Seton against Robert Strachan, 'the leading example of those secular priests whose spiritual counsel continued to influence women... during the opening decades of the [eighteenth] century'; it was alleged that these ladies were swayed in favour of the reputedly Jansenist devotional styles of the Scots College, Paris.[20]

In the early eighteenth century Catholic women shared in a more general migration of Scottish females to Edinburgh, where the recusant women in two parishes outnumbered men in the proportion of 73 to 25. Even within this metropolitan Catholicism, though, aristocratic female leadership remained marked, as in 1722, when 11 lay Catholics and a priest were arrested in the presence of their protector Lady Huntly. By the late 1720s Edinburgh Catholicism had also taken on a tone of fervour, especially over Confession and Holy Communion, reminiscent, perhaps, of the emotionalism of the Jansenist-inspired 'prophets' of Saint-Médard in Paris in the same decade. The manifestations of zeal in Edinburgh were associated with Catherine Duncan, under whom, the priest Patrick Leith suggested, there was collusion between 'female Devotees' and priests to allow women to say Mass. Nor was it only in Edinburgh that Scottish Catholic women were displaying exceptional spiritual gifts at around this time, for in Gaelic Lochaber the alumnus of the Scots College, Rome, Iain MacDonald, was persuaded into staying at his mission station – for 40 years, as it was to turn out – by the pious eloquence of the dying Holy Woman of Insch. Other women in the Gaelic west played essential roles in baptisms, as on those occasions when a 'knee woman', supported by a choir of 'watching women', would administer three drops of water to the forehead of a newborn infant 'in the name and in the reverence of the kind and powerful Trinity'. In Aberdeenshire in the 1720s the midwife who 'threw a little water at the chyld's head' when the infant 'was weak and in danger to dye' was also performing a form of baptism: it was one that, though heavily imbued with folk magic, was at least derived from baptism, in a version of the sacrament canonically administered by women as mid-wives. Indeed, by the beginning of the nineteenth century, increased control of baptism by midwives, at least when the child's life was in danger, gave them a kind of spiritual power, as with a midwife who 'aye blessed the child and the hoose wi' the cross when she cam' to a birth'. One of the results of the scarcity of priests in the Scottish mission in the period under review, then, was to highlight the claims of women in the roles of midwives to deploy religious, including, at baptisms, sacramental, power, bestowing on them sacerdotal traits such as blessing a house on entry. That emergence of feminine spiritual power had a class as well as a gender dimension. Between the mid-seventeenth century and the 1720s the patronal role of women such as Ladies Rothiemay, Frendraught, Aboyne and Murray within Scots Catholicism rested on their secular social status as great ladies. The conversion to Protestantism of the duchess of Gordon in 1728 is viewed by Alasdair Roberts as a watershed closing the period of noble female patronage; it opened up, though, a new and interesting period featuring plebeian feminine religious potency, whether among the charismatics of Edinburgh or with the baptising midwives of the north and west.[21]

The period in Scottish Catholic history between the mid-seventeenth and the mid-eighteenth centuries had dismal features, including unhelpful theological rifts over the issue of Jansenism. Hopeful signs, in contrast, included vigorous female leadership and Vicar Apostolic Gordon's initiative in 1716 setting up a seminary within the kingdom, at Scalan, in the Braes of Glenlivet, within the largely Catholic Gordon lands in Banffshire. This venture and its timing are all the more significant in that in the very year of the foundation it was Bishop Gordon himself who warned Propaganda Fide of the danger of the extinction of the Scottish Catholic tradition in the wake of the '15. The little seminary was poor and remote and its regime necessarily austere, but it taught the 'French and Irish or Highland languages', and indeed provided a Tridentine seminary curriculum, forming much of the Scottish priesthood for the remainder of the century. Thus, at one of the lowest points of their post-Reformation fortunes, Scottish Catholics showed themselves capable of making the provisions that would eventually issue in a remarkable renaissance.[22]

Ireland, c. 1635–1745

The Kalends of January, ... anno Domini 1636. Brian Og, son of Brian, son of Ruaidhri, son of Tadgh, son of Ruaidhri Og, ... lord of Magh-Luirg, ... the best man of his age, and estate, and high lordship,

that came of the Gaeidhel of the West of Europe in his own time
[died]; . . . it was he that presented and dispensed most to ollaves and
poets, and to men of science; . . . to devout persons, and to pure
orders; to noble minstrels. . . . After going to Ath-Luain, where the
chieftains of Connacht were before him, . . . his mortal illness . . . seized
him . . . after the triumph of unction and penitence . . . and from the
hands of very many orders and ecclesiastics; . . . after assuming the
habit of St Dominic.[23]

Down to the mid-1630s, and in the years following the arrival of a new
Lord Deputy, Wentworth, whose coming would precipitate a quarter-
century of shattering disruption in Ireland, the obituary of a Gaelic
notable indicates that, despite all the changes that had taken place in
Ireland in the Tudor and early Stuart periods – the vast extension of
crown control, the suppression of rebellion and even the Plantations –
the ancient religious and cultural assumptions of a Celtic aristocratic
society remained intact. Brian Og's panegyric celebrated a tribal society
still held together by threads of honour, of lordly gift-giving and of
intense personal loyalty to chiefs; these latter, in the religious sphere,
functioned as donor-patrons within an essentially pre-Tridentine set of
arrangements in which entourages of priests, assembled in large numbers on ceremonial occasions, conferred further prestige on their spon-
sors; clerics occupied, that is to say, the roles of dependent spiritual
specialists and dispensers of vicarious purity and virtue, on a level of
service approximate to that of 'ollaves' – bardic scholars. From the
1640s onwards the stabilities of that kind of society and those kinds of
assumptions were about to be exploded not only by political and civil
disturbance but also by the fuller adoption in Stuart Ireland of Counter-
Reformation styles of Catholicism. In particular, a new wave of bishops,
who were intensely European in their formations, fully conscious of
their episcopal dignity and imbued with the Tridentine drive to change
and reform, brought Catholic Ireland fully within the orbit of the
Counter-Reformation. By 1648 the country had a full quota of 27
Catholic bishops in residence, forming the large nucleus of a total of
37 examined by Donal Cregan for the period 1618–60. It is worth
examining the collective profile of this group in a little detail, not least
because they formed not a random collection of clerics but an episcopate, with a common and shaped purpose. Obviously, the family backgrounds of the group reflected the wealth necessary to send boys
abroad for protracted education. This mid-seventeenth-century Catho-

lic episcopate also embraced key strata of Irish elite society. It contained eminent representatives of the Gaelic aristocracy, including the primate, Hugh O'Reilly, and a further four colleagues who were eligible for clan chieftainships. Gaelic culture as well as nobility was also well represented: two of the bishops, both named Boethius MacEgan, came of the stock of the *brehons*, the ancient custodians and interpreters of Irish law. This group within the wider cohort emerged from Irish-speaking backgrounds and were bi-lingual in Irish and English, though the Ulstermen amongst them tended to be hesitant in English.

Beyond these element from the tribal and scholarly upper echelons of old Gaelic society, Dr Cregan's group of Irish Tridentine bishops were linked to other strands in the island's Catholic establishment: four of his total group of 37 were sons of peers, and more of them were related to noble families, giving these bishops vital liaisons with the traditional ruling class, providing financial endowments and making Irish Catholic bishops less unacceptable than they might otherwise have been in the eyes of a rank-conscious government in Dublin. Links existed with sometimes vast estates: Bishop Niall MacGeoghegan's brother held over 4000 acres in Westmeath, while Viscount Clanmalier, brother of Edmund Raymund Dempsey, OP, bishop of Leighlin, had over 20 000 acres in the King's and Queen's Counties. Reflecting the nobility's traditional choice of the religious orders rather than the secular clergy for entry of their sons into the priesthood, this group of bishops had seven or eight Franciscans, four Dominicans, two Cistercians and an Augustinian. One of the Dominicans, Ross MacGeoghegan, named bishop of Kildare in 1629, provides a case of a man with origins in that Gaelic aristocracy that was ennobled as Irish peerage: 'a Gaelic aristocrat, a descendant of the MacGeoghegans of Cinél Fhiachach, a branch of the southern Uí Néill, whose genealogy has been traced from the thirteenth century'. As for his culture, Ross MacGeoghegan grew up in a Gaelic-speaking, but probably also bi-lingual, home, and was subsequently immersed abroad in Iberian Dominican ideals and in 'the Tridentine tradition in the Castilian mode...in scholarship and the university world of Salamanca'. He was typical of the group studied by Cregan in the strength of his relationships within it, for his cousin the Franciscan Anthony MacGeoghegan was to become bishop of Clonmacnoise and later of Meath. Such close interelationships within this bench of bishops – a cluster including two brothers, an uncle and a nephew and several cousins – and a kin network that was centred on the Roman-based 'bishopmakers', Peter Lombard, Archbishop of Armagh, and the

Franciscan Luke Wadding cemented a strong *esprit de corps*, as did the cohort's recruitment, noticeably from the south-east of the country. Though one of the group, Archbishop Thomas Walsh of Cashel, aroused snobbery as 'a merchant's son', it was an additional source of strength in this group that, alongside the Gaelic and Anglo–Irish nobility, it drew in Old English elements from burgess and office-holding stock in Galway (whence came two episcopal Lynches) and the southern towns, a class all the more crucial for the fortunes of Irish Catholicism on account of its traditional loyalty to the crown. Indeed, a detectable criterion in these appointments was the avoidance of offence to the crown, even though one of them, Bishop McMahon of Clogher, whose County Monaghan family lost heavily in the Ulster Plantations, retained a sense of grievance. Generally speaking, though, the most strident voice of resentment, that of the exile rebel earls, who sought to exercise ancestral territorial rights by submitting nominees to Rome, went unheeded in these promotions, as Lombard and Wadding selected relative political moderates whose priorities were Tridentine reform rather than Catholic political hegemony. Coming from pious Catholic homes, trained in Latin grammar and literature, all these men proceeded to seminaries abroad (and most graduated). Cosmopolitan, polyglot in a range of up to four languages, yet thoroughly Irish in culture, they were formed in a rigorous regime of early rising, hearing Mass, prayer, frequent reception of the Sacraments, sermons, silences, fasting and devout reading, to emerge 'prayerful, ascetic, exact in the performance of... religious duties, and zealous to improve the quality of faith and practice in Ireland'; they were, indeed, models of Tridentine reformism, the first Counter-Reformation episcopate in Europe.[24]

During their education, these bishops in the making and especially the Dominicans amongst them partook in the revival of the theological system of St Thomas Aquinas then under way, markedly in the Spanish universities. Political theories stemming from the Spanish Thomist Vitoria on the moral illegitimacy of land confiscations from the American Indians may have given rise, in the minds of the Irish seminarians, to reflections on parallels closer to home, just as the ideas on political resistance of the Italian Bellarmino and the Spaniard Suarez – the writings of both of whom were freely available in the Continental seminaries – may have contributed to a certain political intransigence on the part of some of the Irish bishops in the highly polarised 1640s. Dr Cregan, though, points to another strong intellectual influence, that of the disciple of Bellarmino and Suarez, the Vienna professor, Martin

Becanus, who dwelt on the invalidity of royal supremacy in religion but who also developed views, which were potentially applicable to Ireland's religiously mixed society, on the possibility of mixed marriage. At the same time, exposure to Jansenist influences abroad, including personal contacts with Cornelius Jansen himself, was likely to stimulate severity towards Ireland's admixture of folk culture and Catholic religion: it was to be reported in Rome that 'Jansenism has lately crept in' to Ireland. However, the programme of this group of bishops was Tridentine rather than Jansenist. As such, it involved an ambitious educational drive directed at the laity in which, for example, from 1668 onwards Luke Wadding II, pastor of Wexford, made himself an educational patron of 'poore Gentry', the provider of the newer French, Spanish, Italian and Flemish works of piety. Inevitably, the social relations of clergy and laity were reversed, certainly when compared with the state of affairs in which, in the obsequies of Connacht's Brian Og clerics were regarded as members of a chorus of dependents. Noble as he was, Ross MacGeoghegan, when bishop of Kildare, treated the aristocracy as subjects, suitable cases for Tridentine re-education: 'He found that the nobility were more given to the pursuit of worldly pleasures than concerned with the Christian education of their sons. By means of admonition and correction many eventually returned to lives of righteousness.' This should be seen as part of the shift towards clerical leadershp within the social relations prevailing in post-Reformation Ireland's Catholic majority.[25]

If the Irish Counter-Reformation looked to Continental Europe, the country's nearest neighbour was its Protestant master, and English mastery was brought home ever more forcibly to the island with Strafford's 'thorough' policy of subjugating the Irish, involving new plantations. Pent-up Gaelic fury at these exploded in the rebellion of 1641, which coincided with and fully exploited England's political breakdown in the period leading to the outbreak of civil war. The Irish Rebellion's savageries, ferocious by any seventeenth-(or even twentieth-) century standards, confirmed and perpetuated a loathing and a dread of 'popery' amongst Protestants on both sides of St George's Channel, for the Rebellion seemed to be a popish plot realised and, as a consequence of it, renewed vigilance was directed at recusants in England and Wales, with what Clarendon described as 'new jealousy and sharpness...as if they were privy to the insurrection in Ireland and [planned] to perform the same exploit in this kingdom'. As Dr Lindley shows, citing as one instance the Sussex recusant squire who loaned £500 to the crown to help suppress the Rebellion, 'the reports of a link-up between Irish ... and English and Welsh catholics ... in a grand conspiracy are completely without foundation'; nevertheless, tales of numbers of English Catholics crossing over to help the rebels, with a reputed 300 priests and Jesuits sailing to the island to foment rebellion, did much to fuel English anti-popery and to heat the pre-civil war atmosphere of panic. In Ireland itself Protestants became suddenly aware of a new vulnerability. Indeed, the role of the Rebellion and its massacres was crucial in stoking Irish Protestant anti-popery throughout the period surveyed in this chapter, and, indeed, well beyond it. The anti-popish propaganda work, Sir John Temple's graphic *History of the Rebellion* was regularly reprinted and, alongside annual commemorations – such as the one held in Dublin in 1732, with 'Ringing of Bells, Bonefires, Illuminations, and other Demonstrations of Joy' – contributed to keeping the memory of 'Papal Cruelty' fresh in the Irish non-Catholic consciousness: in 1714 the strongly pro-Hanoverian Deist (and ex-Catholic) John Toland deplored a reputed Tory-supported Catholic revival taking place 'to the inexpressible terror of the protestants who are in daily fear of a massacre'.[26]

Though the terror induced in Irish Protestant minds by the 1641 Rebellion and fixed there by a reiterated propaganda of recollection was to prove over the course of almost two centuries damaging for Catholic hopes of emancipation, in the shorter term Charles I's desperate need for allies in the civil wars opened up possibiltiies of a Catholic–royalist coalition on which a secure position for the Catholic Church in Ireland might be built. Exactly what that position might be on a spectrum between tolerance and hegemony depended on a range of considerations. These included: the firm Anglicanism of Charles I and his lord lieutenant Ormonde; the goal of the papal nuncio, from 1645, Archbishop Giovanni Battista Rinuccini, of securing a Catholic establishment; and the balance of power between the 'old Irish' and the 'old English' Catholics – the latter tending to disparage some of the Gaelic clergy and to be less enthusiastic than the old Irish for an independent and financially well-endowed Church. Organised, even before the outbreak of civil war in England, in their Confederation of Kilkenny, the Irish Catholics put forward in 1642 a programme of Catholic restoration which was based on pre-Reformation, and, indeed, thirteenth-century, models and which assumed an unquestioned ascendancy for their Church: 'That the Roman Catholic Church in Ireland shall ... have ... the privileges and immunities according to the great charter, made and declared within the realm of England, in the ninth year of King Henry III'. However, an alternative view of a Catholic restoration as a result of a royalist victory focused not so much on the formal, institutional and exclusive re-establishment of a medieval-style *ecclesia hibernica* as on a free and open exercise of Catholic worship; a statement of the 'Confederate Catholique' position on this possibility did not seem to leave out the possibility of pluralism:

> First proposition. That the exercise of the Roman Catholique religion be in Dublin, Drogheda, and in all the kingdom of Ireland, as free and publick as it is now in Paris, in France, or Bruxells, in the Low Countreys.

Yet whether the vision was of a restored Catholic sole dominance or of a co-existence, the political and military price of any such gains was a royalist commitment and, indeed, victory. Urban Catholic Ireland was to the fore in promoting Catholic royalism. The mayor and corporation of Galway, the city which, it was to be claimed, was the first to come out in arms for Charles I and the last town in the two islands to surrender to his enemies, in 1652, voiced this ideology when, in 1647, it spoke of the 'bounden and dutifull allegiance and obedience to their undoubted and lawfull Soveraigne' to be found in 'the hartes of his Majesties faithfull Catholique subjects of Irland'. The more specifically religious side of the equation is evident in the corporation's favourable reception of a petition from the abbess and convent of St Clara 'resident in Galway' for 'sufficient roome for building a monasterie and roomes convenient thereunto a garden and orchard'.[27]

In Waterford, too – the home town of Luke Wadding I, whose cousin Patrick Comerford was bishop during the Cromwellian siege of 1649 – 'a strong Catholic fervour' was combined with royalism, though in the case of that town there was support for Rinuccini's more ambitiously Catholic Roman policies, rather than for Confederate stategies of negotiating with the Protestant crown. It was in the towns, also – 'strongholds of the counter-reformation movement' – that, in the disturbed 1640s, any continuation of Tridentine reformism could be expected. Inevitably, then, they were the prime target in Cromwell's campaign against the Irish Counter-Reformation, for, as the Lord General himself said

> if by liberty of conscience was meant liberty to exercize the mass, he judged it best to use plain dealing and let him [the governor of the

town of New Ross] know, where the parliament of England have power, that would not be allowed.

The campaign to obliterate the Mass inevitably struck at priests. Thus, in the arrangements for the surrender of the town of Clare in November 1651 amnesty for 'all persons . . . who desire to live in protection . . . , submitting themselves to all acts and ordinances of Parliament' was expressly witheld from 'Romish preists, Jesuits and friers'. And it was in the towns, which had been pinpointed by the Confederates for the implementation of their plan of open Catholic worship, that executions of priests were pursued most relentlessly. Mgr Corish estimates that up to 1000 priests left for the Continent; by the time of the Restoration, and even allowing for some recovery in clerical numbers as the 1650s wore on, numbers of priests fell to an abysmal level – between four and eight in some dioceses: there is no denying the efficiency or the efficacy of the Cromwellian campaign to reverse earlier successes of the Counter-Reformation in Ireland.[28]

Though the towns were the key to the success or failure of the Irish Counter-Reformation, land ownership was the determinant of power in Ireland, and the Cromwellian 1650s were decisive in worsening the territorial position of Catholics there, vastly accelerating that 'massive discontinuity in landownership' taking place between 1600 and 1800 in which the 'Gaelic order . . . was progressively overwhelmed or pushed to the periphery by Elizabethan soldiers of fortune, Cromwellian adventurers and Williamite planters'. In the 20 years before the Restoration one estimate is that the proportion of Irish land in Protestant hands went up from 40 to 78 per cent, the Cromwellian revolution sweeping 'away a catholic proprietary class of both Celtic and Anglo-Norman descent': 'whole counties were swept clean of ancient proprietors producing a geographical *tabula rasa* unprecedented in British history'. Though revolutionary procedures were used to accomplish these results during the Interregnum, their effects, despite the professed desire of Charles II and Ormonde to achieve a 'substantial catholic restoration' were not reversed with the accession of Charles II, in whose Stuart cause Irish Catholics had enlisted, as one of their leaders, Viscount Gormanstown, put in in 1667 'at the sacrifice of their lives, estates and fortunes'. In fact, the alteration in the balance of landownership was, after 1660, 'institutionalised and its transformation made permanent by the legitimist monarch Charles II'. It is true that in many cases Catholics survived economically, as tenants, but it was the ownership of land that provided the key to political power and as a result of the radical but unreversed changes of the 1650s, the political power to defend their Church was denied to Ireland's Catholic elite. Further, loss of lands, and, in particular, the way that Catholic suits coming before the Irish Court of Claims were simply left unheard, created a deep and lasting sense of grievance, 'a major source of catholic discontent'.[29]

In view of such disastrous losses in land ownership, it is all the more remarkable that the Irish Catholic Church was able to begin its own institutional reconstruction after 1660. For example, faculties given by the Holy See to Edmund Teighe, Vicar Apostolic of Meath, made provisions for expected, and indeed largely realised, substantial numbers converting 'from heresy', provided for the re-use of 'profaned' churches and equipped Teighe with extensive matrimonial jurisdiction. Rome also recognised the recovery in the numbers of priests, with 117 men suitable for appointment to Irish dioceses. Though it took a long time for clerical numbers to get back to where they had been in 1640, in half a dozen dioceses totals doubled in the course of the 1660, so that by 1673 the Archbishop of Armagh, Oliver Plunket, was even complaining that there were too many priests. The renewed vigour of post-Restoration Catholicism was accelerated by the departure of the firmly Anglican Ormonde in 1669, in which year a wave of appointments to Dublin, Cashel, Tuam and Ossory renewed the Irish Catholic episcopate. Such factors made the reign of Charles II seem, in the grim retrospect of a renewal of persecution following the Revolution, a Catholic golden age, so much so that in the 1691 Limerick Treaty between William III and the Catholic Irish the latter sought 'such privileges in the exercise of their religion as ... they did enjoy in the reign of King Charles the Second'. Such nostalgia notwithstanding, the reality was that, at around the time that Plunket was bemoaning an excess of clergy, the security that Irish Catholics enjoyed depended on the operation of a delicate power balance between Charles and his Protestant Parliaments in London and Dublin. Thus, in 1672, when the king issued his Declaration of Indulgence, Plunket noted the opening of Catholic schools in Drogheda and toleration, even from the stoutly Protestant lord lieutenant, the earl of Essex. However, in the following year, when Charles was forced by Parliament to cancel the Declaration, Archbishop Peter Talbot of Dublin recorded the expulsion of Catholic bishops and of other ecclesiastics from the country. Predictably enough, the Popish Plot crisis beginning in England in 1678 further endangered the precarious security of Irish

Catholics under Charles II. They were extensively disarmed, religious houses were dissolved and bishops and members of religious orders were exiled. In Dublin the period when Mass centres were 'as publicly frequented as [Protestant] churches' was followed by an official campaign to forbid Masses and expel Jesuits and leading clerics; the capital's main church, in Francis Street, built by the Franciscans, was, for discretion's sake, handed over to seculars for the duration of the scare. In Wexford, where, in 1674, Luke Wadding II had built a new chapel, with subscriptions from some Protestants of the town, Catholic marriages declined sharply in the period of the Plot and Mass was suspended at its height, at Christmas 1678.[30]

We should not, though, over-emphasise the disruption occasioned in Ireland by Oates' allegations made in London. The south-eastern port town of Wexford provides a clear example of Catholic social integration and relative tolerance during Charles II's reign. During the Interregnum, a recession followed the enforced withdrawal of experienced Catholic seamen and traders who were subsequently brought back into the mainstream of the life of the port, often rising to positions of considerable influence, so much so that the town's large and well-knit Catholic community came to include leading merchants families. In a conscious post-Restoration retreat from the militancy of the 1640s, Luke Wadding encouraged the development of a system in which Catholics 'accommodated themselves to the state church within the context of fairly harmonious relations between members of the Protestant and Catholic elites'. Prudently, and even when their religion was public knowledge, Catholic couples in the 1670s were marrying in both their own and in Protestant churches, though having their children baptised as Catholics. Bishop Luke Wadding (1633/4–91/2) colluded in these evasions in his (probable) role of recorder and sought to avoid offence by withstanding, until 1684, pressure from Rome to be consecreated bishop. He may have been arrested in 1678, though it seems likely that powerful connections prevented his banishment and it was undoubtely in large measure as a consequence of his policies of discretion that 'as soon as the hysteria generated by the plot had subsided, there was a return . . . to the *modus vivendi* which had operated in the years leading up to it'. The continued pursuit of prudent policies allowed Wexford Catholics modest political gains – as when five of them sat of a jury in 1683 – and enrichment, as with Wadding's cousin, the merchant Anthony Talbot, who amassed extensive property and became an alderman in the borough's 1685 charter. In Dublin, too, a new

Catholic middle class, including a group of eminent barristers, was emerging even before the end of Charles II's reign; Catholics were being admitted to the College of Physicians, entry into which required no religious test and, by becoming 'quarter brothers' of the commercial Holy Trinity Guild, gained access to its trading privileges. It is true that Catholics were as yet only a 'small minority' amongst Dublin merchants and that the role of Catholics in the capital remained that of a a 'labour force' for its trade and manufacture. Nevertheless, the numerical, if not social, rise of Catholics in the country's capital – perhaps from a third to a half between 1685 and 1689 – confirms the importance of urban Catholicism in late-seventeenth-century Ireland.[31]

We may say that a limited Catholic restoration took place in Ireland in the quarter century preceding the accession of James II in 1685. James's Irish policy has been described by Professor Miller as being divided 'between a desire to maintain England's dominance over Ireland and his zeal to advance the Catholic religion', his primary aim being that of obtaining the repeal of the Test Acts and other penal laws in England. As in Scotland, so in Ireland the king proceeded slowly at first, supporting the English interest, apppointing the Anglican Clarendon lord lieutenant and maintaining the pro-Protestant land settlement that had been in its essentials confirmed at the Restoration: indeed, Charles O'Kelly of Screen, Catholic high sheriff of County Roscommon in 1686, member of Athlone corporation in 1687 and of the Jacobite Parliament in 1689, criticised James for neglecting to 'assert the hereditary rights of the [Catholic] natives, or restore their estates'. The clergy's moves were as circumspect as the king's: they continued to abstain from wearing clerical dress in 1685, though in the following year James allowed bishops to wear cassocks and cloaks. More boldly, Dublin's Archbishop Russell held a meeeting which asked James to establish the Catholic Tyrconnel in Clarendon's place. In 1686 rumours of a plan by James to draft Catholics into the Council, the Irish commission of the peace and the borough corporations were being reported.[32]

Though it can be said that Catholic 'Ireland continued to be a source of strength to James, even if an embarrassing one', its most dramatic political initiative on his behalf came not during his reign but after his fall in England, with the Jacobite Parliament of 1689, summoned following his invitation by Tyrconnel to Ireland, where he arrived in March 1689. Reflecting the continuing centrality of landownership in relations between the religious communities, 'the repeal of the Restoration land settlement was the primary object of the parliament'. James himself, who held vast estates in 16 Irish counties, was opposed to a radical settlement, but in the event the Jacobite Parliament passed an Act of Repeal which swept away the post-Restoration Acts of Settlement and Explanation, so injurious to Catholic territorial interest; it also made provisions to establish a new court of claims, and provided for the return in the provinces of Leinster, Munster and Connacht of land lost to Catholics since 1641. Needless to say, the implementation of this intended revised land settlement depended utterly on Catholic–Jacobite success in James's war of recovery against William. On the more purely religious front, there is some evidence of tension between James II – who called Protestant, not Catholic, bishops to the Parliament and who took his stand on the retention of the royal prerogative in matters of religion – and the overwhelming Catholic majority in the assembly; what seems to have emerged (the text of the agreement is lost) was a measure providing for equality and liberty of worship for both Protestants and Catholics, without a Romanist ascendancy, though Catholics were to be freed from paying tithes to any church but their own. As for the constitution, a declaratory Act maintained that 'his majesty's realm of Ireland is and hath been always a distinct kingdom from that of his majesty's realm of England' – a view of Ireland as, in equal measure with England, one of the king's various dominions, a kingdom in its own right. The existence of this semi-autonomist view, as against James's opposition to the repeal of Poyning's Law, which guaranteed the subordination of the Irish Parliament to the English, indicates that on the constitutional, as on the religious and the land-tenurial fronts, this assembly of 1689 was more than simply a forum for James's comeback but provided rather a voice for a distinctively Irish Catholicism – albeit that of a privileged elite within the majority community – having a national political voice of its own.[33]

The events of the 1690s in some ways repeated those of the 1640s as far as Irish Catholics were concerned. Pledged to a doomed Stuart king, in both periods Catholic Irish people resorted to actions which were bound to bring down on them further Protestant recriminations if their liege-lord failed in his ambitions, as James II did in the early 1690s. Far less brutally than in 1641, through still ill-advisedly, Catholics committed acts of aggression based on ill-founded triumphalism in 1689: in Wexford, for example, Luke Wadding's carefully nurtured legacy of eirenicism was threatened, if not shattered, by the action of the Catholic mayor, Edward Wiseman, in confiscating the town church from the Protestant minister. Not surprisingly, Wiseman himelf subsequently suffered heavy losses of property as a consequence of that seizure and the Wexford Catholic merchant class underwent a collective banishment in 1691. More widely, Catholics were politically penalised for their support of James and gradually, but very effectively, were excluded from Parliament, with an Act of 1691 requiring from candidates abjurations of the pope's authority and of Transubstantiation. However, in the October of that year, after months of negotiation following James' crushing defeat at the Boyne, the Treaty of Limerick guaranteed possession of property to the people and garrison of Limerick and to the remaining forces in the west, in return for the surrender of the surviving Jacobite armies; to Catholics at large religious concessions in line with Irish law and with privileges extant under Charles II were awarded. Whereas, as we have seen, the status quo under Charles II came to be accorded, as J.G. Simms wrote, the status of a 'standard by which their future treatment should be regulated', the Limerick Treaty itself was soon to become an icon of Catholic nostalgia – not surprisingly, since William III was entirely serious about honouring it, so that by 1695 the vast majority, 483 out of 491, of land claims covered by the Treaty had been settled in its beneficiaries' favour, and, as Dr Simms wrote, 'from 1692 to 1699 nearly 1,200 Limerick claims were admitted and the successful claimants included representatives of almost all the leading Jacobite families'. Even so, in 1697 a diluted version of the Treaty was passed by the Dublin Parliament, without the clause promising Catholics privileges that had prevailed under Charles II. In point of fact, since any such privileges as had been extended during that reign were informal or extra-legal, the clause in the Limerick Treaty meant little in terms of identifiable rights, and even the letter of the pro-Catholic clause did not stand in the way of such measures of the Irish Parliament as the Bishops' Banishment Act of 1697. The latter was indeed, as it was intended to be, a calamitous measure for the Irish Catholic Church, ordering the expulson of all Catholic clerics exercising ecclesiastical jurisdiction and of all regulars.[34]

As a result of the Act, 153 members of regular orders were transported from Dublin, 170 from Galway, 75 from Cork and 26 from Waterford (James II's wife, Mary of Modena, claimed that 700 in total had been forced to leave); of the eight bishops present in Ireland in 1697 six remained following the passage of the Act, though in hiding, as fugitives, in danger of arrest and concealed 'in cellars and cisterns, in

mountains and caves', as Cashel's Archbishop Comerford reported in
1698. However, it was the regulars, seen as coming directly under
Rome's control, who took the brunt of the banishments and under
this measure designed to exterminate the Irish priesthood in point of
fact 'nothing of consequence seems to have happened to secular dignat-
ories other than bishops'. It is also true that the events of the 1690s were
not as disastrous as they might have been for the Catholic laity, and that
the land settlement was relatively benevolent to them. Catholic refugees
from Wexford were already returning by 1694. Even so, the view that
the faith pledged in the Treaty of Limerick was betrayed in the Bishops'
Banishment Act – 'broke by a Parliament in Ireland summoned by the
Prince of Orange... [which]. ... made a law for banishing in perpet-
uum the Catholick bishops, dignitaryes and regular clergy' – became a
new article of faith in the credo of bitterness accumulated in the Irish
Catholic consciousness in the course of the turbulent and tragic seventeenth century.[35]

As we saw, by the middle of that century Catholic Ireland had beeen
equipped with a model Tridentine episcopate. What was the character
of Irish Catholicism in the years down to the end of the century, how
had the progress of the Irish Counter-Reformation fared amidst massive disruptions and what was the nature of the relationship between
Tridentine and extant pre-Tridentine Catholicism in the country? On
that last point, we have conflicting reports. Government accounts were,
predictably enough, dismissive of a religious culture seen as being
characterised by ignorance, illiteracy and priest-ridden superstition:
thus Clarendon portrayed Irish Catholicism in 1686, describing

> the wonderful stupidity of the common people... it is scarce possible
> for any that have not been here to believe the profound, ignorant
> bigotry the natives here are bred in by the priests, who to all appear-
> ances seem as ignorant as themselves.

A picture of timeless – and certainly pre-Tridentine – superstition is also
conveyed in a report from Wexford of a 'wooden idol in the shape of a
man, called St. Iberian' before whom oaths were sworn and to whose
shrine a priest was accustomed periodically to go to take up offerings.
Even so, another English Protestant, the projector of Irish modernisation William Petty, observed, in the same town of Wexford where Luke
Wadding distributed classics of Counter-Reformation Continental
literate piety, a form of faith and practice amongst 'the richer and

better-educated sort' who made up the local Catholic bourgeoisie which was entirely comparable with standards maintained elsewhere in Europe: 'they are such Catholics as are in other places'. Thanks to Wadding, Catholic Wexford had a new chapel by 1694. In the County Wexford countryside, also, and allowing, perhaps, for a degree of description of actuality in terms of (Tridentine) ideals, the inhabitants were depicted in the 1670s as leading Christian lives of exemplary yet moderate restraint, marked by peace, neighbourliness, sobriety, hospitality, sacramental order and great regularity in the due observance of feasts and fasts:

> The native inhabitants celebrate with singularlie pious devotion the yearlie festivities...in the several parishes..., esteeming him profane ...who doth not on such dayes penitently (by confession to his spiritual pastor) purge his soul from mortal sinne, be reconciled to his neighbours, and reverently receive the sacred Eucharist. Of such festivals, they mutually invite theire neighbouring friends and alliance into their howses, whom they cheerfully, piouslie and civily intertaine, with variety of the best accommodation the country can afford; not without incentive facetiousness and Musical Instruments...They are very precise and exact in the observacion of Ecclesiasticallie injoined fasts, never eate flesh on Fridayes or Saturdayes, few use eggs, butter or milk on Fridays,...They are not inclined to debauchery, nor excessively addicted to the use of any liquor.[36]

The political prospects for Ireland's Catholic community as the seventeenth century gave way to the eighteenth seemed the dismal ones of a powerless majority. As the Attorney-General Dudley Ryder put it in 1715, 'though the number of papists is vastly superior to that of Protestants, yet the Protestants are able to keep them in order and prevent any trouble or danger from themselves'. Further statutes confirmed this state of subjugation, and in particular the Act of the Irish Parliament of 1704 'to prevent the further growth of popery', identified by Lecky as the most injurious of the penal laws and dealing with a wide range of religious and civil issues including conversions, pilgrimages, land purchase and inheritance, education and voting. The Act was tightened up further in 1709, from which year Simms dates the real beginning of the penal period as far as Ireland was concerned; in 1728 Irish Catholics were deprived of the parliamentary vote. We should, though, try to assess the exact amount of harm done to most Irish Catholics by deprivations such as that of the franchise. Loss of the vote was not the worst of their tribulations. Even if the Irish Parliament's franchise and membership had reflected the numerical preponderance of Catholics in the kingdom's population, the truth is that it was dependent on the government in London, had little scope for initiative and met seldom and briefly: for example, the Parliament of 1703 was the first since 1698 and that of 1713 sat for one month only. If the vast majority of Irish people were excluded from their Parliament's deliberations on grounds of faith, so most 'mainland' British people were also excluded, on grounds more or less of social class, from involvement with the West-minster parliament. It is not that the Dublin Parliament was irrelevant to the lives of Irish people; it is, rather, that in a search for evidence of power or influence exerted by Catholics in Georgian Ireland, of subtler freedoms co-existing with and evading the simple rigours of parliamentary statutes, we should turn away from the Dublin Parlia-ment as a protected species upholding Protestant ascendancy and look at the political and social nuances operating in the Irish provinces and especially in the towns.[37]

Conditions for Catholics in Ireland's towns in fact varied widely. In Wexford an influential Irish Catholic bourgeoisie re-emerged in the early eighteenth century and by 1708 the town had as mayor a Catholic, or at least the husband of a Catholic wife, and at least two Catholic aldermen, one of them almost certainly Edward Wiseman, the combative mayor of 1689. In Galway, in contrast, Catholics enjoyed every social asset except political power. In common with neighbouring Limerick, Galway was reported in 1703 to be 'in great part inhabited by Papists', and in 1709 it was said 'The inhabitants are most Roman Catholics.' With this numerical superiority went control of the western city's trade, 'wholly in their hands'. Indeed, it may have been the case that, as with the Nonconformists in England, the Galway Catholics throve commercially, undistracted by the pleasures and pains of civic office. For this was an avenue closed to them, ever since the military occupation of the Cromwellian 1650s. A local convention regulating entry into the seat of local government encapsulated the Catholics' degradation in the city in which they formed a majority: 'no Catholic durst enter here with its hat on but should remain uncovered, as a mark of subjection to his Protestant towns-men . . . a Catholic clergymen durst not at all enter the exchange.' As far as Parliament was concerned, the presence of Galway members in the Jacobite Parliament of 1689 was followed by a local ruling of 1703 to the effect that only freeholders 'being Protestant' could vote, anticipating the nation-wide withdrawal of the franchise from Catholics in 1728.[38]

In Galway, though, all was not as it seemed. If, officially, Catholics could not vote, nearly 10 per cent of those qualified to do so in a list drawn up in 1727 were entered with the formula 'Popish wife' or some variant of it. Clearly, cross-confessional families were a feature of the Galway scene, and were no doubt a factor in bringing about the evasion and *de facto* relaxation of the penal laws in the western city. Indeed, corporate non-compliance with those laws could be splendidly brazen, as was the case in 1731, when the mayor and corporation reported that a search for friars in the 'reputed friary' in the city had been fruitless, while the brothers' own accounts itemise the purchase of a bottle of wine – to entertain the sheriffs. More zealously Protestant outsiders were less patient with the Galway mens' tricky ways: the city's new governor in 1731 demanded, 'No sham searches, Mr sheriffs, as to my knowledge you have lately made. Your birds are flown, but they left you cakes and wine to entertain youselves withal.' However, as Mgr Corish comments, such attempts to obstruct a drift into social acceptance of Catholic worship were 'like trying to keep out the tide'.[39]

It is true that the laws remained savage in their intent, particularly against the clergy. Following on the heels of the Banishment Act of 1697, the 1704 Registration Act opened up the possibility that 'within a generation at most there would be no Catholic priests left', while a statutory requirement in 1708 to abjure the Stuarts faced recalcitrant priests with banishment. Yet despite all this legal ferocity, numbers of priests rose steadily in the eighteenth century – to the point at which purists were once again deploring a surplus – and by 1730 most dioceses had bishops. The orders were back in business, the friars were expanding their operation (until Benedict XIV stepped in to control them in 1751) and by 1721 the Dominicans had established themselves in Dublin, Limerick, Cork, Cashel, Drogheda, Sligo and Galway. The capital's increasing Catholic population, in large part Irish-speaking, had 13 Mass-houses by 1731. A memorial of 1729 was signed by 10 priests who confidently styled themselves with the full canonical titles of a diocesan clergy – 'Priest and Dean of the Cathedral Church of St. Patrick, Dublin ... Priest and Canon of the same Church', and so on; confirming 'the strength of the Catholic middle class in Dublin city at this time', the signatories to this memorial included seven Catholic physicians, an apothecary, a lawyer and three merchants. There were even hints that Catholicism in the capital was becoming chic and aesthetic, not least among Protestants. Nuns came to Dublin in 1712 and the 'nunnery in Channel Row' operated a boarding school by 1731, but by 1727 this 'famous convent in Channel Row' was the venue 'where the most celebrated Italian musicians help to make the voices of the holy sisters more melodious, and many Protestant fine gentlemen have been invited to take their places in a convenient gallery to hear the perform-ance'. It was clear that, the laws notwithstanding, Catholic intellectual, literary and devotional, as well as musical and fashionable, life throve in the Irish metropolis before the mid-eighteenth century. In the 1730s Bishop O'Gallagher of Raphoe published 17 sermons in Irish in Dublin. As a result of publishing activities within Ireland, literate Dubliners were becoming acquainted with translations of devotional classics by the likes of Nicholas Caussin and Francis de Sales, though it may be revealing of Anglo–Irish Catholic empathies that Richard Challoner's writings were the firm favourite. Devotional life in the capital now took on more of the richness of Continental Catholic practice: with vespers, sermons and congregational Rosary available in the afternoons, along with Exposi-tion and Benediction of the Blessed Sacrament, it might almost have seemed that Georgian Dublin had achieved the dream of the Kilkenny Confederates of Catholic worship 'as free and publick as it is…in Paris,…, or Bruxells'.[40]

Even so, this opulent and overtly displayed, yet officially illegal, Catholic worship was under recurrent threat and more specifically of proclamations to close the Mass-houses, especially during periods of war or rumours of war and invasion, in 1714–15, 1719, 1723, 1739 and 1743–4. Alarmed at a 'growth of popery' in 1732, the Church of Ireland Archbishop Boulter pressured the House of Lords to set up an inves-tigative committee empowered to take evidence from Protestant clergy on the situation; the results might, in fact, have discouraged rather than prompted a drive against a religion so well established in the island: there were 892 Mass-houses (229 of them built since 1727), 54 private chapels, 1445 priests, 51 friaries, 254 friars, nine nunneries and 549 Catholic schools. In the face of such entrenched Catholic provisions, the work of priest-hunters, essential agents of repression, was becoming impossible to perform: their role confirmed the almost stereotypical abhorrence of the figure of the informer in Irish popular culture, while at the same time magnifying the status of priests as folk heroes. In 1718 the informer John Garzia was responsible for the arrest of Archbishop Byrne of Dublin and six of his diocesan priests, but for his own safety Garzia had to be given a room in Dublin Castle; earlier, in

1716 a priest-hunter had complained of being attacked by mobs; in the Irish tradition of verse satire they were pilloried:

> God is pleased when man doth cease to sin,
> The devil is pleased when he a soul doth win,
> Mankind are pleased whene'er a villain dies,
> Now all are pleased for here Jack Cusack lies.[41]

In the countryside, meanwhile, landownership remained the most pressing issue of inter-confessional division, for the eighteenth century was decisive in confirming the process whereby in Ireland 'landownership became almost the exclusive preserve of members of the established church'. Even the odd exception to this rule seemed to confirm its overall validity. Thus the O'Hara Boy family of County Sligo appeared to defy the apparent destiny of those of their Catholic faith and Celtic stock, and Charles O'Hara of Annaghnore (c. 1705–76) became the personification of 'the independent county gentleman of the eighteenth century'. Even in his case, though, political influence was not to accompany landed substance, for Charles O'Hara's Gaelic–Catholic antecedents and connections barred his way to occupying what might otherwise have been his accepted place in Sligo politics. And direct ownership of land was not the only issue, for although Catholics might have the use of farms as intermediate tenants, in the south-eastern counties at any rate the dominance of Protestant 'middlemen' was marked and 'Catholic sub-tenants occupied a position in the social hierarchy of the area that was markedly less favoured than their Protestant counterparts', so that the countryside contained dangerous potential for inter-confessional rancour on tenurial grounds and for the explosion of the 'furious sectarian passions which seethed below the surface of Irish society'. Violence presented a serious challenge to a Catholic episcopate devoted, as Challoner was in England, to a quest for peace within the Catholic community and between it and its neighbours. Indeed, the condemnation by bishops of a Catholic population bent on 'raising a quarrel, or revenging a real or imaginary insult, offered to their relations, friends and partisans', and inclined to the 'shedding [of] their neighbours' blood, by murder, and the transgression of every law' indicates that, as a result of the deprivation under which the Catholic community suffered, a social Tridentine agenda highlighting pacification had a good way to go to achieve realisation in Hanoverian Ireland.[42]

5

CATHOLICS IN ENGLAND AND WALES, c. 1745–c. 1829

England

Our final period in the history of the Catholic communities of England and Wales between the Reformation and Emancipation is in some ways the most intriguing. The decades in question are punctuated with clear marks of transition: the Catholic Relief Act of 1778 as the first breach in the wall of penal legislation; the Gordon Riots as a violent reminder of the stubborn persistence of popular anti-popery; the impact of the French Revolution in softening national anti-popery; the Second Relief Act of 1791, licensing Catholics' worship by, in effect, extending to them the benefits that Nonconformists enjoyed under the 1689 Toleration Act; the arrival of refugee French priests in the 1790s, bringing refreshment to the faith, especially in its newer urban centres; and, finally, after protracted political struggle, the achievement of full civil rights in 1829.[1]

Despite the fact that English Catholics of the later Georgian age patiently built the foundations of the edifice that their Victorian heirs inherited and developed, the period of Catholic history whose moving spirits were Challoner and Lingard was not on the whole well regarded in nineteenth-century English Catholic thinking. Across a wide denominational spectrum, earnest Victorian Christians did not admire what they saw as the rationalistic lukewarmness of Georgian religion, and for Catholics looking back from the vantage point of the splendid growth in numbers and quality in their own time, the period between the second major Jacobite rising and Emancipation seemed one of timidity, decline and retreat. From a Victorian perspective, even the architecture of the pre-Emancipation Catholics seemed to echo their decadence, for in the 'chapels' they they built, illegally before 1791 and legally thereafter, the Catholics adopted a classical or baroque style that was viewed as debased and pagan by the dominant Victorian school led by Pugin, who upheld the sole claims of Gothic architecture alone to be a Christian style; a typical Catholic intellectual product of the Georgian age, John Lingard, with his English patriotism and 'Cisalpine' view of the relative independence of national branches of the Catholic Church from Rome, came by the time of his death in 1851 to be regarded by the ultra-orthodox Romanists of the Victorian age as little more than a crypto-heretic. The Georgian Catholics lacked the heroism and romance of their Tudor and Stuart predecessors and their guiding spirit, Richard Challoner, was little regarded until quite recently.[2]

If Victorian Catholics tended to look back on the history of their faith in England in the eighteenth century as a narration of decline, the demography of the community as we can now assemble it may, at least partly, bear them out, especially in those parts of the country in which Catholicism had never been strong since the Reformation and where, in the second half of the eighteenth century, extinction must have seemed at last to be be a real possibility. Such a prospect must have seemed likely, for example, in the Diocese of Exeter which covered Devon and Cornwall and where, in 1767, 235 of the enumerated 291 recusants were located in Devon, giving Cornwall fewer than 60 recusants; the situation in the west hardly justified Anglican fears of 'that most dangerous pernicious Sect' and of 'these restless, artfull, and ambitious people'. It is true that in the late eighteenth century there were some signs of growth in West Country Catholicism, including the establishment of a new school near Exeter in 1792: the inclusion of mathematics and the sciences in its curriculum suggests modernisation, while the fact that only 25 per cent of the students went on to the priesthood indicates that this was a new foundation for the Catholic community's lay elite. Evidence also comes from the West Country, though, to the effect that the Catholic faith was being relegated to the status of a picturesquely archaic cult, as with the Protestant farmer advised – rewardingly, as it turned out, – to drink as a cure for asthma water at Glastonbury 'out of Holy Ground where a great many Saints and Martyrs had been buried'. The early Romantic revival and its love of ivy-clad ruined abbeys may have added to the image of Catholicism as a poetically attractive 'gothick' ruin.[3]

To set against a picture of numerical decline and social marginalisation in pre-Emancipation English Catholicism, we have evidence of
demographic growth, albeit steady rather than spectacular: from
about 60 000 to 70 000 from the begining of the century to around
1780. Perhaps even more sinigificant than this demographic increase
was the unfolding geographical and social re-orientation of the Catholic
community within this period of extensive urbanisation in English
society. The urban focus of the Catholic community that was already
perceptible in the first half of the eighteenth century was even more
marked towards the end of the period under review – assisted, for
example, by the endowments of chapels by well-off entrepreneurs in
Birmingham in 1786 and 1809 and of a group of Mass-centres in New-
castle-on-Tyne and its satellite towns. Lancashire's recusancy was now
beginning to take on an increasingly urban flavour,with numbers in the
four main towns – Manchester, Liverpool, Preston and Wigan – rising
five-fold betwen 1780 and 1810 and increasing to a total of 32 000 by
1820; as in London, a further pointer towards a future in which most
Catholics in Britain would be plebeian Irish townspeople was the sharp
increase in the proportion of Irish-born in the total of Catholics
enumerated.[4]

We should not make too much, though, of trends in the direction of
the 'modernisation' of the English Catholic community – its relocation to
towns, the formation of a proletarian social base, the emergence of
middle class and priestly, rather than aristocratic, leadership, the reduction of the importance of the 'upper crust lay elements in Catholicism...with the lightening of persecution and the growth of urban
missions outside gentry control'. In fact, characteristic features of English Catholic sociology since Tudor times – gentry and noble patronage,
village locations, and relatively large communal concentration of rural,
native English tenants – remained in place as the eighteenth century
gave way to the nineteenth. It may even have been the case that the old
gentry and noble families were instrumental in helping to guide the
Catholic community into its new urban locations. The noble family of
Molyneux were archetypes of the traditional patronal Catholicism in
recusant rural Lancashire, sheltering, the historian Gillow calculated, 15
priests between the 1620s and the 1770s and protecting a Catholic
community of around 750 in the Sefton parish of Liverpool's hinterland. The family's connections with the Jesuits were especially strong, Fr
William Molyneux, SJ, inheriting the viscount's title in 1745. Then came
what might have amounted to disaster for the Molyneux links with the

Jesuits in particular and for their ancestral patronage of local Catholicism more generally for, brought up largely by Protestant guardians, and marrying the daughter of the earl of Harrington in 1768, in 1769 Charles William Molyneux renounced 'the errors of Rome' and in 1771 became earl of Sefton. On the face of it, this should have represented a severance of habits of patronage that had nurtured recusancy in the Molyneux satrapy for generations. In point of fact, this was far from being the case, for Lord Sefton, and subsequently his son the second earl, instituted and continued a generous £40 pension to the Jesuit fathers at nearby Gillmoss and the second earl was emphatic in maintaining provision for a 'resident Minester' in the surrounding villages. As late as 1824, when the Gillmoss chapel, housing 700 people, was built with handsome Molyneux assistance, it was clear that, 'apostasy' notwithstanding, patterns of rural patronage going back to the beginning of the recusant period were still being maintained in this West Derby heartland of Lancashire Catholicism. As for the urbanisation of the Catholic community, it was rural, seigneurial Gillmoss, where the priest in charge farmed his eight acres in a rural idyll like a small-scale Romanist squarson, that formed the nucleus for the Jesuit mission to bustling Liverpool. Such instances may suggest a need for some caution in describing a swift transition from rural–patronal–peasant to urban–bourgeois–proletarian social patterns in the social profile of the English Catholic community between the eighteenth and nineteenth centuries.[5]

Elsewhere in England's most Catholic county durable structures of gentry support for recusant dependents continued to operate. In 1767 94 Catholics around Birchley in south-west Lancashire nestled under the protection of the gentry Andertons, who had sponsored a secret press in the seventeenth century. The ancient family of the Gerards of Bryn, in the coalfield of Ashton-in-Makerfield, have a *beatus* and a canonised saint in their ancestry; from funds in the estate of the coal-rich eleventh baronet, at a cost of £1400, the church of St Mary, Birchley, was opened in 1828. In 1783 in Claughton-on-Brock, lying between Preston and Lancaster, James Hesketh, of the Brockhole family on his mother's side, made over part of the estate to the district's mission, while William Brockhole's mother-in-law, Elizabeth Heneage, donated £200 to the splendid chapel that was built in 1794. Up the Lune Valley from the county's second port, Lancaster, Ann Fenwick, Edmund Burke's 'lady of condition beyond the middle of life', set up a priest at Hornby Hall in 1762 for the area's 78 Catholic families and made the endowments that were later to furnish John Lingard's living as priest in residence at

Hornby. Though Ann Fenwick was the gentrified daughter of a wealthy attorney, her imperious way with the clergy – 'if he is a young man I wld have him to be very regular in every point belonging to his Function & particularly diligent in reading Pious Books' – and her regular acts of charity to the local poor indicate a continuing assured leadership of the community exercised by the rural elite.[6]

Of course it is true, as Dr Gilley comments, that the first (1778) and second (1791) Catholic Relief Acts fostered the ascendancy of middle-class and urban attitudes within the Catholic community. However, with regard to the first Act, it is worth noting that its passage was activated by the plight of a distressed landed gentlewoman, Ann Fenwick, and that the second Act was in large part the achievement of the head of one of the great noble recusant clans, Lord Petre. Indeed, the Petres, with six out of nine Essex missions recorded by Challoner under their care, were the principal Catholic patrons in the south east. Wealthy enough to build in the grandest Italianate style, the ninth Lord Petre echoed the old relationship between lordly patron and subordinate priest: in his accounts, he provided £40 to his cook, £26 to 'My Lord's gentleman', £25 to the butler, but £20 to 'Mr Lucas', the Jesuit household chaplain. No clearer signal of old leadership for new Catholic causes could be given than the proposal at the time of the opening of negotiations with the government for a second Relief Act that Lord Petre should be elected chairman – unless the duke of Norfolk should wish to occupy the position. If we needed any further confirmation of the centrality of the traditional recusant ascendancy, it would lie in the identities of the 130 signatories of the loyal subscription which preceded the first Relief Act, over a hundred of them belonging to families which for generations had been in possession of substantial landed estates.[7]

Apart from political guidance, financial aid and continuing assistance to rural recusant congregations, religious, liturgical and artistic leadership of the Catholic communitiy was provided by the great houses in the second half of the eighteenth century. Between 1770 and 1776 the eighth Lord Arundell paid for the building by his architect, the leading English Palladian, James Paine or Payne, of the new Wardour Castle, with a chapel able to accommodate the 'most numerous Catholic congregation outside London'. Following its opening by the Vicar Apostolic Bishop Walmsley in 1776, Wardour Chapel, with its vast size, became the venue for a richness of ritual that was perhaps deliberately designed to advertise its Catholic owner's self-assurance at a time when many of his co-religionists might have been persuaded to adopt a more timid

profile during the ferocious anti-papist Gordon Riots of 1780. Arundell
showed a confident, lordly approach to this crisis, insisting that he be
provided with of a 'party of guards' to defend Wardour and its great
Mass-centre; while, in June 1780 in Bath (which was not under Arundell
protection) the chapel was 'burning with a fury that is dreadful' and the
resident priest was in terrified flight, Lord Arundell's 'request' for
protection was 'immediately complied with' by the local authorities.
Subsequently he had notices posted at Wardour warning would be-
assailants of the legal penalties for malicious trespass, and, just for safety's sake, a 'keeper of the peace', a liturgical bouncer, was placed in a
handy pew in the Chapel. There were other benefits from Arundell
patronage: a chapel in the Arundel locality serving 540 Catholics; a
boarding and a day school operating peacefully under Wardour's
walls; and the accommodation of a congregation of 40 or 50 in Salisbury
'at a Mrs Arundell's... – a relation of his Lordship's'. More generally,
with popular anti-popery still current in later eighteenth-century England, the recusant community enjoyed the protection of peers of the
realm that the Nonconformists largely and the Jews entirely lacked.[8]

The charitable benefits to the English Catholic community dispensed
by its traditional landed leadership during this period included Lady
Stourton's education charity; Lady Mary Yate's and Nicholas Salvin's
poor relief; the Webb baronets' subventions to the Vicars Apostolic, to
converts and to the Jesuit; Lady Mary Webb's bequests in favour of
'compassion to the poor'; Sir Thomas Dereham's endowments for training converted clergymen for the priesthood; and Lady Peterbrough's
provision of a Mass-centre for Bedfordshire. All these cases confirm that
the late Georgian Catholic community continued to rely on the kind
hearts of those who wore the coronets. And if the centre of gravity of the
community's life was moving towards the industrialising urban centres,
with their urgent social problems, we should note that one of those
addressing those problems – dying heroically, ministering to epidemic
victims in Preston in 1813 – was the Jesuit Philip Darrell, born amidst
privilege, educated choicely at Liège and Stonyhurst and of a Kent
gentry family traceable to the fifteenth century.[9]

Far away in spirit and in miles from the horrors of industrialising
Preston was the harmless, indeed idyllic, rural world of the Dominican
estate priest Dominic Darbyshire (1690–1756) at the Cliffords' south
Devon home, Ugbrooke. This priest's pleasant and innocent routines –
teaching birds to sing to the viol, the care of the dogs, the birth of the
year's first fawn, the planting of broccoli, beans, artichokes and tulips,

jam-making, brewing and drinking its products, the administration of the Sacraments, small purchases, hunting, angling, a trip to see the fleet at Torbay – suggest an interval of calm between the sanguinary heroisms of the full penal period and the earnest endeavours of the Victorian age. The tolerance of English people depended indeed upon the maintenance by English Catholics of a modest and unthreatening demeanour. This in detail involved the absence of energetic schooling to raise up new generations of 'papists'; the lack of any episcopal pastoral care that would challenge the supremacy of the Established Church; low rates of activity on the part of priests and their practical invisibility as such; and low and declining recusant numbers, with slow rates of conversion. Such characteristics were to be found in the recusant cell which enjoyed Lord Petre's favour in Essex in 1766, of which an Anglican incumbent reported,

> if there is any Popish Priest resident or who resorts to these reputed Papists, it is done in so secret a manner that I cannot possibly take it upon me to declare it as a truth; there is no School for Popish Children; neither hath any Visitation or Confirmation been ever held.

The Petres' household, Ingatestone, was depicted as a small, quiet, well-established, inoffensive, and non-proselytising Catholic community made up of tenants of small farms, retired servants and other dependents and clients: 'none have been converted to popery... within twenty years'; the chaplain was so discreet 'an old Gentleman' that the fact that he was a 'Popish Priest' was only something that might be 'supposed by many'; there was 'no Popish School, nor has there been a Popish visitation'. Other reports confirmed the disposal of Petre charity, including an almshouse. The authorities did not object to the existence of this low-level Catholic activity or to the weekly celebration of Mass.[10]

Numbers were also kept low through the deliberate avoidance of proselytising in another Essex parish where the parson knew 'not of any Persons that have been perverted since my admission, nor of any means made use of in order to convert them'. Such inactivity in evangelism facilitated Anglican clerical attitudes of indifference, acceptance or even benevolence towards local recusants. Conversely, as Dr Haydon shows, any sign of a Catholic revival was sure to alert anti-Romanist clerical vigilance, and indeed the surveys we have been considering were occasioned by alarm that 'popery' was once more developing into a threat to the Church of England. Quiet and unexpanding clusters of Essex recusants overseen by an aristocratic co-religionist were safe enough, but Essex formed part of the diocese of London, whose bishop, Richard Terrick, alerted his clergy in 1765 to

> The visible Increase of Papists in the Cities of London and Westmin-ster,...a matter of serious Reflection to all, who wish well to the Safety and Happiness of this Protestant Country....[The bishop recalled his clergy to]...a more particular Zeal and Attention at a Time, when...the Emissaries of the Romish Church...appear to have for-got, that there are Bounds, which our Constitution has set to the Exercise of their Religion.

Thus the re-awakening of investigations of 'popery' in England in the 1760s arose from a perception that it was reviving, especially in London. Earlier in the same year that Bishop Terrick instigated his diocese-wide investigation, the London informer William Payne mounted his own campaign, which resulted in the convictions of Bishops Challoner and Talbot, along with priests and a schoolmaster, and when he did so, he had recourse to the 1700 Act for Preventing the Growth of Popery. Challoner himself referred to 'a kind of persecution, raised by some of the bishops under pretence of stopping the growth of popery'; the year 1767 saw the conviction at Croydon assizes of John Baptist Maloney for the offence of 'exercising the functions of a popish priest'. Seeing the 'first part' of George III's reign as a period in which 'the Catholics suffered a considerable degree of persecution', the near-contemporary Charles Butler noted the trial for his life in 1769 of the Hon. James Talbot for saying Mass and catalogued further incidents of 'great vexa-tion and contumely': perhaps, though, Butler spoiled his own effect somewhat by adding to his list of oppressions the way that a 'roman-catholic young lady of very high rank' had been reduced to tears when 'treated with marked slight by the lord chamberlain' at a court ball.[11]

The perceived revival of Catholicism of the 1760s was particularly linked with London. In other cities and towns around the country also a resurgent Catholicism challenged any comforting Protestant view that the Catholic faith was safely declining in rural backwaters. With demo-graphic growth, the towns also saw new social patterns of Catholic patronage and leadership. In its old north-western nuclei urban Cath-olicism was acquiring an especially powerful new numerical momentum through industrialisation. Wigan's Catholic population rose from 900 in

1783 to 1200 (out of a town total of 11 000) in 1800 and 3000 in 1819, putting heavy pressure on chapel provisions. In fact, the building of two rival chapels exposed social cleavages within Lancashire Catholicism between the old rural–patronal and the newer urban–bourgeois and proletarian elements. To John Barrow, the priest who operated under traditional gentry patronage in the hamlet of Claughton-on-Brock, the Wigan Catholics were 'ragamuffins' who ought to 'mind their tins pans, brass kettles, their looms and their bobbins' and not challenge priestly authority. However, industrial Wigan's Catholic sociology and ecclesiastical politics were more complex than Barrow depicted them as being, for the Catholic proletariat apart, a middle class, represented by a cotton manufacturer, a canal agent and a land-surveyor, had led a successful congregational revolt against the control of the Stonyhurst Jesuits who were allied to a Walmesley squire.[12]

A report by the Vicar Apostolic Bishop Petre in 1773 on the situation in Preston confirmed that the town's Catholic community were at that stage still reliant on gentry provisions, for 'Our oratories or places set aside for Mass and prayers are normally part of some mansion'. In 1768 the town chapel in Friargate became a victim of the borough's highly volatile electoral politics and was 'scandalously and impiously plundered and violated by a band of unprincipled ruffians'. By 1793, though, Preston had secured a permanent and imposing chapel in Fishergate, the centre of what was to become by 1829, in Mr Warren's words,'a great industrial parish'; already by 1813 so rapid, it was said, 'has been the increase of Catholics in the town of Preston only, that this Chapel (the largest in England) can no longer contain them'; this required the reopening of the closed Friargate premises. Like Preston, Leeds was a northern town having 'a consistent tradition of recusancy...from the end of the sixteenth century'. There, too, the period between the mid-eighteenth and the early nineteenth centuries saw a shift in the leadership of the Catholic community from the old gentry and peerage to the new middle class. Traditionally, the dukes of Norfolk had sheltered Catholic worship at Red Hall, Roundhay; then in 1776 sponsorship of what was to be the last of the patronal Yorkshire Mass-houses came to be shared between Lord Stourton and Leeds merchant converted to Catholicism, John Wade; the subsequent initiative of the cotton-spinner Joseph Holdforth to set up the town's mission in 1786 tells us that, before the end of the eighteenth century, key tranformations had taken place, not only in bringing Catholic populations into the industrialising towns, but in establishing in those towns structures of bour-geois, as distinct from gentry and noble patronage.[13]

In Bristol, by way of contrast, the identity of trustess of a new chapel built in 1786 in Trenchard Street – Lord Arundell, Sir John Lawson, Sir John Webb – suggests a continuity of gentry and noble leadership. Served by the Jesuits from the 1740s (and, following the Society's suppression, by an ex-member priest), the Bristol mission maintained a modest presence, with an extra-urban chapel at Baptist Mills, near a brassworks whose Quaker owners provided work for Catholics. As Dr Little shows, the 1778 Relief Act, allowing Catholics to own property legally, tended to come to mean that 'What they did in those properties was apt to be conveniently disregarded, so their "Prayers" (i.e. Mass) regularly occurred in the buildings concerned'. A chapel set up in a warehouse in the middle of Bristol in the 1770s was, however, prudently taken down so as to avoid a repetition of the scenes of pillage taking place in nearby Bath, themselves a re-enactment of the London Gordon Riots. By the later 1780s, though, the Bristol Catholics were once more anticipating advantageous changes in the law and in 1786 laid the foundations for the chapel that was to be completed in 1790 and was described in 1791 as 'a spacious Gothic building'. We have already seen that Bristol Quakers looked after the city's Catholics, and a kind of practical ecumenism was further evident in the city in the shape of donations made to the Trenchard Street chapel by 'papists and Protestants'. In Preston a new Catholic school received sub-scriptions from the earl of Derby, Sir Robert Peel, and the Bishop of Norwich.[14]

In Bath, though, the devastation dealt by the local version of the Gordon Riots provided an object lesson to the effect that conspicuous Catholic growth was likely to invite a popular backlash. The planning for growth on the part of Bath Catholics may have been too bold and premature. As J. Anthony Williams writes, full 'fourteen years before the second Catholic Relief Act permitted the existence of Catholic cha-pels', the resident priest, Dom Bede Brewer, was planning what he called 'a more spacious and convenient building' for Mass, and Dr Williams comments that it may have been 'the more public nature of the chapel' that brought down destruction upon it in 1780. Additionally, there may have been a strand of populist anti-popery in the attacks on the part of a mob led by a coachman and a milkman on the wealthy and fashionable style of Bath Catholicism: carriages arriving from London had 'No Popery' chalked on their doors and a gentleman attracted hostile notice for the reason that 'he must be the Pope, because he lodged in St James's Parade, and had a nightgown with gold flowers in it'. The Bath riots of 17 June 1780 made a lasting, terrifying impression on a very young member of the old recusant establishment: Charles Stonor recalled, 'In the dead of night I was obliged to get up hastily and was led by my father to York House, where we all passed the remainder of the night, and early next morning we set off for Stonor, leaving the Catholic Chapel in flames.'[15]

Even so, the Catholics in the western centre of fashion and leisure quickly recovered their collective composure and their property. Dom Bede was back in the town and administering the Sacraments before the month of the riots was out and was joined by his eventual successor in 1781 and by a third priest in 1784. The Benedictines successfully sued the Hundred of Bath and Wells for damages amounting to over £3000 and by 1786 the city's Catholics had acquired the

> Chapel, in Corn Street, ... well furnished with seats, [it] has a gallery with commodious pews; a fine altar, with an elegant painting of Our Saviour dying on the Cross over it. Here is Divine Service every Sunday at seven, nine and eleven.

Bath had become 'a veritable Mecca for Catholics'.[16]

Bath was one of a number of eighteenth-century British towns devoted to one specialist function or another. Other 'specialist' towns were the garrison bases of that belligerent nation, and in these, too, Catholics abounded, especially Irishmen serving in the forces – the category, in fact, for whom the laws were relaxed in 1778 to allow them to fight for the crown in the American War of Independence, though they were not to hold commissions and must swear an oath of allegiance. Catholic garrison congregations expanded accordingly in the years following. By means of 'private subscriptions', the 'extensive communion' in Sheerness in Kent acquired in 1790 a chapel seating 400; the 'neat building' of what may have been the even larger chapel of Woolwich, another Kent garrison town, was near the Royal Arsenal, and soon became 'quite inadequate ... to the numbers of Roman Catholics of Woolwich and its vicinity. . . . The congregation consists chiefly or soldiers and labouring men employed in the congregation.' In Portsmouth the mission based at Portsea opened its chapel in 1796, when the rector reported, 'Yesterday I had 200 Irish Soldiers at prayers, with their officer at their head drawn up in order publically.'[17]

If the demands of war helped produce the first Relief Act, the war consequent on the French Revolution again increased the recruitment of Catholics into the forces, creating the beginnings of a chaplaincy system, the first known Catholic chaplain to a British regiment, Alexander MacDonnel, being appointed to the Glengarry Fencibles in 1794. The French Revolution, though, through creating a large-scale migration of French priests into the country, had an even more dramatic effect in fostering Catholicism in England in the period following the passage in 1791 of the second Relief Act which legalised Catholic worship, subject to careful limitations. The garrison towns lying near the points of entry from France and needing reinforcements of priestly provision were particular beneficiaries of the flight of *curés* from the Revolution; at Woolwich two *Blanchardistes* (priests who repudiated the 1801 French Concordat) were reported to be at work in 1801, while in Dover, where the mercenary-sounding local priest thought that 'his only obligation [was] to serve Sir Edward [Hales]', it was émigré French priests who turned the Catholic religious provisions of the area from those of a traditional recusant household chaplaincy to those of a parochial-style mission, focussed on the Irish laity serving in the forces.[18]

The role of the French priestly exiles, coming at a fortunate moment of opportunity, with the statutory licensing of Catholic worship in 1791, deserves appreciation. Indeed, the 1790s formed a most hopeful period for real Catholic growth in English Catholicism, and if not a Newman-esque spring, then at least an end of winter. Dominic Bellenger quotes the encomium of J. H. Darnton on the special role of the French priests in this renewal:

> If the French Revolution was a terrible blow to the Church of France, Divine Providence was quick to turn to good account the misfortunes of the exiled priests who crowded every packet-boat that reached the English Channel ports.

Clearly, out of this large-scale exodus of French clerics, much would depend on individual priests' sense of a missionary commitment to England, on the length of their stay, and on their ability to learn the English language and English ways. Perhaps little was to be looked for in terms of pastoral zeal from such an elegant worldling as Arthur de Dillon, the émigré Archbishop of Narbonne who had once magnificently countered Louis XVI's rebuke over his distinctly un-Tridentine gambling debts with the promise that he would 'direct [his] steward, sire, to enquire into the matter'. More typical, though, of the usefulness of the refugee priests was the experience of the Yorkshire coastal town of Whitby, where the arrival of three dedicated French *curés* made an indispensable contribution to the survival and subsequent rapid expansion of the Catholic community. Of this trio, Nicholas Alain Gilbert, who arrived in 1794, became an active controversial journalist in English, his position that of a staunch royalist who set out to remind his English co-religionists of their loyal duties; Gilbert was also a liturgist, whose *Method of Sanctifying the Sabbath at Whitby, Scarborough, &c. With a Paraphrase on some Psalms, &c.* provides an excellent example of the vogue within this period for locally adapted 'congregational' forms of service. Though joining in the mass return of the exiles to France that took place in and after 1815, Gilbert left behind him in Whitby solid foundations on which his successor, the Lancashire Scripture scholar George Leo Haydock, was to build, republishing Gilbert's *Method*, along with a canon of saints linked with that place of holiness. Thanks to this succession of effort Whitby, whose Catholic population had been reduced to 15 in 1774 but which in 1805 opened a new chapel for a Catholic population of 300, by 1825 had three Masses each Sunday, 'with singing accompanied by the organ, and a discourse [sermon] at the morning and evening service. High Mass in every first Sunday of the Month...On holidays [holy days] Benediction with incense is given'.[19]

In Reading liturgical enrichment was the particular legacy of a massive encampment in the town of French priests transferred from Winchester and given a home in the King's Arms. As in Whitby, so in the Berkshire county town the Catholic presence had been reduced to a mere pilot light, with Mass said in a rented room, served, infrequently, from Ufton Court. The French priests brought to this stinted Catholic life the full splendours of the Tridentine rite *à la mode française*; they celebrated the full *horarum*, or daily schedule, with Masses from 5 am to noon, High Mass on Sundays and holy days, with Benediction – all in a chapel that could accommodate 400. One of the priests who stayed on when he could have returned to France at the time of the Peace of Paris in 1802, François Longuet, taught French in order to raise the funds to build Reading's first permanent post-Reformation Catholic chapel, dedicated to the Resurrection; it was ready by 1809 and by 1812 was offering Sunday mass at 11('very full'), vespers at 3 and evening prayers at 7, with a 'lecture' at Mass and an 'exhortation extemporary' in the evening. Longuet was able to record, not surprisingly, 14 conversions in just one half of the year 1812. In the far west, too, by 1797 French priests were active in what had been the sterile territory of Cornwall, in Truro, Trelawney, St Austell and St Columb.[20]

Around the country, regular, as well as congregational, life was boosted by the Continental Catholic diaspora occasioned by the French Revolution and its spread in Europe. French priests also played their part in this conventual renewal. At New Hall in Essex, for example, the repatriated English canonesses had as their chaplain for almost half a century a near-martyr to the guillotine, the 'singularly pious' Etienne Chapon, whose white hairs were his personal memorial to the Terror. In the 1790s English female regular life saw a massive return home from the Continent. In 1794, for example, the English Carmelite nuns, formerly at Antwerp, settled at Langhorn Manor, Cornwall, where in 1799 the first clothing of a nun in the western counties since the Reformation took place, along with, in 1800, the first construction of an English convent chapel since the Tudor age; after months of imprisonment, in 1795 Benedictine nuns from Dunkirk accepted an offer from Bishop Douglas, Vicar Apostolic of the London District, to take up accommodation at the Mary Ward convent in Hammersmith; in the north in 1794 other Benedictine nuns, from Ghent, set up a convent in Chapel Street, in the fashionable quarter of Preston. The year 1793 had already seen the arrival from Montargis of nuns who included the Hon. Catherine Dillon, to open a 'fashionable school' in Norfolk. The Bruges canonesses, settled at the Gage family home, Hengrave Hall, Suffolk, established there an imposing repertoire of the office and the liturgy, Sunday and feastday vespers and compline, with Benediction of the Blessed Sacrament, and two daily Masses, one of them open to neighbours. A school was opened following consultations carried out by Lady Gage with the two local members of Parliament and the Archbishop of Canterbury, and in 1795 the full habit of the order was resumed. The combination that these nuns from the Continent brought of social tone with ceremonial enrichment amidst a liturgically still austere Anglicanism proved irresistible to the local Suffolk gentry and the clergy of the area, one of whom cried out, at the Elevation of the Host, 'This is solemn indeed.' It is true that these early restorations of convents were usually temporary – the nuns in Preston left in 1811, those at Hengrave in 1802 – but they undoubtedly paved the way for the vast expansion of English feminine regular life, much of its also fed from the Continent, that took place in nineteenth-century Britain.[21]

The English Catholic community's educational provisions were also enormously expanded by the effects of the French Revolution. A series of moves brought the English Jesuit college in the Low Countries to Lancashire, where its former student Thomas Weld gave it the magnificent house of Stonyhurst in the lovely Ribble Valley. Building extensions followed and the school quickly slotted into place as the principal training college for England's Catholic elite, both of new and old wealth. When the secular seminary at Douai was closed in 1792, it eventually moved to remote Ushaw in County Durham, to open there in 1809. The restitution of its library, from the low point in 1790, when some of its priceless folios were recycled as cartridge cases for the French armies, to a point of recovery at which, acquiring dozens of volumes formerly belonging to the monks of Durham, it rose to 4000, and then to 7000 works by 1827, might be taken as a metaphor for the intellectual restoration of English Catholicism in the decades following the French Revolution.[22]

A leading figure in that academic restoration, even though, in the heat of mid-Victorian Catholic triumphalism he was excoriated as a thinker the moderation of whose historical writing 'made it agreeable to heretics', was the erstwhile vice-president of Ushaw, John Lingard. However, if we had to identify one figure of the mid- and late-eighteenth century who can be regarded as the Georgian architect of Victorian Catholicism it would be the long-serving (until his death in 1781) Vicar-General of the London District, Bishop Richard Challoner. We shall consider Challoner as the pastor and administrator of a Catholic population in the metropolis already having stereotypical 'Victorian' features – partly Irish, very large, heavily proletarian, but also quintessentially urban and heterogeneous in its sociology. To this metropolitan community and its problems, Challoner, always, and rightly, regarded as the 'most English' of English Catholic clerical leaders, not least in his liturgical and devotional initiatives, was also the most 'Roman' – or rather the most Tridentine – of pastoral bishops. The genius of Richard Challoner, though, was that, the Tridentinist reformer through and through that he was, he was also able to align his Catholic faith with the most creative force within eighteenth-century British Christianity, the evangelical renewal.[23]

Challoner's 'parish' was London – Johnson's London, but already in many ways London as Dickens was to know it, Britain and its empire in microcosm, both profoundly and uniquely English and bewilderingly cosmopolitan. With its 20 000 recusants even in 1730, this great city of the Reformation, with more Protestant places of worship than any other city anywhere, had also become, astonishingly, one of Europe's great

Catholic cities. Its aristocratic elements gravitated towards the embassy chapels – the Imperial, the Portuguese, the French, the Spanish, the Venetian, and, above all, the 'Cathedral of London Catholicism', the Sardinian; in these worshippers encountered liturgy 'approaching the baroque splendour of the counter-reformation' and music which delighted non-Catholic visitors, including the Dissenter Richard Kay. Alongside the fashionable and the nobly born was a bourgeois element including converts, and 'made up of professional people, merchants and tradesmen, middle and lower-middle class, London-born and immigrants from the provinces and abroad'. The proletarian stratum included weavers, both in the City and more widely dispersed, and dock-workers. The immigrants included Germans, but had a broad proletarian base of 'poor Irish and poor Italians': by 1780 there were already 4000 Irish worshipping in Wapping alone. The social profile of Georgian metropolitan Catholicism already pointed towards the opportunities and challenges for a priestly apostolate in urban Britain in the nineteenth century.[24]

Challoner's contribution to this evolution, though, as much looked back to Trent as forward to the nineteenth century. His Tridentine disciplinarianism was imposed, in the first place, on himself, for his Wesley-like 'iron regime, never relaxed, part of the discipline, regularity and poverty he believed to be fundamental to the priestly life', was specifically grounded in the Council's exacting requirements of the bishop: that he be apostolic, vigilant, diligent, resident and exemplarily austere. From that personal foundation, Challoner set up a sytem of regulation of his priests strongly reminiscent of the measures taken by the great Catholic reformers of the Counter-Reformation period, above all Borromeo; Challoner, for example, implemented for his priests weekly conferences designed to 'cultivate in their souls an Ecclesiastical Spirit', by keeping up habits of theological study and by discussing perplexing lay cases of conscience that had arisen in the Confessional; they were to conduct daily meditative prayer and follow an annual retreat, and to stay at home of an evening – Challoner was fully aware of the magnetic rival attractions of the capital's theatres, clubs and taverns – 'so that we may be found by those who shall want us for the sick ... or ... come for instructions': the conversionist dynamic. Ministry to the poor must be given gratis and priests must catechise children, hear Confessions, 'reconcile those that are at a variance' and preach at every evening service having a congregation. His approach was paternally solicitous, and in his regular conferences he dealt with the pastoral

care of his own clergy. That said, though, his fatherly care was undoubtedly authoritarian, as can be seen in his strict supervision of the regular
orders. Towards the Jesuits, in particular, Challoner, like his contemporaneous Irish colleagues, showed the typically Tridentine approach of
episcopal disciplinarianism *vis-à-vis* regulars, deriving from the Council's Chapter XIV in its 25th session which placed members of orders, or
at least their delinquent members, under episcopal control. Challoner,
insisting on high-quality education at the English College, Rome,
showed himself prepared, in 1759, to move Rome to end the *Venerabile*'s
control by the Jesuits. He had further difficulties with an Irish Dominican whom Dr Duffy calls 'a loud mouthed drunk' and whose uncon-
trollability – 'passing his time in public houses, with very improper
company, drinking to excess,... sometimes vulgar swearing etc.' – was
compounded by his semi-exempt status within the Sardinian Embassy
chapel. Other ambassadorial exemptions to Challoner's episcopal
authority to carry out regulation of the clergy included the diplomatic
immunities of the Portuguese and Bavarian missions, where the challenges to the Vicar Apostolic's powers that he had to surmount were
complicated by Jesuit and Capuchin claims to autonomy. In asserting his
rights in these matters, Challoner calls to mind contemporaneous
Continental Tridentinist diocesan reformers such as Muratori and
Scipio de Ricci; in securing ratification of his powers from the Holy
See, in the Bull *Apostolicum Ministerium* of 1753, Challoner won
papal backing for his determination to overcome challenges to his
episcopal rule so as to confirm the scope of bishops' jurisdiction as set
out by the Council of Trent. Looking back to Trent, though, he also
pointed forward to the full restoration of the English hierarchy in
1850.[25]

It would be grossly misleading to present Bishop Challoner as simply
an administrative disciplinarian, for he was particularly attentive to his
sacramental function and brought Confirmation to a large area of the
London area after a period of its absence over some years. His work in a
wide arc in Kent, Sussex and Buckinghamshire recalls the heroic Catholic itinerants of the earlier penal period, but also puts us in mind of his
contemporary John Wesley. In Catholic circles, though, Challoner was
most enduringly known as a devotional writer, one who, as Patrick
O'Donovan wrote, 'gave England back to prayer' – though we might
ask, 'What sort of prayer?' John Bossy reminds us that 'prayer' in
eighteenth-century English Catholic usage was code for the Mass.
And, as Professor Bossy adds, what Challoner provided, within his

devotional classic *The Garden of the Soul* (1740), was 'a detailed commentary on what was taking place on the altar, and . . . a series of meditative prayers appropriate to successive actions'. Direct congregational participation was not envisaged, for Mass was essentially a sacrifice offered by the priest, though, of course, on behalf of the congregation – 'by the hands of this thy minister'. Following a 'commentary' was one of the things congregants could do during Mass, another special favourite being the recitation of the Rosary. However, such optional activities tended to reduce congregants to the status of atomised individuals present *at* Mass. With Challoner, this individuation continued the emphasis, much earlier seen in the *Imitation of Christ*, on the Mass-goer as a private *dévot* only ostensibly present at a public event. Thus where the *Imitation* advised 'That he who is about to communicate with Christ ought to . . . shut out the whole world . . . remain in some secret place, and enjoy thy God', Challoner used the same second-person-singular voice to advocate private union with Christ – a 'private' Mass, within the appearance of a congregational structure:

> Imagine that you hear within you the sweet voice of your Saviour, inviting you to come to his sacrifice and to unite yourself to him . . . - Choose as much as you can a place to kneel in, where you may be more recollected and least disturbed.[26]

In the *Introduction to the Devout Life* St Francis de Sales extended the interiorist tradition of the *Imitation of Christ* into the seventeenth century, addressing, conversationally, an imagined single reader who prepares for Communion the night before reception. The tone is richly emotive and its muted erotic flavour perhaps cloying to the modern reader: 'If you should awake during the night fill your heart and your mouth straightaway with some fragrant words by means of which your soul might be perfumed to receive the Beloved.' Challoner was a disciple of de Sales: his *The Garden of the Soul* includes 'Ten meditations out of the first part of St Francis de Sales's Introduction to a Devout Life', the work of which he has been credited with 'the most important English translation'. However, there were limits to Challoner's indebtedness to de Sales, who was a Frenchman of the high baroque, while Challoner was an Englishman from an eighteenth-century culture that admired plainness and restraint. Plainness was the epitome of Challoner's literary style, a style that Dr Luckett rightly calls demotic – and we might add, didactic and homiletic. We can see this didactic approach – and contrast it with de Sales' emotive and devotional tone – when we consider a passage, also on the Eucharist, in which the sobriety of Challoner's language is ancillary to his educational task:

> Thus in His Incarnation and birth, he made Himself our companion; in His passion and death, the price of our ransom; in the banquet of His last supper, our food and nourishment: and in His heavenly kingdom, our eternal reward.

Dr Luckett illuminatingly compares Challoner, in his use of this plain language of 'explication' and 'intelligibility', with the Anglican Bishop John Pearson, whose *Exposition of the Creed* (1659) was much reprinted: note, for instance, how Challoner's teaching aims induced him to use Anglo–Saxon synonyms, or near-synonyms–'Incarnation and birth', 'food and nourishment' – to clarify latinisms and gallicisms. The difference of method between de Sales and Challoner was that the former was assuming in his reader doctrinal knowledge on the foundations of which he could develop arabesques of piety, whereas Challoner had himself to build a base of instruction. This elementary pedagogy was also his technique in his *Catechism*, in which he started from the most basic data – 'Who made me? God made me' – successively working up to more advanced doctrinal levels. In Lancashire, another priest-teacher, John Barrow, of Claughton-on-Brock, used Challoner's catechism as his pedagogic *vade mecum*.[27]

Challoner, then, represented the bishop as teacher, in a vital episcopal role reaffirmed at Trent. Thus, when Challoner explained the meaning of the Eucharist, he was carrying out to the letter the instruction of the Council that bishops must 'in a manner adapted to the mental ability of those who receive [the Sacraments], explain their efficacy and use'. He used his clerical conferences as seminars and opened his school at Sedgeley Park, near Wolverhampton, in 1763. His educational, or catechetical, programme strongly influenced his approach to the Eucharist and the Mass and, as we have just seen, his exposition led him into a pedagogic outline of the whole redeeming action of Christ. It is true that Challoner's 'Devotions for Mass' within the *Garden of the Soul* do form, as Professor Bossy says, a 'commentary', but it is specifically an instructive commentary, setting out doctrine; to give one example, 'A Prayer after the Elevation' expounds the doctrine of the Atonement, in a slightly awkward way, in the form of a reminder to the Almighty to the effect

that thy only begotten Son, for us poor sinners, was conceived and
born into this world; that for us he suffered a bitter agony and sweat
of blood; for us he died, and for us he triumph'd over death by his
resurrection, and opened heaven for us by his ascension.

Challoner's educational purpose was enhanced by the adoption of a
vivid exclamatory prose, though one perhaps more reminiscent of the
Evangelical Revival than of de Sales' lusher rhapsodies:

O look not on our sins, but on the infinite ransom paid for them . . . -
May all heaven and earth bless and praise thee for ever for all thy
mercies. O pardon me, dear Lord.

That kind of language can be heard with particular clarity in Challoner's
celebration of 'Christ's incomparable mystery of love, which will aston-
ish men and angels to all eternity'. And that talk of astonishment
reminds us in turn of Charles Wesley's amazement at the fact of his
redemption:

Amazing Love! How can it be
That Thou my God shouldst die for Me.

Were there, though, any deeper levels of similarity between Challoner
and the Wesleys beyond some stylistic resemblances?[28]
    On the face of it, there can have been few points of sympathy between
Challoner's Catholicism and the Wesleys' Methodism. While Challoner
attacked Methodism in his 1760 *A Caveat against the Methodists*, Wesley
condemned Catholicism in *Popery Calmly Considered* of 1779. Even so,
there were strong similarities between these two men, and not only in
their passions for work and routine, their abstemiousness and their care
for the poor. For one thing, the devotional writer John Gother, who
received Challoner into the Catholic Church, was read by Wesley before
his conversion of 1738. In addition, both Challoner and Wesley strongly
upheld celibacy and both observed fasting, Wesley actually keeping
Wednesday and Friday fasts. However, it was in the field of soteriology
– the doctrines of salvation – that Wesley and Challoner had most in
common, so that Dr Butler speculates that if Wesley and Challoner 'had
met and understood one another properly', the result might have been
'a consensus document on Justification'. Challoner's soteriology was that
of the Council of Trent, which insisted on the absolute indispensability

of divine grace flowing from Christ's sacrifice in winning the redemption of sinners, securing 'for us justification by His most holy passion
... and [making] satisfaction for us to God the Father'. In Challoner's
rendition, this Tridentine doctrine of justification by merits won outside
of ourselves, for us, vicariously, reads:

> neither mercy, nor grace, nor salvation, either can, or ever could,
> since Adam's fall, be obtain'd any otherwise, than through this death
> and Passion of the Son of God ... We must believe also the necessity of
> divine *grace*, without which we cannot make so much as one step
> towards heaven. And that all our good, and all our merits, are the
> gifts of God.

Thus Challoner restated the Pauline–Augustinian theological tradition,
inherited both by Luther and by Trent, of stress on grace and faith,
rather than on works, in the achievement of salvation. Meanwhile, on
his side of the divide that is usually thought to distinguish Reformation
from Catholic soteriologies, the Protestant John Wesley stated a formula, usually associated with Catholicism, that brought together faith,
grace and works in a triple salvific formula: 'We have also received it as a
maxim, that "a man is to do nothing in order to justification." Nothing
can be more false.' Such were the points at which the 'evangelical'
Challoner complemented the 'Catholic' Wesley. Neither in Wesley nor
in Challoner, though, was there a predestinarian conclusion to be drawn
from a soteriology of justification coming initially from outside ourselves. Central to Challoner was the view 'That Christ died for all
men.' This anti-predestinarian outlook made of Challoner what Wesley
was, an active, conversionist missionary at large.[29]

Challoner resembled John Wesley also in his congregational view of
the church, balancing the devotional individualism of the *Imitation of
Christ* tradition. 'We' and 'us' are Challoner's pronouns in 'Devotions for
the Mass' and his congregational ethos is encapsulated in the prayer he
recommended to prepare for the Elevation of the Host: 'We present to
thee, O Lord, this bread and wine, which being composed of many,
reduced into one, are symbols of concord and unity'. Beyond the
particular congregation, Challoner was concerned with society and the
community of the nation at large, with prayers for the king and for 'all
magistrates and men in power, ... in this nation'. His sense of sin and
morality was equally social. He did not manifest what is sometimes seen
as an obsession with sexual matters in the post-Reformation Catholic

Church and was laconic on the subject of 'uncleanness of thoughts, words, and actions, beyond the lawful use of the marriage bed'. He was, though, insistent on observance of the practical details of Christian civics – on 'the laws of the church and state', on 'due care of our children, and of others that are under our charge'; Catholics must avoid

> all injuries to our neighbour's person, . . . must not steal, cheat, or any
> other way wrong our neighbour in his goods and possessions; . . . pay
> our debts, . . . make restitution . . . .We must not wrong our neighbour
> in his character or good nature, by detraction or rash judgment.

Challoner's strong sense of Christian good neighbourliness and the tentative ecumenism evident in his view of the Scriptures 'received and admitted by all Christian' must have contributed to fitting his co-religionists to the requirements of a 'polite and commercial' Georgian society. As Dr Rowlands writes, Challoner's co-religionists were becoming less and less

> a separate or besieged group, cut off from the community at large, but
> [were becoming] a minority, close-knit indeed, but participating in the
> whole community and influenced to some extent by the same devel-
> opments.[30]

In its worship, the English Catholic community was utterly distinctive, alone having the Mass, which by the later eighteenth century was available weekly to most and daily 'to a considerable proportion'. The rite was, though, also partly assimilated to some styles of worship prevailing elsewhere in the wider community, especially in Independency's latitude of liturgical choice for individual congregations. Local adaptations of forms of prayer for particular Catholic congregations or towns included Nicholas Alain Gilbert's Whitby cycle looked at earlier. The fugal effect of embroidering the standard 'Tridentine' Mass with variety for local congregations was achieved through weaving prayers before and after Mass around the celebration itself. Thus in Wolverhampton a printed set of congregational prayers, based on an edition of Gother's devotions and designed for congregational recitation before and after Mass, consisted of psalms, the Our Father, Acts of Faith, Hope, Charity and Contrition, the Litany of the Saints, the *Te Deum*, along with prayers for the dead, the sick and (after 1778) the king. From a point of view of Tridentine uniformity, these local variations, designed, especially through 'bidding' prayers for the sick and departed to answer to the special needs of the congregation, were repugnant, as they were to the Vicar Apostolic Bishop Milner who, in 1803, when he established himself in Wolverhampton, complained of the various versions of prayers for before and after Mass being published by priests: he suppressed them. Nevertheless, the way the Mass operated as the focus for additional services and instruction, including vespers and catechesis, undoubtedly allowed for 'missions' to develop into identifiable local congregations, and, indeed, into proto-parishes. Meanwhile, liturgical facilities were by no means stinted, least of all at gentry houses such as the Giffards' Staffordshire Chillington Hall (before its owners' apostasy), where there were 11 sets of Mass vestments, servers' cassocks, plentiful altar-plate and three missals; at the Astons at Tixall and at Bellamore the complete liturgy of Holy Week was observed, the Blessed Sacrament was exposed for veneration and nuptual and requiem Masses were celebrated.[31]

The lightening of penal conditions must have allowed for closer observance of the season and feasts. In Staffordshire Holy Communion was received on the principal feasts – about half a dozen of them a year, though in 1745 the pious squire of Chillington Hall vowed to receive about once a month. The Host was taken to the sick and those in danger of death; children made their First Holy Communions between the ages of 12 and 15. Easter Communion represented 'the climax of the liturgical year', when the number of communicants was carefully logged – as they were, for instance, at Hornby by Lingard, who in 1813 recorded 114 Easter communicants – and checked for comparison with earlier years. Communion was always preceded with a strict fast, as ordained by Challoner, and Confession was made before Communion, in general conformity with the requirements set out at Trent that 'no one conscious to himself of mortal sin . . . ought to receive the Sacred Eucharist without previous sacramental confession' (or, in Challoner's version, 'we go to confession before communion, in order to clear our souls from the filth of sin'). As for Confession itself, the more perfectionist routines required fasting, 'meditation and prayers . . . more particularly the night before . . . communion'; however, in one Lancashire community in 1780 what may have been a congregational preference for a more unbuttoned, or less Salesian, Saturday night followed by traditional Sunday-morning Confession immediately before the Mass at which Holy Communion was to be received led to conflict with a mission priest.[32]

Rigorous penitential self-scrutiny was observed by Peter Giffard at Chillington: 'What guard do you keep upon your thoughts, words, actions and senses? How do you perform your prayers and acts of piety? What self-denials do you practise?' Such searching self-examination was recommended by Challoner, who warned against 'too much anxiety and scrupulosity', but followed this wise advice with 11 pages of a sample examination of conscience. We have, then, the sense of a religious community in which perfectionist norms were upheld – or, as Dr Rowlands puts it, 'Regularity and discipline [were] the keys to spiritual progress.'

Abstemiousness was central to the penitential regimes, Challoner highlighting strict observance of the 'days of abstinence commanded by the church' – 'Have you...eaten more than one meal on fasting days?' – which comprised all the days of Lent, almost all Fridays and the vigils of major feasts. (The Vicar Apostolic Bishop Hornyold relaxed the rules during a dearth in 1758 and in 1781 Pius VI drastically reduced the swollen number of the English fast days.)[33]

Confession and Holy Communion apart, Dr Rowlands' Midland Catholics had regular access to most of the Sacraments. Baptism was administered promptly, or even pre-promptly, John Giffard being christened *in ventro*. By way of comparison, Bossy's survey of a group of Catholic missions from the 1740s to the 1800s shows that 'nearly all the community's children were baptised within a week of birth'. Confirmation was dispensed, by the Vicars Apostolic, with remarkable regularity: Bishop Stonor confirmed four times at Chillington Hall between 1724 and 1731, with as many as 29 recipients at a time, while Bishop Talbot conducted a systematic tour to confer the Sacrament over a three – four year cycle. In contrast, the 'Last Sacrament' of Extreme Unction is not recorded in the Staffordshire sources, though Catholic burials did take place, with parish incumbents often collaborating, and sextons and bellringers taking fees from Catholics to perform the parts they would have taken in legal internments. Richard Challoner himself was buried with deference to the parochial proprieties of the Established Church, recorded in a curious and inaccurate entry, 'Anno Domini 1781, January 22 Buried the Reverend Richard Challoner, a Popish Priest and Titular Bishop of London.' As for marriage, special difficulties were raised with Hardwicke's 1753 Marriage Act which made all non-Anglican weddings except those of Quakers illegal: Catholics adopted an arrangement, which Challoner observed in the London District in1760, of legal marriage in the parish church followed by nuptual ceremonies of their own, often held, in Staffordshire at least, after Sunday Mass.[34]

English Catholics traditionally observed an exceptionally full calendar of feast days, when, Challoner insisted, the faithful must 'rest from servile works'. These, apart from folkoric and local observance kept by Catholics, such as lighting bonfires in the Bowland Forest of Lancashire on All Souls' Eve, included Easter Monday and Tuesday, Whit Monday, the Annunciation, St Michael, St John the Baptist, St Ann, St Thomas of Canterbury and St George. Mr Hilton considers the 'holy days of obligation' to have been 'burdensome' to working and wage-earning people, and their reduction to 12 by a papal decree in response to a petition, while it reduced the eccentricity of the English Catholic community within English society, can also be interpreted as recognition of the fact that a typical member of that community might now be an urban artisan.[35]

Private and family prayer continued to be cultivated at home: Peter Giffard took a vow to devote one day every day to the practice. Confraternal prayer re-emerged in the form of a sodality set up in honour of St Francis, in Edgbaston. Pious literature featured stock favourites: *The Garden of the Soul*, and some Douai Bibles or New Testaments. More ambitiously, the library of 60 works left by a Worcester lady included three copies of *The Garden of the Soul*, a Kempis, Gother, James II's *Memoirs*, and the Roman rite for Sundays and holy days. Dr Rowlands finds evidence in Staffordshire of a retreat from mysticism in favour of the same kind of 'solid regularity of practice' which Professor Bossy observes in this period in Lancashire. Education was expanding rapidly in the Midlands, where the school opened at Sedgeley Park by 1763 as a outcome of planning by the Vicar Apostolic Bishop Hornyold was aimed at middle-class boys and future seminarians, with a predominantly utilitarian curriculum, along with the inculcation of devout and gentlemanly habits; in the last four decades of the eighteenth century it produced 1000 scholars, laying foundations for English Catholic middle-class leadership in the century to come, the age of emancipation and assimilation.[36]

Wales

The second half of the eighteenth century, in which Methodism took Wales by storm, saw the continuing erosion of a Catholic tradition which in areas such as the south west of the Principality had become folkloric practices focused on the cult of saints and on visits to therapeutic holy wells:

> many times in their ejaculations [they invoke] not the Deity but only the Holy Virgin and other saints; for Mair Wen [White Mary], Jago [James], Tailaw Mawr [Teilo the Great], Celer, Celynnog and others are often thus remembered as if they had hardly yet forgotten the use of praying to them. And there being not only churches and chapels but also springs and fountains dedicated to those saints, they do at certain times go and bathe themselves in them and sometimes leave their small donations behind them either to the keeper of the place or in a charity box prepared for that purpose by way of acknowledgement for the benefit they have, or hope to have thereby.[37]

Welsh Catholicism was both rural in its distribution and found in a very few pockets within the Principality. A survey of the Diocese of St David's carried out in 1767 covered Radnorshire, five parishes of Herefordshire, one parish of Monmouthshire, and Breconshire and returned only 52 male and 62 female recusants, with a low social profile – 'poor labourers', small farmers, and widows, with a Brecon apothecary, converted in Flanders. Indigenous Welsh Catholicism saw little of the urban growth that we have noted in London, Staffordshire and Lancashire. In Monmouth, county town of the Principality's most Catholic shire, the Catholics were treated with suspicion and behaved with timidity: in 1792 they opened a chapel up a 'narrow passage' behind a gaggle of poor houses, a siting that may have been responsible for the local tradition that the mayor and corporation insisted that the building not resemble a church and be entered one person at a time. The little Monmouth community which, though nourished by some Irish immigration in the 1820s, fell from 120 to 100 over the course of the nineteenth century, should be regarded as an offshoot of the patronage of the Herbert cadet house of nearby Perthîr. Under this protection the Vicar Apostolic of the Western District, the Franciscan Bishop Matthew Prichard took up residence at Perthîr, where he established the Franciscans, whose novitiate it became between 1808 and 1818. There was continuity and some growth in the Catholic community in the locality, with an annual average of 2.3 baptisms in the period 1761–6 and 5.6 in the years 1799–1806. At Llanarth, also in Monmouthshire, the continuity of the Catholic circle was attributable 'to the Catholic fidelity of the family of Herbert', lords of the manor. Mass was said within Llanarth Court and subsequently in a chapel near the house, most, if not all, of the priests also serving as household chaplains. However, the demolition of the manse with its chapel at Perthîr in 1830 might be viewed as a symbol of the disappearance of these patterns of gentry patronage. Landownership and the political power that went with it were, obviously, essential elements in patronal protection. The Morgans of Tredegar in Monmouthshire were extensive landowners in three Welsh counties and Whig magnates. On the death of William Morgan in 1763, the Catholic William Jones, Clytha, claimed the estate in right of his wife, a Morgan descendant; its possession, writes Dr Dowden, would 'have allowed Jones – long … prominent in the sizeable Catholic community of Monmouthshire – to rise above the disabilities stemming from his family's adherence to Catholicism'. In 1774, however, the dispute over the inheritance was settled in favour of the Protestant Charles Morgan and a major opportunity to improve the fortunes of Catholicism in south-east Wales was thereby lost.[38]

The Joneses of Clytha also played a part in the Catholic life of North Wales, with its powerhouse in Flintshire, where the succession, going back to John Plessington (d. 1679), of secular priests serving the Holywell mission and its St Winifrid's shrine from the Cross Keys Inn was continued through the long priestly ministry, from 1763 to his death in 1800, of Philip Jones, Clytha. The Jesuits at Holywell also operated from an inn and maintained a strong presence at the shrine, opening a new chapel in 1833. From 1763 Irish names appear on the registers at the shrine, increasing strongly in the 1820s and 1830s. They represent the harbingers of the waves of Irish immigrants who were to resuscitate Catholicism, especially in the ports, Cardiff, Newport and Swansea, and the industrial valleys of Victorian South Wales.[39]

6

CATHOLICS IN SCOTLAND AND IRELAND, c. 1745–c. 1829

Scotland

The period from 1745 to 1829 cannot be categorised in any simple terms of growth or decline for the Catholic Church in Scotland, even though it may be possible to detect the early signs of a 'second spring' from around 1790 onwards. Yet for some commentators 'a severe judgment on eighteenth-century Scottish Catholicism is deserved'. Some might see the symptoms of a more general malaise in the failure of the Scots College, Rome, a key institution set up for 'the provision of a steady and regular supply of secular clergy who would spend their lives working in Scotland amongst Scottish Catholics': the early nineteenth-century historian of the College, the Abbé Paul McPherson, claimed that amidst 'disorders', serious ill-discipline and chronic financial mis-management 'the college had failed and failed lamentably and culpably in fulfilling that purpose'. A further sign of contraction in Scottish Catholicism on the Continent was the secularisation in 1744 of the much-reduced ancient Benedictine foundation at Würzburg. While these erosions of the Scottish Catholic presence abroad might, arguably, have had the effect of concentrating attention on the task of the mission within Scotland itself, there was a further problem of Catholic ecclesiastical authority within the country. From the retrospect of the firmer episcopal control prevailing from the time of the restoration of the Scottish hierarchy in 1878 the Georgian Scottish Catholic Church appeared virtually leaderless, its Vicars Apostolic friendless and unrespected: 'Vicars apostolic were in a most unenviable position', writes Fr. Anderson, 'and they had no defender. There were no halcyon years for a Scottish vicar apostolic in the eighteenth century.' Not only did the Vicar Apostolic of the Lowland District, Bishop Hay (appointed 1778, d. 1811) have to put up with the unorthodox approaches to Scripture of Alexander Geddes (1737–1802) but the '45 and priests' involvement in it did lasting damage in highlighting Catholic clerical Jacobite militancy, in some cases displayed by difficult characters, such as the contentious John Tyrie, wounded at Culloden, or Allan MacDonall, who featured in the rising as 'Captain Graham' and who was subsequently deported to the Netherlands. The migrations of priests with their congregations to Canada in the 1770s and 1780s did nothing to redeem the serious under-provision of priests in the Gaelic Highlands. The administrative problems of the Scottish Catholic Church and its clergy were compounded by continuing divisions, which were more acute than in England, between seculars and regulars, and the weakness of the Vicars Apostolic in the face of these conflicts was exacerbated; in 1755, when the Jesuits' superior in Scotland was writing to Propaganda Fide complaining of the hostility of Vicar Apostolic Bishop Smith (1746–66) towards the Society, the bishop himself was reported to be seeking recognition of his authority over the religious orders through the application to Scotland of Benedict XIV's decree *Apostolicum Ministerium*.[1]

As with its church order and priestly provisions, so in its worship and piety, in the retrospect of the period following Emancipation the Scottish Catholicism of the later eighteenth and early nineteenth centuries seemed impoverished, its liturgy shabbily enacted, its devotional life tarnished with a Jansenistic preoccupation with guilt and personal unworthiness, and all marred by a joyless asceticism. There was:

> no glamour or romance about Catholic worship in Scotland to attract Protestants, for this was the last thing anyone wanted to do. First Communion was often postponed for years because of fear of irreverence and lack of true understanding of the august nature of the Sacrament. The laity were discouraged from making their Confessions or receiving Holy Communion more frequently than at the time of the so-called 'Indulgences', i.e. the greater festivals....Devotional life centred around the weekly Sunday 'Prayers', a weekly simple low Mass; the observance of the many abstinence and fasting days; the reading of a few well-known spiritual books, and more rarely the Bible.

The general air of timidity obtaining in the community was reflected in Bishop Hay's determined resistance to the introduction of liturgical music, lest it ignite smouldering anti-popery. As had been the Scottish tradition since the Reformation, the Rosary made up for the deficiencies of liturgical provision and indeed remained at the centre of the devotional life of the nation's Catholic community. The beads were recognised by the authorities as Romanist contraband, as when a ship was seized in 1746 with a cargo of Rosaries; Rosaries were also impounded from Vicar Apostolic Hay's parcel of gifts from Rome in 1782; Hay himself in 1799 prescribed the Rosary for the hour and a half's prayer to be said each evening at his seminary at Auquhorthies in Aberdeenshire; and the Abbé Paul McPherson strongly recommended the Rosary to the Catholic people of Glenlivet following his return there in 1826.[2]

If there was a recovery of confidence and, in particular, of liturgical life in the 1790s, especially following the pasage of a Scottish Relief Act in 1793, it was stimulated by the traditional Catholic nobility, as was the case with the opening in 1792 in Huntly country of a chapel dedicated to St Gregory, a building said to be bigger than 'the best Roman Catholic chapels in London', where High Mass was sung in 1792, for the first time in Scotland since the Reformation, it was claimed. The evidence of these stirrings in the 1790s, fostered, as in England, by the arrival of French priests, has encouraged Dr Anson to see the last decade of the eighteenth century as indeed 'the dawn of a "Second Spring" of Catholicism in Scotland'.[3]

Despite the importance of noble patronage in this revival of Scottish Catholicism, despite the major contribution of French royalist clergy to that renewal and the presence of the Catholic Bourbon bother of Louis XVI at Holyrood House from 1796, despite, above all, the traditional links between the faith and Stewart royalism, there were Catholics, such as William Maxwel of Kirconnel, who took up the Jacobin sympathies of other Scottish radicals. Amongst these Scottish Catholics who gloried 'in the fall of the Bastille and [shared] the opinions of Robert Burns on Louis XVI and Marie Antoinette' was a leading member of the Edinburgh Catholic congregation, David Downie, sentenced (but not executed) in 1794 for the high treasons of storing weapons, raiding arsenals and inciting troops to mutiny. Alexander Geddes, a pioneer of modern biblical scholarship, was another Catholic who joined in radical Scotland's chorus.[4]

If the French Revolution allowed some Scottish Catholics to identify with those of their compatriots who struck up a Caledonian *Marseillaise*, literary romanticism created, even more forcibly, perhaps, than it did in England, a vogue amongst lovers of the picturesque and the sublime for all that was numinous, mysterious, in short 'medieval' in Catholicism. Indeed, in the 'age of Ossianic romanticism and Strawberry Hill Gothic', Catholicism had the capacity to recall a Scottish historical identity constructed before the Reformation and the Union, before the advent of anglicisation, commercialism, urbanisation and industrialisation. The pioneering historical work of Thomas Innes (1662–1744) as archivist of the Scots College, Paris, and author of *A Critical Essay on the Northern Part of Britain or Scotland* (1729) was continued by a line of eighteenth-century antiquaries who developed interest in Scotland's pre-Reformation, medieval and Catholic past. Typical of this orientation of interest was George Henry Hutton (d. 1827) who in 1789 submitted a plan to the earl of Buchan to compose 'the monastical history of this country'. In the height of the Romantic revival, the craze for respectfully visiting medieval ruins – 'monuments of our forefathers' piety,... sacred precincts' – was stimulated by Charles Cordiner's *Remarkable Ruins and Romantic Prospects of North Britain* (1795). Even the quintessentially Romantic Fingal's Cave was likened to medieval and Catholic cathedrals. While the pseudo-archaic Ossian texts also helped to 'prepare the ground for the Catholic revival', the fate of the Bourbons awoke nostalgia for the Stewarts and above all for Mary Queen of Scots and for the whole chivalric cult associated with the Catholic Church of the middle ages. Despite his own anti-Catholicism, reverence for Our Lady may have been fostered by Sir Walter Scott, with his 'romantic image of women'. Thus in the period 1780–1830, in which legislative Catholic Emancipation was being forged in Scotland, cultural sympathy with Catholic values was also becoming widespread and, Bernard Aspinwall writes, in the fields of 'philosophy, sense of community, architecture and liturgy, Catholicism seemed to be at its most advanced evolutionary point. Scotland provided the emotional outlet and the intellectual equipment for a Catholic revival.' At the same time, the scholarship and suavity of the likes of Vicar Apostolic Bishop Geddes (1780–97) did much to endear Scottish Catholics as individuals to a wider Scottish public. Changes in perception of Catholics and Catholicism amongst that wider public were such that 'In a few years ... they who before could scarcely see a Catholic without horror' were to become unanimous 'to have the whole of that infamous [penal] code buried forever in oblivion'.[5]

However, and even while incidental cultural factors and temporary political circumstances may have improved the climate for Scottish

Catholicism in the late eighteenth and early ninteenth centuries, we should not write too euphorically of the longer-term prospects for the Catholic faith, for, as Fr Ross wrote, in the Victorian age 'the growth of understanding between different religious communities in Scotland would come almost to a standstill'. The fact is that, romantic medieval antiquarianism notwithstanding, Scotland's more immediate post-Reformation history had given the nation an identity largely synonymous with Protestantism, and all the more so in that it had lost the constitutional edifice of its separateness in the Union of 1707. Indeed, in contrast with England where, following the 1689 Toleration of Nonconformists, it had become impossible to assume that 'English' meant exclusively 'Anglican', in Scotland, popular political and religious culture, supported by academics and clergy, held on to the idea of a covenanted and Reformed crown and nation. The talisman of that godly national identity was the Calvinist Westminster Confession of Faith (1646) which repudiated essential features of Catholicism including religious vows, the authority of the pope, Transubstantiation and the Mass. Therefore, a formidable obstacle to acceptance of Catholicism in nineteenth-century Scotland, writes Dr Muirhead, was the assumption that

> Religion was essentially a community responsibility; [that] the happy fulfilment of national destiny involved obedience to the truth (with its consequent blessings showered upon a faithful people covenanted with God); the governors of the community were, *ipso facto*, also involved in responsibility for the nation's faithfulness to its religious calling. In such a context, religious unfaithfulness was more than individual error.[6]

In that intellectual climate, one in which Scotland's Calvinist legacy came to be reaffirmed, with a renewed cult of the seventeenth-century Covenanting martyrs, it would be difficult to assemble a simple graph of linear overall progress for Scottish Catholics betwen the eighteenth and nineteenth centuries. Instead, our picture of Scottish Catholic history betwen 1745 and 1829 must be a complex one, complicated by differences between areas. In study of the variety of patterns between different areas, our attention will continue to be focused on the Highland heart of Scottish Catholicism, but it must also be directed at the new nuclei of Catholic expansion in what was soon to become one of Europe's most dynamic regions of urbanisation and industrialisation.

In the course of the eighteenth century the special opportunities presented to Catholic evangelism in the Highland zone received recognition in administrative reforms. In 1732 Propaganda Fide divided the Scottish mission into two districts, or vicariates, the Highland and the Lowland, giving Catholics in the former region the option of their own Gaelic-speaking priests and episcopal Vicar Apostolic. Hugh Macdonald was the first Highland Vicar Apostolic, consecrated in 1731 and serving until 1778 – working, that is to say, throughout the period in which the Highlands experienced the disastrous sequence of rebellion, 'pacification' and depopulation. The Highland–Lowland partition, albeit as a shifting linguistic hedge rather than a rigid frontier, continued in existence until 1828, when a new rescript reorganised the Scottish mission into three zones, at a point in time when the Highlands' Catholic strength had become gravely depleted with the erosion of their population, culture and language. Before that point was reached, however, close attention to the Highlands and Islands – to their intractable problems from the point of view of the Kirk and of the Scottish and British political authorities, to their bright opportunities from the point of view of the Scottish Catholic Church and of Rome – has bequeathed us a remarkable series of statistical profiles of Gaelic, Highland and Island recusancy over the course of the eighteenth century. A common official assumption was that in parts of the Highlands Protestantism had never been introduced: in 1720, for example it was reported that 'There are some places where the Reformation never yet had footing.' Official reports also focused on the geography of Catholic persistence; the work of Jesuit itinerants; the propagation of Catholicism amongst youth, especially through schooling; and the missioners' exploitation of the resources of Gaelic culture, in particular song:

The Popish Preists [reside] in … Moydart, Knoydart, Arisaig, Morer, Glengary, Braes of Lochaber,…the Western Isles of Uist, Barra, Benbecula, Canna, Egg…where nothing is professed but the Roman Catholick Religion … Popery is prevailing dayly in the forsaid places. The number of Preists there is considerable … trafficking Papists, and Priests, all of the Society of Jesuits …. The youth in the above mentioned Countrys, are early byassed & tainted in their principles with the Popish Books,… and songs put into their hands by the Preists … a number of Popish Schools [operate] in the within mentioned Countreys.[7]

It should be realised that such descriptions of the persistence and augmentation of Catholicism in the Highlands, whose effect, if read in Rome would surely have been to gladden hearts, were inspired by the need to raise an alarm about the dangerous links between popery and the Stewart cause, for those 'trafficking Papists, and Priests' were perceived as giving 'great encouragement to the revival and progress of Jacobitism and disaffection in Scotland'. The military threat, even after Culloden, was thought very real, exacerbated by the presence in the north and west of the country of a group of army officers exempted from the Act of Indemnity passed following the rising; all of these were 'Roman Catholicks, and in the Irish Brigades'. Weapons abounded to re-launch a Jacobite Catholic bid – 'many Guns, Blunderbushes, Pistols, Durks, & Targets [shields] in Caves [,] Bens, Pits dug deep in the Earth,... as will compleatly Arm Six thousand men'. The shipmasters of the east coast ports were said to be 'disaffected' and to be bringing in fresh Jacobite recruits. The threat from the Continent lay in the continued support for the Stewarts of the Catholic monarchies of France and Spain, abetted by Protestant Prussia. Priests in these circumstances were viewed as the ideological commissars of Jacobitism, preaching up the 'Jure divino Hereditary Right of the Stewart family' and circulating 'Rebellious and Scurillous pieces... merely to create a dislike... to the present Royall ffamily'. The persisting social structures of the Highlands was seen as aggravating the religious and political problem, for the power of the 'Chieftains or heads of familys of the disaffected Clans' remained intact, shored up by the 'Tie of Clanship, and attachment' which was 'so firm and strong' because it was reinforced by paternalistic arrangements for leasing and mortgaging land. Indeed, from a Protestant and Lowland point of view the Highland problem was even more deep-seated, for it was made up of primitive attitudes and lifestyles, shored up by popery and perpetuating

> the idleness of the people, who not being brought up to Mechanical Trades or other Occupations loiter away their time in dancing, attending on their Chiefs... and in stealing from other people in order to Support them in their idleness.[8]

Yet even though we should make every allowance for the effect of politically-induced panic in magnifying accounts of Catholic strength within these reports, especially in the immediate aftermath of the '45, we may find adjustments for the bias of politically motivated reportage by consulting parallel data, those compiled for the Vicariate Apostolic, for where returns drawn up by reporters as hostile to one another as the Kirk and the Catholic mission are in close accord on the statistical picture, we are surely entitled to conclude that the 'agreed' figures returned are reliable. And indeed there is a remarkably close alignment, allowing for some changes over time, between a census of 'the numbers of the faithful' in his Vicariate returned to Propaganda by Hugh Mac-donald in 1763 and figures drawn up in 1774 by the Scottish SPCK (SSPCK) on the basis of a survey of the Highlands conducted between 1759 and 1772. In the first place, there is a close correspondence between the two overall sets of returns, Mcdonald enumerating 13 166 (and Hay 12 900 in c. 1780) and the SSPCK 12 000 (incorporating Dr Roderick Mcdonald's re-calculation of the figures so as to exclude mountainous parts of the Lowlands included in the orginal returns). When we consider the returns from particular districts and islands, the comparability of the two compilations is even more striking, as Table 6.1 shows.[9]

Their impressive scale apart, there is a solidity about these figures which indicates the perpetuation over time of clearly defined dissident religious communities, neither expanding nor contracting too specta-cularly in numbers. There are also signs that populations of particular islands were, if not entirely, then overwhelmingly Catholic, perhaps as a kind of subscription to community; for example, of South Uist in 1720 it was said that the Kirk minister who had been in post for 40 years had never had more than 18 in a congregation, while of the people of Barra in 1764 it was reported 'They are all [1285 inhabitants] Papists, except 50'. In turn, the reality of the persistence of Highland popery presented the authorities with the challenge of mounting an educational mission. Indeed, the SSPCK survey was drawn up in the first instance on the basis of reports made to the General Assembly of the Kirk by visitors

Table 6.1   Numbers of Catholics, 1763 and 1774

	Mcdonald	SSPCK
Barra	1200	1250
Uist	2503	2300
Moidart	894	848
Arisaig	739	824
N.Morar and Knoydart	1409	1340
(Crathie and) Braemar	900	832

sent into areas in which catechists and missionaries were working under the auspices of the Committee for Managing the Royal Bounty, George I's proselytising charity originally set up in 1723–4. And the aims of the SSPCK were, of course, intensely educational. In 1774 it was setting up schools in areas already identified as having substantial Catholic populations, such as South Uist, Canna, Eigg, Rhum, Muck, Glengarry, Knoydart and North Morar, the areas in which, Dr McHugh writes, up to that point in time the Catholic 'Mission had fulfilled its task of retaining the allegiance of those districts gained by the earlier missionaries of the first half of the seventeenth century'.[10]

Needless to say, the provision of priests was absolutely indispensable to this relative success story of the Highland mission. The survey by the Vicar Apostolic Macdonald in consequence took particular note of the apportionment of priests to districts or groups of districts – a bishop and a priest in Barra and Uist (with a combined lay total of 3703), a priest in Glengarry and the Braes of Lochaber (1670 laity), a Jesuit in Strathglass (1321): the average for six priestly districts can be calculated at a priest for roughly every 1250 laity. The commitment of these priests to their region and its needs, though, was not always of the highest, for 'several Lowlanders heartily disliked the Highlands and, . . . some Gaelic-speaking Highlanders seem to have preferred the Lowlands . . . Some Gaelic-speaking priests became bishops in the Lowlands.' The '45 and its aftermath hit the priestly mission hard; several priests were imprisoned and exiled and Mcdonald was himself arrested in 1755. Two of the priests linked directly with the rising showed some of those factious traits that handicapped the Catholic Church in Scotland at large and in the Highlands in particular. Colin Campbell was a quarrelsome personality who, as we saw, petitioned Rome against 'Jansenising' clergy in 1735, who may have taken part in the fighting in 1745 and whose character, as Anderson and Forbes tactfully say, is a matter of differing opinions. John Leslie was another stormy petrel: sent first to Uist, 'which he disliked', he petitioned to be allowed to work in the Lowlands, was accused of libelling the Jesuits, was at Prestonpans in 1745 and eventually, despite possessing a character described as 'extremely dubious', became a canon of Courtrai. Other priests brought scandal to the Highland mission through their human failings: one had a 'bad and scandalous' record, apostasised in 1743, became a Kirk catechist and was 'accused of gross immorality'; another 'got into trouble through intemperance' and had his priestly functions suspended in 1750; a third was accused of 'a serious moral delinquency'; and yet another was the subject of a 'shocking scandal' in 1781.[11]

Needless to say, the careers of a few notorious individuals should not distract attention from the quieter achievements of the Highland priestly mision: its steady growth in numbers, from 10 in 1750, 11 in 1760, 14 in 1770, 17 in 1780, 20 in 1790, 21 in 1800 and 22 in in 1810; and the heroism of the overwhelming majority that evoked from Hugh Mcdonald praise for priests who were

> truly worthy, simple and good..., of burning zeal for the salvation of souls,...very prudent, and full of the Apostolic Spirit..., of long-standing repute, simple and upright,...[enduring] incredible hardships.

Of all those hardships the Highland landscape itself formed the hardest. Bishop Macdonald himself described it, not in the language of Romantic appreciation of its sublimities, but with the repugnance of a man of the Enlightenment at its 'terror' and 'horror'. The terrain formed a massive practical impediment to the efficacy of an itinerant mission conducted along a line of 'stations'. In fact, amidst 'rough mountains,...terrible sea, wild and very mountainous country', a typical missionary might 'scarcely ever [spend] two consecutive nights in one place' and soon become 'worn out with toil and advancing age;...the burdens of the...region could not be borne for much longer'. To add to these natural difficulties, the Highland mission from as early as the 1740s had to withstand an assault on the position Catholicism occupied within Gaelic culture. In 1741 the Presbyterian Alasdair MacDonald compiled a Gaelic–English dictionary with the aim of bringing about 'the Reformation in the Highland and Islands of Scotland', opposing the influence of 'Popish Emissaries in many Places in those Countries'. MacDonald's programme was of one of modernisation and acculturation designed to improve 'the Situation of the Inhabitants' by eradicating 'the Customs, Fashions and Supersititions of their Forefathers'. Bilingual book-learning was to be the means to lead to the supremacy thoughout the kingdom of a Protestant anglophone Lowlands culture and the creation of a class of educated Protestant Gaels fitted for careers 'in the Navy, or Army, or in any other service in the Commonwealth'. The Kirk and the establishment were indeed responding with mounting vigour to the challenge of Protestantising the Highlands and Islands. From the mid-1760s, for example, it was reported from Catholic sources in Moidart that, unprecedentedly by the authority of the Government, a [Kirk] minister was sent ... to take up residence and try to lead the faithful people into the errors of heresy. (This is now [1764] done in all the Catholic parts of this Vicariate.)[12]

Highland and Gaelic Catholicism was capable of adaptive responses to such challenges. Anchored in a collective oral tradition, it found powerful expression in the collection *Ortha nan Gaidheal/Carmina Gaedelica*, a compilation, in essentially poetic and almost bardic form, of scripture, doctrine and hagiography. However, through the work of the chaplain to the Edinburgh Gaels, Robert Menzies, in the later eighteenth century Catholic Gaeldom gained a new literary voice, devised for the individual reader, for whom Menzies provided digests of Tridentine doctrine and interiorist spirituality. Menzies' *Aithghearradh N A Teagaisg Chriosduidh* (*An Abridgement of Christian Doctrine*, London: Coghlan, 1781) was followed in 1785 by his translation, or rather, perhaps, his Gaelic version of Challoner's translation, of *The Imitation of Christ, Leanmhuin Chriosa*.[13]

Priestly education for the Highlands also underwent fruitful developments within the period covered by this chapter. The junior seminary set up on an island in Loch Morar in 1712 had been suppressed in the aftermath of the '15, but the Vicar Apostolic Bishop Gordon (1708–46) opened a new seminary in the place that came to be known as Scalan in the Braes of Glenlivet in Banffshire in 1717, with later ventures such as in Glenfinnan and Lismore, followed by the establishment of the new seminary at Blairs College in Kincardineshire in 1829.[14]

At the end of the eighteenth century Gaelic and Highland Catholicism continued to exhibit vigour and distinctive social, ecclesiastical and religious features. These included: a tendency towards exogamy resulting in numbers of mixed-faith families in certain areas; the attachment of priests to 'their traditional people', rather than to anything resembling territorial parishes, along with a marked lay reverence for the authority of the priest, evident in ready acceptance of his peace-making role; and a high level of devotion, seen in extensive reception of Holy Communion at Mass. Even so, a relative contraction of Catholic Gaeldom eventually came about: through official missionary efforts; through the general erosion of Gaelic life and culture; through the demolition of the clan system; through the introduction of a new landlord class; through the depopulation of the Highland zone and the emigration of its people; and as a result of the general shrinkage of the area that could be considered *Gaidhealtachd* and the retreat of its linguistic sphere, especially in the north-east of the country. Our next concern, therefore, will be with the emergence of new non-Gaelic, extra-Highland centres of Scottish Catholic life; with the the the shift in the centre of gravity in Scottish Catholicism away from the Highlands and Islands and towards the Lowlands and their developing industry and towns; with the effects of Irish immigration; with the emergence of renascent Catholic nuclei in Aberdeen, Edinburgh, Glasgow and Dundee; and with 'the balance of the Catholic population [which was] to weigh heavily on Clydeside and the south-west'.[15]

Initially, the prospects for Catholicism in the heavily Calvinist south-west were not promising, for in 1755 the entire counties of Wigtown, Bute, Ayr, Renfrew, Lanark and Dumbarton numbered only five recusants. Within the same decade, eastern districts showed more potential for Catholic growth: Bishop Smith administered Confirmation in Brechin in Angus, Stobhall in Perthshire, and Drummond in Stirlingshire, while Brechin itself, along with St Andrews, were classed as missionary 'out-stations'. Over the period 1732–1829, 118 priests can be counted as serving in the non-Highland region. Their major mission stations included: Aberdeen (from 1709), Deeside (from 1730 grouped in the 'Lowland'region), Drummond Castle (from 1706), Edinburgh (from 1709), Glasgow (from 1792), Glenlivet (including Scalan and classed in the Lowland district), and Stobhall (from 1734). A pattern is traced by Dr Johnson over a century of steadily diminishing repression:

> As ... fear of persecution receded priests were able to settle down, to begin with often living on small farms, but tending more and more by the end of the period [to 1829] ... to move into neighbouring towns and villages.

During this gradual progression, the protection of nobles and lairds remained indispensable and rural locations salient in the overall profile of the community. In Aberdeen, for instance, the growth of a genuinely urban Catholic community was slow, overshadowed as it was by the Huntly estate of the Enzie and the rural seminary at Scalan: in 1763 there were 260 communicants, including gentry, between Aberdeen itself and the lower Dee valley, while in the city itself George Gordon looked after two chapels. In 1780 a total Catholic population of 470 in Aberdeen and its hinterland could be enumerated, with numbers of communicants rising healthily to 276 in 1786 and 316 in 1798. Proper records begin in 1782, with the arrival in Aberdeen of Bishop Hay, who had already made a substantial contribution to the urban revival of Scots Catholicism by rebuilding one of Edinburgh's pair of Mass centres, attacked during the anti-popish rioting of 1779. Hay's six years in Aberdeen, working peacefully on his *The Sincere Christian* and, probably, on his version of the New Testament, may be taken as epitomising the shift in the Scottish Catholic experience away from the great estates – in Aberdeen's case the Huntly [Gordon] estates – and towards the towns and cities. Further reinforcement for Aberdeen's emergent urban Catholic circle came with the migration during the French Revolutionary Terror of what was left of the Scots College, Paris. The most significant of these exiles for Abderdeen's Catholic community was George Gordon, who was ordained in 1795 and whose service in the city over the next 50 years pointed towards the urban future of the Scottish Catholic Church in the nineteenth and twentieth centuries. Charismatic and glowingly confident, 'Priest Gordon' began in 1799 the building of St Peter's chapel, whose opening in 1804 was celebrated with High Mass. In its 'Gothick' styling, with choir and organ, St Peter's anticipated the Victorian passion for the medieval mode, but the building was in fact transitional in its architecture for, with its galleries in the Georgian fashion it was very practically equipped to contain a rising number of Mass-goers, having 610 Easter communicants in 1835.[16]

The case of Edinburgh reminds us that, though the dispersal of Gaelic Catholics weakened their faith in its Highlands and Islands heartland, the same diffusion strengthened Catholicism in the first city, as it did in Glasgow and, indeed, in the Empire at large. Six priests and the Vicar Apostolic Bishop Gordon were already active in Edinburgh in 1747 and by the second half of the century the city had a sizeable Gaelic-speaking, but (of necessity) bi-lingual, Catholic population spread across a wide social spectrum and including Highland chieftains and lairds with their ladies, members of the City Guard, sedan-chairmen, and servant girls. Robert Menzies, whose work as a Gaelic translator has already been mentioned, became the protégé of Bishop Hay and was sent to Douai, returning in 1775 and probably being ordained by the Vicar Apostolic, in Edinburgh, there to take on the care of the 'Highland Chapel', a small room in Blackfriars Wynd that was to be sacked in the city's anti-popish riots in 1779. When its replacement was completed in 1786, it was described as 'a good chapel for [Robert Menzies'] congregation and now the Catholics of Edinburgh found themselves very well situated as to places of worship'. Before the end of the century, Catholicism had been successfully re-implanted in Edinburgh, largely as a result of Highland immigration.[17]

The principal beneficiary of Scotland's commercial and industrial revolutions, Glasgow, shows how urban growth, including the impact of Highland and Irish immigration into the towns, fuelled the regeneration of Lowland Catholicism from a demographic low point in 1762–3, when the Lowlands returned a population of just over 6000. The Glasgow Catholics acquired their first post-Reformation priest with the arrival in 1792 of Alexander MacDonnell, who was to serve a community whose social base was made up of evicted Highland crofters, a workforce for the cotton factories whose owners MacDonnell successfuly approached for donations for building work. He thereby put 'the Glasgow congregation on a sound financial footing at an early point in its history', providing as a chapel

> a very large hall taken from the Duke of Hamilton and the Provost for the publickly avowed purpose of being a Catholic Chapel. The principal manfacturers are actually placing 300 seats in this hall and are cautioners [guarantors] for the rent.

This financial support provided an extraordinary indication of the newfound acceptability of Catholicism in a city where, but a few years before, as a correspondent of Bishop Hay noted, Protestant Glaswegians had 'burnt our houses and our chapels'.[18]

Not all these favourable auguries were reliable. While MacDonnell's quixotic energies took him off to form Scotland's new Catholic regiment, the Glengarry Fencibles, quarrels with lay managers and deepening financial difficulties led to the apppointment in 1796 of a new priest, John Farquarson, who set about building a new chapel in Boarhead Lane and putting its finances on a new footing by opening a fresh subscription list in 1797. This listing of 157 names, much longer than the 27 donors of 1793, and made up 'mainly of small-scale business men and members of the Catholic community', provides us with a fascinating insight into an emergent Scottish Catholic urban circle made up of upwardly mobile registered burgess subscribers of a guinea apiece; of half-guinea subscribers from amongst the better-off artisans and tradesmen; and of five-shilling contributors from amongst the day-labourers. Tailors and weavers abounded in the Catholic congregation, along with a quill manfacturer, a stationer, clerk and so on. Also noteworthy is the success of the appeal in attracting funds from British Catholics from far beyond the Clyde, and from another town undergoing contemporaneous industrial transformation, Preston: the Lancashire town's priest, Joseph Dunn, having built St Wilfrid's Chapel there, became the 'Channel' for contributions to the Glasgow plan from old north-west English recusant gentry, the Blundells and Daltons. The Scottish Catholic gentry was also represented on the donors' list, with the inclusion of James Maxwell of Kirconnell. French refugee priests added their pounds. The largest single contributor, the Archbishop of Dublin, with £50, made up part of what was – if names such as Quinn, O'Rourke, Sheridan, Donachy, Docherty, O'Neill, McCartney, Gallagher and Kelly are anything to go by – a substantial Irish funding of this scheme. Indeed, the fund to re-launch the Glasgow Catholic community can be regarded as a venture supported by co-religionists in three kingdoms.[19]

The Glasgow mission sailed into what were prospering seas for southwestern Catholicism, which expanded rapidly in the early nineteenth century when, between 1808 and 1822 new missions opened in Paisley, Dumfries, Greenock and Ayr. Catholic education flourished, too, partly encouraged by French priests in Ayr, Greenock (where St Mary's parish and school were opened in 1816), and Paisley, where the one school, also opened in 1816, had increased to three by 1830. In Glasgow financial sponsorship of working-class Catholicism was renewed by donations on the part of 'A number of employers of Irish labourers in the city', pointing unmistakeably to the rising prominence of the industrial Irish in the future fortunes of urban Catholicism in Scotland. Though tolerance of the doctrinal content of Catholic schooling in Glasgow was limited and 'no formal creed was to be taught', expansion continued vigorously: the Glasgow Catholic Schools Society opened four buildings between 1818 and 1822 and by 1825 five schools were running day and evening classes for 1400 pupils.[20]

Over in Dundee, the urban congregation, like that of Aberdeen, had its genesis in noble patronage, for the local Catholic group was provided for during much of the eighteenth century by domestic chaplains from the Drummonds' Stobhall, about 15 miles up the Tay. The delicate balance between official repression and limited unofficial tolerance was caught in a report of 1776 which revealed that Dundee had 'a congregation of papists or those of the Church of Rome who have a priest, . . . but keep not open door, these having no tolleration, though they are winked at'. Three years later this precarious equilibrium was endangered by 'some symptoms of bad blood among the populace', but by this

time the authorities were in no mood to countenance mass anti-popish
rioting, and a Major White, who commanded 400 men in the city,
warned 'he would let loose the soldiery with fixed bayonets among
them if he perceived the least inclination to riot'. As for the Kirk,
while the minister Mr Small 'declared for moderation', his successor,
Mr Raith, told the city baillie that 'Mr [Dom Kilian] Pepper [the Catholic
priest in residence] and I will agree nicely.' In these circumstances,
growth in the Dundee Catholic community was resumed following the
upsurge in popular bigotry in 1779: in 1782 the Vicar Apostolic Bishop
Geddes counted 14 communicants and recorded the celebration of
Mass in an upper room. It was in 1787 that the Dundee community
acquired the Würzburg Benedictine Kilian Pepper as its resident priest.
Pepper cultivated a deliberate lordly appearance and style, as 'a perfect
pattern of a well-fed monk, . . . a tall, fine looking man, and wore what
was then called a three-storey powdered wig' – and probably provided
just the kind of stage presence needed to lead a submerged little community into an enlarged life: its numbers rose from 20 or 30 to several
thousands in the period 1787–1836, within a city which had by 1792
itself become plural in its variety of Anglicans, Methodists, Unitarians
and different kinds of Presbyterians. And for all Bishop Geddes' dismissive 'well-fed monk', Pepper proved to be a zealous, strenuous and
effective pastor. Including Protestants in his preaching programme, by
May 1788 Pepper had brought his Mass attendances up from 26 to 54
and by the end of that year, when Bishop Geddes confirmed 10 of his
people, Pepper had built up a congregation of 100, necessitating the
purchase in 1780 of a building for a new chapel and house. By the time
of his retirement in 1803, Pepper had rebuilt Dundee Catholicism from
the ground up, typifying and paving the way for generations of priests
who reconstructed the Catholic Church in Victorian urban Scotland,
aided as they were by waves of migration into and around the country.[21]

Ireland

The last period of our survey of the history of post-Reformation Irish
Catholicism opens on a note close to despair at the time of the '45, when
such a well informed observer as the Archbishop of Dublin could warn
that the Church, 'grievously afflicted with misfortunes and persecu-
tions', faced a real threat of extinction in the country. In 1765 the

prospects for Irish Catholics and their priests still looked extremely perilous when, for example, it was reported that the government had offered a reward of £300 for the Tipperary priest, Nicholas Sheehy, accused of high treason and of involvement in anti-state plots. The end of the next decade, though, saw the dawning of a 50-year-long process of emancipation. Land remaining at the centre of the issue of religious rights in early modern Ireland, the Catholic Relief Act of 1778 allowed Catholics to take 999–year leases and to inherit lands on the same terms as Protestants did. The Irish Catholic Relief Act of 1782 allowed Catholics who took the oath of allegiance to buy and lease freehold land and relaxed laws concerning the registration of priests, the carrying of arms and education.[22]

Such progress continuing into the early the 1790s, with a further Relief Act in 1793, encouraged a quest for Irish Catholic emancipation, as promoted by the Irish reformist parliamentarian Henry Grattan and fostered by William Pitt's government's need for Irish support against revolutionary France. However, when a bill for emancipation was rejected in the Dublin Parliament in 1795 an undertow of agrarian agitation visible since at least the early years of the decade was reinforced. In the North, though, the formation in 1795 of the Protestant 'Orange Society' (later Orange Order) revealed the existence of growing sectarian discord and violence, whose divisiveness was manifested in the French-assisted Rising of 1798; despite the involvement in this of Catholics – indeed of the Wexford priest John Murphy – the 1798 insurrection was, writes Professor Beckett 'essentially a protestant affair', but one which, in the South, took on, as Dr McDowell says, the 'character of a sectarian war'. Indeed, when Ireland was brought into a full parliamentary union with Great Britain in 1801 Catholics and Protestants were, Professor Kerr comments, regarding 'one another with greater suspicion than ever'. Even so, the Union, with the promise of emancipation, which came true in 1829, was by no means unacceptable to most Irish Catholics For all that, and despite its founding and funding of Maynooth, in the years after 1801 the British government steadily lost positive influence over the Irish Catholic Church led by its bishops.[23]

These, treading a delicate line of obedience between the crown and the papacy and forming an increasingly powerful and collegially organised episcopate, worked to re-establish in Ireland a canonically organised national province of the Church and drove through Tridentine reforms that seriously undermined the scope of the religious orders, especially the Mendicants, so that by the end of the period the traditionally strong grip of the regulars on Irish lay Catholicism was much weakened. A peasant religion much concerned with fear, luck and ascetical personal expiation for sin, as well as with indulgence in occasional riotous festivity, was in retreat before the bishops' Tridentine crusade, but the implementation of the norms of the Counter-Reformation should be seen in terms of accommodation rather than of conquest, for there are signs before the end of the eighteenth century of the emergence of a new Irish fusion between popular culture and piety on the one hand and the clerical Catholicism of the late Counter-Reformation period on the other.[24]

Economic progress was in the air in eighteenth-century Ireland, as the country took advantage of Atlantic trade and as industry started up, notably cotton in Belfast in the 1790s. A Catholic middle class, tending to be less deferential to government in Dublin and London, was challenging the traditional Catholic leadership of the likes of Lords Kenmare and Gormanstown, though this bourgeois element also aimed essentially at finding its place within the status quo. In Galway city, for example, which, like its neighbour Limerick, had a long-standing religious background of Catholicism alongside a political legacy of royalism, there was, writes Patrick Egan,

> in addition to the ascendancy group, a large body of loyalist opinion among people of means of Catholic and native stock. Large numbers who had amassed wealth in trade and other ways were enabled by the partial relaxation of the penal laws to acquire property in land and were aiming at advancement in the social scale. Their energies and outlook were directed primarily towards the aggrandisement of themselves and their families. The most they would wish for was repeal of the laws affecting Catholics.

Arthur Young's liberal programme for the modernisation of Ireland through encouraging 'all the personal wealth of the Catholics and ... their industry' involved also the modernisation of Irish Catholics up to the standards of 'the other parts of Europe' and might have had the type of the Catholic bourgeois in mind.[25]

Young's strategy also implied the updating of Irish Catholicism itself, which he thought 'from the ignorance of the people ... more bigoted than any thing known in the sister kingdom'. In fact, the principal agents in the modernisation of Irish Catholicism in the eighteenth century were the country's Catholic bishops, driven on by the reforming spirit of the Counter-Reformation. The ancestral folk Catholicism which the bishops sought to supplant with modernising Tridentine discipline, with its stresses on regularity, self-control, honesty and work, was, as it happened, suspect to the political authorities because of its proneness to encourage disorder and disaffection. In 1803, for example, much to the alarm of the police authorities, 10 000 people descended on Balla, County Mayo, for a traditional, and distinctively pre-Tridentine, 'day of folly' consisting of religious services held around the ancient focus of a holy well; the authorities were again alarmed, in 1810, at the implications for public order of the old rite of swimming horses in the Liffey. If government supected such rites as a threat to law and order, the bishops had every reason to undermine inherited cultic practices which by-passed the sacramental and clerical provisions of the Church and which seemed to foster irregularity and disorder. Meanwhile, Gaelic popular piety and culture, estranged from the status quo, found focus in and took comfort from an Irish-language literary cult of Patrick as a liberator, reinvented as coming from noble Firbolg stock that had been 'in possession of Ireland for 382 years' before he had heard the children of Ireland pleading with him to return to (and convert) his ancestral land.[26]

As well as being politically alienated from the civil authorities, Irish peasant Catholicism continued to exhibit devotional features which rested on theological assumptions at odds with Tridentine canons. In particular, the harsh, self-expiatory techniques of pilgrimage were not consistent with Trent's repudiation of the belief 'that a person can be justified before God by his own works, done...by the resources of human nature'. Rituals enacted at the most esteemed popular pilgrimage site, Croagh Patrick, celebrated the sanctity of the local environment, rather than the reverence of the church, and upheld the redemptive efficacy, not of the Mass and the Sacraments, but of repetitious routines, of complex numerical combinations and, above all, of heroic acts of self-sacrifice by means of which self-induced merit was credited to the individual – as in the case of the son who performed both his and his father's penances, dying in the attempt, and thereby acquiring saintly status, *voce populi*, and a completely unofficial 'crown of martyrdom'.[27]

Although observers assumed that the Croagh Patrick penitential practices were 'inculcated by the Roman catholic clergy' or 'regulated by the confessors', it may in fact be the case that the role of priests in these devotions was at best that of ancillaries to a cult sustained in effect by the laity and with lay priorities which had more in common with medieval Pelagianism than with Tridentine Augustinianism. Other features of Irish popular religious belief and practice that were discrepant from Tridentine norms included the pervasiveness of fear and the prevalence of anxiety-appeasing performances; the use of rituals for securing good, and averting bad, luck; the widespead use of charms and exorcisms; and reverence for water and its curative properties (allowing also for the attendance of one visitor to a holy well in Kerry 'to see the women'). The environment was charged with fear as well as with reverence, and in some parts 'The country people are afraid of cultivating the Danish forts' (the ancient remnants of Viking invasions), while 'certain trees' might not be destroyed for fear of ill-luck. Funereal practices belonged emphatically to the folk rather than to the Church: in County Roscommon, for instance,

> When a person dies...the bed is burned on a height...Burials are not allowed on Mondays, for a burial on that day would bring about the immediate death of someone in the neighbourhood.

Belief in the material, and especially the curative, power of sacramentals, rather than in the spiritual power of Sacraments, underlay the widespread 'possession of a bottle of holy water, to be used as a remedy in all cases of sickness'. Priests themselves were likely to be regarded and employed as thaumaturges and were 'often called in to perform a sort of exorcism of those whose disorders are supposed to arise from spiritual agency'. Priests also dispensed curative talismans – 'the "Gospels", as they are called...they [the peasants] wear them suspended round the neck as a charm against danger and disease. These are prepared by the priest, and sold by him at the price of two or three tenpennies.' Such commercial dependence of priests on laity in a Church still without official standing may have fostered an emphatically unTridentine subservience of the clergy to the people over such matters as Lenten observance, for when the 'people ask permission from the Parish Priest to fast on three days only...the Parish Priest grants it'. Episcopal discipline, the *sine qua non* of the Tridentine system, to be dispensed down the gradations of the hierarchy to the level of the 'parish priest', was indeed difficult to achieve in situations of effective lay control of the priesthood, such as that prevailing in Galway city, where the laity had gained a papal bull allowing them periodically to elect their own

'Warden' and eight vicars. Of course it is true that the Tridentine Church elsewhere in Europe had to arrive at its own organisational and cultic accommodations with lay piety and power: Italy itself, the heartland of Tridentinism, provides numerous examples of official collusion with popular non-Tridentine cults, especially Marian ones.[28]

In Ireland, though, Mariology helped introduce Counter-Reformational norms. At Croagh Patrick 'official' Marian piety was fed, through the integration of the feast of the Assumption into the site's calendar and through the inclusion of a chapel dedicated to Mary as part of the complex, into what was essentially a local cult. The Irish bishops in the eighteenth century seem to have been particularly concerned to foster the international aspects of Marian piety, the Rosary and episcopally directed confraternities, and what Mgr Corish calls the 'important role in Counter-Reformation spirituality' of devotion to Our Lady. In 1750 the Archbishop of Cashel noted with approval 'The beads is duly observed by most of the people'. There is no doubt that the bishops were, consciously or unconsciously, enhancing their own authority, not least their collegial powers, when in 1788 the Archbishops of Armagh, Cashel and Dublin made a request to Rome for what was in effect the re-designation of Catholic Ireland as a national Rosarian confraternity, through the extension to the whole country of the practice 'of reciting the Office and Mass of the Holy Rosary on the first Sunday of October [the month dedicated to the Rosary], and ... the dedication of the Churches of Ireland on the second Sunday'.[29]

During the period c. 1750–1850 Irish Catholics were presented with the Tridentine agenda of the Counter-Reformation, took this reformed faith to their hearts, and eventually came to equate this Catholicism with their post-Gaelic national identity and to form the most convincingly Catholic people in western Europe. The older, thaumaturgic, environmentally-based cult of curses, blessings, luck and holy wells, of arduous pilgrimages and riotous wakes – 'the wakes and patterns, with their hybrid mixture of Christian devotion, traditional magic, ritual observance and festive celebration' – succumbed to the implementation of a Borromean priestly ideal of the Tridentine renewal: an 'extrasacramental' cult, the property very largely of the lay people, in which 'religious observance is irregular and integrated into the cycle of customary practices, [and] religious beliefs have a high syncretic content' made way for the triumph of a sacramental Catholicism, directed by the clergy and emphasising 'the regularity of religious observance'. The more precise dating of this great transformation – whether, as Professor

Larkin tells us, it took place essentially between the Famine of 1846 and the 1870s, or whether, as Desmond Keenan argues, its crucial phase lay between 1800 and 1850, or whether we should look at an even more extended anterior chronology in which, as Kevin Whelan says, 'the Tridentine surge in Irish Catholicism...[was] clearly signalled from the 1770s onwards, with an accelerated period of reorganisation between 1800 and 1830' is open to discussion. It should be clear, though, that a straightforward *chronology*, as distinct from *geography*, of the Tridentinisation of Ireland is not particularly helpful. For instance, those who argue for the inauguration of Ireland's full exposure to Catholic modernisation, indeed, for a 'devotional revolution', taking place well within the eighteenth century need have little difficulty with their case if they concentrate their attention on urban Ireland. In the capital, for instance, a smoothly running episcopal system was in place by 1751, the Archbishop having 'forty five parish Priests in his Diocese, each pays him a Guinea a year'. The Catholic priesthood was by now the most active element within Dublin's clergy, 'their Duties being heavyer than on the Protestant Ministers'. Though shortages of priests required continued reliance on the friars, Archbishops of Dublin were determined to bring the latter under their authority, subjecting them to a characteristically Tridentine diocesan discipline and, in particular, closely controlling their expressed views on the government.[30]

Education, Trent's most urgent desideratum for the priesthood, was making considerable headway, even though the Council's own schedule sounds inverted in the report that priests 'go abroad after [ordination] to finish their studies'. In Galway city, where priests had regular sources of income and fees from the laity, they formed a collegial life, with a library. The collection of over 160 volumes kept in Drogheda by the former Louvain philosophy and scripture professor, the Dominican John Donnelly, allowed him to base his preaching on French and Jesuit material, in good Counter-Reformation fashion emphasising the Sacraments and moral theology.[31]

Eighteenth-century Ireland's progress in achieving Tridentine goals was fully supported, and indeed, supervised by the Holy See: the regular series of reports on the conditions in their dioceses – '*relationes status*' – were sent by bishops to Rome on such matters as the provision of marriage registers, the availability of chalices and the numbers of priests and of candidates for Confirmation. Such meticulous attention to data and detail was entirely characteristic of the methodical 'Tridentine' mentality, while the enforcement in the island of the sixteenth-century reforming constitutions of Sixtus V formed a further example of the delayed Tridentinisation of the Irish Catholic Church. Also entirely in line with Trent's requirements was the series of diocesan and provincial clerical conferences convened by bishops and metropolitans so as to direct policy and maintain standards – just as the English Tridentinist Richard Challoner used conferences of priests in London in the mid-eighteenth century. But the development of these structures indicates that Borromean-style reform in Ireland was certainly not restricted to the more urban east. Irish conferences were held from as early as 1752 in Tuam in the west; conferences were held in Cashel from 1775 and in Armagh from 1775, while the four metropolitan archbishops began meeting together regularly from 1788 onwards.[32]

If we consider in some greater detail the programme of one of eighteenth-century Ireland's clerical assemblies, we shall see the extent to which the aims of Trent were their inspiration: indeed, it was the great Council itself that had ordered such assemblies to be held annually so as to draw up rules for the spiritual benefit of priests and people. The statutes of the diocesan synod conducted by Archbishop Butler at Thurles, County Tipperary, in October 1782 covered the following areas:[33]

(1) *Baptism*: sponsorship; the conditional Baptism of non-Catholics; the Baptism of children in the womb; the keeping of Baptismal registers.
(2) *Confirmation*: conditions for the reception of the Sacrament; instruction, and prayers to be learned before reception.
(3) *Mass and Holy Communion*: episcopal permission for priests (in exceptional circumstances) to say two Masses on the same day; rules on the use of chalices and altar-cloths; the recitation of the Acts of Contrition, Faith, Hope and Charity before Sunday Mass.
(4) *Penance*: regulations on the vestments to be worn by the confessor and on the Confessions of seven-year-olds and women; minimal monthly Confession by priests.
(5) *Holy Orders*: the rigorous scrutiny (in line with Trent's very careful provisions under this head) of candidates for ordination and the close examination of the newly ordained.

All this quintessentially Tridentine discipline, which is also evident, for instance, in the 16 pages of decrees isued by Bishop Nihell's 1789 synod for the western diocese of Kilfenora (County Clare) and Kilmacduagh

(County Galway) represents the application to the south west of Ireland in the late eighteenth century of the kind of episcopal regulation classically set out in Carlo Borromeo's *Acta Ecclesiae Mediolanensis (Acts of the Milanese Church)*. The Irish approach is systematic, orderly, intensely administrative, and also indicates a strong affirmation of Trent's and Borromeo's cherished principal of episcopal government of the Church. Priests were the focus of the concerns set out in Archbishop Butler's 1782 Thurles synod, but it is noteworthy that they were subject to episcopal control and, if necessary, discipline, including restrictions on the number of daily Masses they celebrated and the requirements that they remain resident in their cures, and that they receive the Sacrament of Penance and attend conferences regularly. As well as assuming a high degree of episcopal authority, much of this legislation takes for granted the existence of an *ad hoc* parochial system. As well as being concerned with bishops and diocesan priests as the principal clerical personnel of the Church, the Thurles resolutions are suffused with concern with the Mass and the Sacraments, indeed with the essentially Sacramental Catholicism that has been seen as the key feature of Ireland's 'devotional revolution'. Alongside Sacramentalism, education, in the first place of the clergy, in the second of the laity by the clergy, was to the fore in the Thurles reforms. Priests were to catechise on Sundays and holy days, visit schools and instruct teachers. And by the 1790s in County Galway 'each chapel has a schoolmaster who teaches the Catechism in Irish'. Confraternities were an essential adjunct to the educational programme for the laity in its wider, moral and behavourial, forms.[34]

The behavioural re-education of Catholic Irish people planned by their bishops, along the lines of moral reformations put in place by Catholic authorities in France and the Low Countries between the sixteenth and eighteenth centuries, involved: (1) the extermination of 'disorderly' religious or quasi-religious festivities which were deemed alien to Tridentine norms; (2) control of the politics of the people, especially of the peasants in the interests of non-violence and loyalty to the crown; and (3) the inculcation of habits of thrift, sobriety and industry. This ambitious programme of large-scale overhaul of the habits of a people was already well under way within the second half of the eighteenth century. In 1761, for instance, in the Leinster diocese of Ossory, Bishop Thomas Burke both wielded spiritual sanctions, in the form of declarations of sin upon the refractory, and also assumed functions tantamount to those of civil government so as to regulate, if not destroy, pre-Tridentine festivals and, in the process, impose moral social controls, which were in part designed to improve the image of Catholicism within the wider society:

> Whereas Robbing, Riding, Cursing, Swearing, Thieving, excessive Drinking, and other great Debaucheries are constantly practised at *St John's Well* near Kilkenny, arising mostly from vagrant Beggars, many whereof feign themselves Lame who in Swarms strole thither from divers parts of this kingdom; and who likewise pester the city of *Kilkenny,* and the Roads adjacent, to the great Detriment, and Terror, of the Inhabitants, and the Travellers; whereby many Reflections are cast upon the Roman Catholick Religion and it's Pilgrimages: hence it is, that all Subjects of that Religion are strictly forbid to give Alms to any Beggars whatsoever at *St John's Well* [or its environs].

Bishop Burke's edict evinces an extraordinary extent of episcopal authority, translated into what was in effect policing power, over 'Subjects'. He was not, however, resolved so much on the destruction of the cult in question as on its control and clerical regulation, intending to see it reformed as a charitable fund properly administered by 'Parish Clergy'.[35]

The extent to which such disciplinary controls were actually influencing Irish people in the eighteenth century may be guessed at anecdotally from comments on public conduct, such as that of the priest James Lyons reporting on Sligo town, within the same 1760s as Bishop Burke was ordering his reforms in Ossory; the case of Sligo may lend added support to the view that not only Dublin and the south and east of the country were making progress in Tridentine reform, in priestly pastoral care, in the introduction of a fully 'Sacramental' Catholicism, and in what was now in effect becoming a parish life. Lyons reported on a Sligo with a variety of professions, including Quakers and 'Calvinists', amongst whom Catholics formed an assured majority and the plebeian base of the population. Morally, if not faultless, they seem to have been well on the way to realising some of the targets of civil behaviour set by clerical reformers for adoption by the Catholic laity: they were 'docile and well-disposed and there would not be better in the world if oaths and drunkenness were not their second nature'. As their town curate, Lyons spared himself no pains on the task of improving their moral education, focusing on parochial pastoral care and laying special emphasis on the Sacraments:

> I could not describe how much I have suffered in trying to reform them. I work night and day attending to their calls, assisting them at the hour of death, administering the Holy Sacraments, and helping them in every way according to the duty of a parish priest.[36]

The aim of instilling docile habits of 'industry, sobriety, and a peaceable demeanour in all things' was linked to a programme of indoctrination in political passivity, of 'pure standards of loyalty and attachment', of that 'duty to God and the state' which the bishops of the province of Cashel in 1787 saw as being likely to attract 'further marks of the legislature's kindness and protection'. In Thurles Archbishop Butler, who emphasised loyalty to the king's person, wrote in 1788 to his clergy expressing his concern for George III's health, recalling the gratitude that the Catholic clergy owed to him and commanding prayers to be said before all Sunday and Holy Day Masses for his recovery. Butler's *A Justification* reiterated the theme of gratitude for concessions already made, along with hopes of further favours still be be expected by obedient Catholics from the government. It followed that insurgent movements, notably the terrorist anti-tithe group, the Whiteboys, elicited episcopal condemnation, such as that from Kilmacduagh's Bishop Nihell of 'a very large body of people under the denomination of White boy', who had forced parishioners 'to take certain illegal oaths... contrary to the dictates of conscience, the laws of the land, and even their own temporal interest and advantage'. The same desire for an accommodation with the establishment beneficial to Catholic interests brought forth from the bishops of Ireland a request to Pius VI in 1788 for a 'revocation of the censure of excommunication against freemasons, as the enforcement of this [Church] law involves denunciations of the very heads of state, of most nobles, and civil and military administrators'. The success within this period of the bishops' policy of loyal accommodation was the setting up, with a partial grant under a 1795 Act of the Irish Parliament, of a Catholic seminary for Ireland, The Royal College of St Patrick, Maynooth, County Kildare.[37]

If Irish bishops tended to emphasise government power, their Tridentine–Borromean ideology made them fully conscious also of their own authority. An aspect of this authoritarianism can be seen in Bishop Nihell's drive in 1794–5 to bring the lay-elected wardenship of Galway into line with episcopal control and financial contribution. However, the principal battle in the campaign by the bishops to subject the Irish Church to episcopal mastery was with the religious orders, especially the Mendicants. Thus in 1747 Nicholas Sweetman, Bishop of Ferns, County Wexford, wrote to the Irish Franciscan Provincial, in language of heavy menace ('I had other things to settle with ye') imposing his terms for the unconditional surrender of the friars in his diocese: a levy of 50 per cent on every Sunday and Holy Day collection, precedence to be accorded to the bishop or his coadjutor, plus 'some other little grievances or incroachments that...I am determined to remedy'. Sweetman's offensive was part of a wider episcopal campaign to subjugate the orders conducted from the mid-eighteenth century onwards. In about 1750, for instance, Patrick MacDonnagh, Bishop of Killaloe (County Clare) referred to one regular who had presumed to say 'Mass the next day after that he was suspended by my orders', and went on to deliver a high statement of *jure divino* episcopal authority according to which 'No power under heaven can take away from [a bishop] the care of the souls intrusted to him by Jesus Christ.' Rome gave its backing to the authority of the bishops, as when Cardinal Antonelli wrote in 1789 from Propaganda Fide to the effect that 'though the Sacred Congregation regards regular clergy with merited affection and esteem, the present state of affairs in Ireland makes it desirable that secular rather than regular clergy be promoted to vacant sees'. If the phrase 'the 'present state of affairs' represents an allusion to the delicacies of the political situation at that juncture, the Cardinal may have had in mind the likelihood that a a settled episcopate staffed by political conservatives might be more acceptable to government than the Mendicants, with their traditional links to popular attitudes.[38]

For there is no mistaking the continued popularity of the orders with the laity: it was their great source of strength, one that the bishops would need to undermine if they were to bring the regulars fully into line with the episcopal principle. Catholics in Waterford were in fact so attached to the friars that in 1750 they seem to have rioted on behalf of the Franciscan Felix Clery (or Cleary) in his allegedly violent resistance against the nominee of Bishop Creagh. Indeed, the orders' presence in the towns of Georgian Ireland was both impressive and, seemingly, expanding. In Galway city, where the Franciscan community numbered five priests and two novices in 1720, a return of 1782 gave eight priests in residence, and, probably, some novices. In 1820 a new friary was opened in the city, its chapel 'a spacious, convenient and handsome place of worship 120 feet long and 30 feet broad, and is capable of accommodating upwards of two thousand people'. Building progress was also recorded by the Dominicans in Dublin where, in 1767, 'Our chapel and house of Bridge Street are almost finished. They will far surpass in beauty and strength any in this city'. In the capital by the middle of the century, taken together 'The Regulars have six Chappells and six or seven Fryars in each . . . [there were] Dominickans Franciscans Carmelites and two kinds Augustines and Capuchins. They live by Collections'. In Wexford, the solidity of the Franciscan presence was made evident both in their splendid vestments and church furniture and also in lay endowments such as that of Anne Lamport, who provided 40 guineas to commission 800 Masses in a chain of requiem provisions spread across much of Ireland and reaching up to the Carmelite convent in Dublin.[39]

Yet despite their being so firmly anchored in lay loyalty, the security of the orders' future may in fact have been illusory. For example, a survey of the Dominicans conducted in 1767 gave the appearance of a solid establishment across the whole island, with as many as 12 friaries in Connacht and populations per house in the region of nine – in Dublin and Roscommon, County Roscommon – and up to 13 in Athenry, County Galway. This numerical prosperity, though, conceals the underlying weakness that the average age of 117 Dominicans in three Irish provinces was just over 54 and, while septuagenarians were not uncommon, friars in their 20s and 30s seem to have been thin on the ground. This aging profile may help explain the longer-term decline within the country of this order into whose hands for so long so much of the missionary fortunes of Catholic Ireland, as of Catholic Scotland, had been entrusted. Fr Fenning shows an overall drop in numbers from 155 in 1767 to 77 in 1817 and explains that the Order of Preachers was displaying a malaise common to the other Irish conventual orders: they were all unable to receive and train sufficient candidates and their members were poached for parish work by the bishops.[40]

The establishment of the seminary at Maynooth was a response to the collapse of Irish clerical education on the Continent, evident in the first place in the 'very precarious state of decadence' of, and especially of chronic discord in, the Irish College, Paris in 1787, a process of decline preceeding collapse in the French Revolution. In turn, the closing of the long Continental phase of post-Reformation Irish Catholic priestly educational history and the replacement of overseas outposts by a domestic seminary can be seen as ushering in a parochial, diocesan, territorial, and indeed canonical rather than missionary, era in the history of the modern Irish Church. The setting up of Maynooth, in short, represents a key stage in what we might term the 'patriation' of the Irish Church – for all its strong Romanism. Before the end of the eighteenth century Maynooth had begun sending out waves of secular priests for the dioceses; it had produced 400 ordained men by 1826 and by 1853 was educating half of Ireland's priests. It was, writes Mgr Corish, 'the biggest single factor in ushering in a new age of reform' in the Catholic Church in Ireland.[41]

All we would add to that observation is that the 'new age of reform' – meaning in essence the possibility of introducing into Ireland (or re-introducing, after the earlier, seventeenth-century endeavour) Tridentine reforms which the Council itself could not have envisaged for a church operating under penal conditions – began with the thawing of repression in the eighteenth century. It is fitting, though, that Maynooth is taken as the symbol of the post-penal phase of modern Irish Catholic history, for the theme of that phase is education, of the clergy, of course, and crucially of the Catholic laity. Bishop Keeffe of Kildare and Leighlin was another of our group of Irish Tridentine reformers of the second half of the eighteenth century, visiting all parts of his large eastern diocese during his long episcopate between 1752 and 1787, assiduously recruiting and training priests, convening, and himself consistently attending, clerical conferences, drawing up regulations for priestly standards, preaching 'incessantly', indoors and out. It is on Keeffe's contribution as a teacher, educationalist and catechist that we should concentrate here: himself the author of a catechism (though he himself preferred Archbishop Butler's version), he undertook the building of Carlow College and encouraged his disciple, and eventual successor (1788–1814) at Kildare, Daniel Delaney, to establish Sunday schools in Tullow, County Carlow, in 1777. While still a priest, Delaney also took on not so much a reform of traditional popular culture, as a kind of compromise with it, focusing on young people and their recreations. Finding that the youth of Tullow in the County Carlow were addicted to the traditional Sunday, featuring, no doubt, misbehaviour of one kind or another, Delaney began, with a policy of Jansenist-sounding puritanism, 'to correct these evils'. Learning, though, by experience, and, perhaps, failure, he next determined on a more negotiated approach and, in the process, can be seen to have hit upon a formula for a new amalgam, and a new sociability, indeed even for a new Irish Catholic popular culture, one combining recreation and piety:

it occurred to the good priest to try the attractions of music....He
knew that the reformation he aimed at must begin with the young, so
he induced the younger children to attend at the Parish Chapel on
Sundays and Holydays, and taught them to sing the beautiful hymns
of the Church. He afterwards formed an amateur band which soon
attracted a large number of children to divine worship. He then
formed the young people, boys and girls, into classes and taught
them their catechism.

Skilfully, Delaney drew in collaborators, recruited from the better-educated elements of his people, 'who gave valuable aid in training the
choirs he had formed and in teaching the Catechism', the progenitors,
as it were, of the countless numbers of pious Irish lay men and women –
schoolteachers, choral instructors, sodality leaders, and the rest – who
were to act as the natural allies of the clergy in the programme that over
time resulted in the intense Catholicisation of modern Ireland. Coming
into a passionately musical culture, Daniel Delaney in the first place
taught song and formed bands and then moved on to catechesis. But
music in itself was central to the Church's own celebration of its Sacramental liturgy, often directed at that focus of Counter-Reformation
congregational piety, the reserved Blessed Sacrament. Delaney
arranged eucharistic devotions around music in the following way in
Tullow:

> On Sunday morning the people flocked to the Chapel at an early
> hour. The Blessed Sacrament being kept in the Chapel, they began
> the devotions of the day by singing the *O Salutaris* in honour of the
> Blessed Sacrament, and to invoke the light of the Holy Ghost in the
> schools, they sang the *Veni Creator*; then standing, sang the hymn of
> the time [*proprium de tempore*] in English.[42]

The whole religious atmosphere – an orderly, clerically orchestrated,
carefully programmed liturgical action, contained within a church interior, using Catholicism's own rich musical resources and centring on the
international Sacramental and latinate devotions of the Tridentine
Church – seems aeons away from the lay-directed, extra-mural, auto-
penitential routines of Croagh Patrick, expressive as they were of an
essentially regional cult. An early-nineteenth-century Wexford schoolmaster also recalled elaborate musical (and processional) accompani-
ments, with bassoon and 'clarionet', of devotions to the Eucharist, and

also to Mary; such services, following the 'Church's year', were, of course, common to the whole of post-Reformation Catholicism:

> We do have great work here on festivals. On Corpus Christi [the June feast of the Body of Christ in the Eucharist] we have a procession of the Blessed Sacrament, on Palm Sunday, a procession of palms, on 15th of August [the Assumption into Heaven of the Blessed Virgin Mary] our patron day, a grand solemn Mass and procission of candles. Every Sunday in Lent we sing round the Stations [of the Cross, a processional commemoration of the Passion of Christ], and on other festivals we have a benediction of the Blessed Sacrament, all of which serve very much to excite devotion in the people.

Incidentally, the Wexford teacher also seems to point forward to an aspect of moral or behavioural, as well as devotional, revolution that was also promoted by the Church, in the person of the Capuchin temperance campaigner Fr Mathew (1790–1856): 'I have completely given up drinking and can now see the complete folly of it.'[43]

The final ingredient to be considered, alongside the cultural and, in particular, the musical, integration of recreation with Catholic worship and the internationally oriented Tridentinisation of Irish devotional practice, is the rising level of lay religious education between the eighteenth and nineteenth centuries. In the western diocese of Kilfenora and Kilmacduagh the learned philosopher and controversialist Bishop Laurence Nihell (1726–98) was also an energetic sponsor of the catechism, probably Archbishop Butler's version in the Archbishop's own abridgement, over 400 of which Nihell ordered for distribution to his flock who, he anticipated, would 'find them useful in their families'. By the early nineteenth century the schools of Catholic Ireland were providing students with copies of Challoner's *Think Well On't*, with Archbishop Butler's *Catechism* and the *Imitation of Christ*, with the Douai New Testament, as well as 'Bible Histories', along with preparations for Confession and Holy Communion and de Sales' *Introduction to the Devout Life*, with St Augustine's *Confessions*, Tertullian, Madame de Maintenon, 'Prayers of the Liturgy', eucharistic meditations, and so on. If this literature was having any effect, a devout and reflective Catholic laity would already be well advanced in formation. More externally, a Church that was now confidently led by its episcopate was rapidly acquiring the building stock appropriate to a canonical establishment, with cathedrals in Waterford (1793), Cork (1799), Dublin (1815), and

Carlow (1829). Obviously, vast progress had to be made in the fuller achievement of a 'devotional revolution' under Cardinal Cullen betwen 1850 and 1870 – not least because the 1846 Famine itself did untold damage to the religious consolidation achieved before its impact was felt. However, the evidence suggests that some years before the Famine the Catholic Church was already poised to occupy the dominant position it would assume in the social, cultural, religious, educational and political life of most of the island of Ireland until the concluding years of the twentieth century.[44]

CONCLUSION

The status of Catholicism in England, Wales, Scotland and Ireland within the period of this survey was odd, if not unique. In the great lands of the Reformation elsewhere in northern Europe, and certainly in the Scandinavian realms, where Protestantism was established Catholicsm became extinct, and only the United Provinces of the Dutch Republic existed as a Protestant state harbouring a Catholic minority. If anything, though, that comparison functions better as a contrast, for the United Provinces formed a federal republic, loose, devolved and unmonarchical, exactly the kind of libertarian polity in which people might expect such irregularities as toleration to prevail. The British, or at least the English, state was different – a royal and highly centralised regime, of the kind in which, as in late Bourbon France, the monopoly of a single state church was supposed to prevail. I have offered no grand explanatory scheme in this book for why British Catholicism endured, except to say that it did and that that made it highly unusual. I can hardly question the view that noble and gentry support in England and Wales was crucial in providing protection in the most dangerous periods within the sixteenth and seventeenth centuries; in the Scottish Highlands and Islands, the successful integration of Catholic faith with Gaelic speech and culture obviously fostered Catholic durability; in the case of Ireland, it is almost a cliché to write that national or proto-national identity supported and drew support from Catholic resistance to Protestantisation.

The doctrinal, institutional and liturgical forms of the faith prevalent within the period of this book were of the type labelled 'Tridentine', shaped by the Council of Trent and formed by the political exigencies of

197

surviving or expanding within a credally polarised Europe. For its most successful operation, the Tridentine species of Catholicism required (1) majority comunal membership of the Church within identifiable political units; and (2) broad support from and alliance with the political authorities in any given state. In the 'British' cases, although we can identify majority attachment to the Catholic Church in Ireland, the hostility rather than the alliance of the state was to be expected over most of our period. And even though the Irish Catholic Church set itself ambitious Tridentine goals in the eighteenth and nineteenth centuries, and though in eighteenth-century England Bishop Challoner introduced a Tridentine programme of reform, the Catholic Church in the 'British' realms within the Tridentine period was emphaticaly un-Tridentine in its status, but rather for the most part occupied a position unusual for Catholics over most of their history, that of a social heresy. It was little the worse for it.

Notes and References

Preface

1. Eamon Duffy, 'Mary', in Peter Marshall (ed.), *The Impact of the English Reformation 1500–1640* (London, New York, Sydney, Auckland: Arnold, Arnold Readers in History, 1997), pp. 102–229.
2. Conrad Russell, 'Composite monarchies in early modern Europe: The British and Irish examples', in Alexander Grant and Keith J. Stringer (eds), *Uniting the Kingdom? The Making of British History* (London and New York: Routledge, 1995), p. 135

1   Catholics in England and Wales, c.1558–c.1640

1. For the background to the emergence of Elizabethan recusancy, see Adrian Morey, *The Catholic Subjects of Elizabeth I* (London: George Allen & Unwin, 1978); Edward Robert Norman, *Roman Catholicism in England: From the Elizabethan Settlement to the Second Vatican Council* (Oxford: Oxford University Press, 1985); Arnold Pritchard, *Catholic Loyalism in Elizabethan England* (London: Scolar Press, 1970); Elliott Rose, *Cases of Conscience: Alternatives Open to Recusants and Puritans under Elizabeth I and James I* (Cambridge: Cambridge University Press, 1975); William Raleigh Trimble, *The Catholic Laity in Elizabethan England 1558–1603* (Cambridge, MA: Belknap Press, 1964); Alexandra Walsham, *Church Papists, Catholicism, Conformity and Confessional Polemic in Early Modern England* (London: The Boydell Press for the Royal Historical Society, 1993).
2. Stonor, in Alan Dures, *English Catholicism 1558–1642* (Harlow, Essex: Longman, 1983), p. 94.
3. Richard Challoner, *Memoirs of Missionary Priests and other Catholics of Both Sexes That Have Suffered Death in England on Religious Accounts* (published as *Martyrs to the Catholic Faith*, 2 vols in 1, Edinburgh: Thomas C. Jack, 1878), pp. ix, xxxv, l.

4. A.G. Dickens, 'The First Stages of Romanist Recusancy in Yorkshire, 1560–1590', *Yorkshire Archaeological Journal*, XXXV (1940–3), 161, 166–9, 180–1.

5. J. Stanley Leatherbarrow, *The Lancashire Elizabethan Recusants* (Manchester: Chetham Society, NS, X [1947]), xi, 152–7.

6. John Bossy, 'The Character of Elizabethan Catholicism', quoted in Patrick McGrath, 'Elizabethan Catholicism: A Reconsideration', *Journal of Ecclesiastical History*, XXXV (1984), 414–15.

7. John Bossy, *The English Catholic Community 1570–1850* (London: Darton, Longman and Todd, 1975), pp. 11–74; Eamon Duffy, 'The English Secular Clergy and the Counter-Reformation', *Journal of Ecclesiastical History*, XXXIV (1983), 214–7.

8. Christopher Haigh, 'The Continuity of Catholicism in the English Reformation', *Past and Present*, XCIII (1981), 37–69.

9. Christopher Haigh, 'From Monopoly to Minority: Catholicism in Early Modern England', *Transactions of the Royal Historical Society*, 5th series, XXXI (1981), 129–30.

10. Haigh, 'From Monopoly to Minority', 132, 146–7.

11. Thomas Wright, *The Disposition or Garnishment of the Soule To receiue Worthily the blessed Sacrament*, in John R. Roberts, *A Critical Anthology of English Recusant Devotional Prose, 1558–1603* (Leuven: Nauwelaerts, 1966), p. 244: by 'solafidean erroure' Wright meant assumptions, allegedly derived from the Reformation doctrine of justification by faith alone, that works of charity were not necessary for the Christian to perform.

12. Christopher Haigh, *Reformation and Resistance in Tudor Lancashire* (Manchester: Manchester University Press, 1975), Chapter 5; J.J. Scarisbrick, *The Reformation and the English People* (Oxford: Basil Blackwell, 1984); Eamon Duffy, *The Stripping of the Altars Traditional Religion in England c. 1400–c. 1580* (New Haven, CT: Yale University Press, 1992); J.J. McConica, *English Humanists and Reformation Politics under Henry VIII and Edward VI* (Oxford: Clarendon Press, 1965), Chapter 4; Dermot Fenlon, *Heresy and Obedience in Tridentine Italy: Cardinal Pole and the Counter-Reformation* (London: Cambridge University Press, 1972), pp. 1–6.

13. Roberts, *A Critical Anthology*, pp. 297, 62–6. For the fortunes of the confraternities in the Counter-Reformation, see John Bossy, 'The Counter-Reformation and the People of Catholic Europe', *Past and Present*, XLVII (1970), 58–60; for the English Carthusians and the circulation of devotional themes in the later middle ages, see Michael G. Sargent, 'The Transmission by the English Carthusians of Some Late Medieval Spiritual Writings', *Journal of Ecclesiastical History*, XXVII (1976), 225–40; see also Roger Lovatt, '*The Imitation of Christ* in Late Medieval England', *Transactions of the Royal Historical Society*, 5th series, XVIII (1968), 96–121.

14. Anna Jean Mill, 'The Stations of the York Corpus Christi Play', *Yorkshire Archaeological Journal*, XXXVII (1948), 492–505; Dr Duffy writes (*The Stripping of the Altars*, p. 67), 'Few communities could match [York's] sort of commitment to the task of [religious] instruction and consolation'.

15. Richard Rex, 'Thomas Vavasour MD', *Recusant History*, XX, 4 (1991), 436–54; Christopher Haigh, 'The Continuity of Catholicism', 48.

16. David Loades, *Revolution in Religion: The English Reformation 1530–1570* (Cardiff: University of Wales Press, 1992), p. 10.

17. Haigh, 'The Continuity of Catholicism', 37–69.

18. John O'Leary, 'Prisoners in the Clink Prison in 1586', *London Recusant*, IV, 4 (1974), 94–6; John O'Leary, 'Prisoners in the Gatehouse in June 1586', *London Recusant*, IV, 4 (1974), 96–7; Patrick McGrath, 'The Elizabethan Priests: Their Harbourers and Helpers', *Recusant History*, XIX, 3 (1989), 204.

19. Leo Warren, 'The Catholic Community in the North West', in Michael Mullett and Leo Warren, *Martyrs of the Diocese of Lancaster Beatified on the Feast of Christ the King* (Preston: Diocese of Lancaster, 1987), pp. 11–12.

20. Patrick McGrath and Joy Rowe, 'The Imprisonment of Catholics for Religion under Elizabeth I', *Recusant History*, XX, 4 (1991), 415–35; Patrick McGrath and Joy Rowe, 'Anstruther Analysed: "The Elizabethan Seminary Priests"', *Recusant History*, XVIII, 1 (1986), 1–13; Scarisbrick, *The Reformation and the English People*, pp. 144–5.

21. Patrick McGrath, *Papists and Puritans under Elizabeth I* (London: Blandford Press, 1967), p. 57, n. 1.

22. Scarisbrick, *The Reformation and the English People*, p. 142.

23. Scarisbrick, *The Reformation and the English People*, pp. 139–40.

24. Scarisbrick, *The Reformation and the English People*, p. 140; Sheridan Gilley, 'The Roman Catholic Church in England 1780–1940', in Sheridan Gilley and W.J. Sheils (eds), *A History of Religion in Britain: Practice and Belief from Pre-Roman Times to the Present* (Oxford, and Cambridge, MA: Basil Blackwell, 1994), p. 350; M.M. Nolan, 'A Petition for Aid from the Religious Order of St. Bridget, Formerly Sion House in England', *Essex Recusant*, XI, 1 (1969), 13–15.

25. *The Chronicle of the English Augustinian Canonesses Regular of the Lateran, at St Monica's in Louvain* (ed. Dom Aidan Hamilton, OSB, Edinburgh and London: Sands & Co., 1904), p. 29. For the Council of Trent's rulings on monastic discipline, see Norman P. Tanner, SJ (ed.), *Decrees of the Ecumenical Councils* (2 vols, London: Sheed & Ward, Washington, DC: Georgetown University Press, 1990), II, pp. 776–84.

26. Leatherbarrow, *The Lancashire Elizabethan Recusants*, p. xi; Nicholas Sanders' Report to Cardinal Morone, 'How the People are Affected towards the Catholic Faith', in *Catholic Record* Society, Miscellanea, I (1905), p. 45; Haigh, *Reformation and Resistance*, p. 114; Dures, *English Catholicism*, pp. 4–5; Dickens, 'First Stages of Romanist Recusancy', p. 161; *Depositions and other Ecclesiastical Proceedings from the Courts of Durham Extending from 1311 to the Reign of Elizabeth*, Surtees Society, XXI (1845), 19.

27. *Durham Depositions* 184–5, 188; for a summary of the Revolt of the Northern Earls, see McGrath, *Papists and Puritans*, pp. 65–7.

28. *Durham Depositions*, p. 188.

29. For the erosion of the 'church papist' option, see Trimble, *Catholic Laity*, pp. 45ff; for Elizabethan penal legislation, see G.R. Elton (ed.), *The Tudor Constitution Documents and Commentary* (2nd edn, Cambridge, New York and Melbourne: Cambridge University Press, 1982), pp. 419–42.

30. Patrick McGrath, 'The Bloody Questions Reconsidered', *Recusant History*, XX, 3 (1991), 305–19.

31. Albert J. Loomie, 'The Armada and the Catholics of England', *Catholic Historical Review*, LIX, 3 (1973), 385–403.
32. Michael E. Williams, 'William Allen: the Sixteenth-Century Spanish Connection', *Recusant History*, XXII, 2 (1994), 123–40; William Allen, *A True Sincere and Modest Defence of English Catholics*...(2 vols, London: Manresa Press and Herder, 1941), II, pp. 58–9; Victor Houliston, 'The Fabrication of the Myth of Father Parsons', *Recusant History*, XXII, 2 (1994), 141–51.
33. The Bishop of Carlisle to William Cecil, 27 October 1570, in *Catholic Record Society*, Miscellanea 12 (1921), 116.
34. *Catholic Record Society*, Miscellanea 12 (1921), 1.
35. Rex, 'Thomas Vavasour', p. 439, citing Aveling.
36. A.G. Dickens, 'The Extent and Character of Recusancy in Yorkshire, 1604', *Yorkshire Archaeological Journal*, XXXVII (1948–51), 42–8; J.C.H. Aveling, 'Some Aspects of Yorkshire Catholic Recusant History, 1558–1791', *Studies in Church History*, IV: *The Province of York* (ed. G.J. Cuming, Leiden: E.J. Brill, 1967), p. 110; K.R. Wark, 'Elizabethan Recusancy in Cheshire' (Manchester: Chetham Society, 3rd series, XIX (1971), pp. 130, 137.
37. Alan Davidson, 'Robert Atkinson, a Famous Lawyer', *Essex Recusant*, XII, 2 (1970), 91–7.
38. M. M. Nolan, 'Catholics in England: 1583', *Essex Recusant*, XI, 1 (1969), 16–19.
39. Geoffrey Anstruther, OP, *The Seminary Priests: A Dictionary of the Secular Clergy of England and Wales 1558–1850* (4 vols, 1968–1977: vols I & II, Durham: Ushaw College, vols III & IV, Great Wakering, Essex: Mayhew-McCrimmon), I, p. vi.
40. *Records of the English Province of the Society of Jesus* (ed. Henry Foley, SJ, 7 vols, London: Burns & Oates, 1877, 1875–83), VI, (1880), p. 69.
41. *Records of the English Province* (ed. Foley), VI, pp. 99–100, 69–70; Sanders, cited in McGrath, *Papists and Puritans*, p. 61.
42. *Records of the English Province* (ed. Foley), VI, pp. 72, 80, 117.
43. Aveling, 'Some Aspects of Yorkshire Catholic Recusant History', 110, 114, 120; John O'Leary, 'The Certificates of the Middle Temple, 1577' and 'Recusants in Lincoln's Inn', *London Recusant*, IV, 3 (1974), 90–3: see also John J. Larocca, SJ, 'Popery and Pounds: The Effect of the Jesuit Mission on Penal Legislation', in Thomas M. McCoog, SJ, *The Reckoned Expense: Edmund Campion and the Early English Jesuits: Essays in celebration of the first centenary of Campion Hall, Oxford (1896–1996)* (Woodbridge, Suffolk: The Boydell Press, 1996) p. 257; Dickens, 'The Extent and Character of Recusancy in Yorkshire', 42 and map facing 48; Haigh, 'The Continuity of Catholicism in the English Reformation', 184; Bossy, *English Catholic Community*, pp. 191–2; Aveling, 'Some Aspects of Yorkshire Catholic Recusant History', 110.
44. Aveling, 'Some Aspects of Yorkshire Catholic Recusant History', 117–9; Dickens, 'Extent and Character of Yorkshire Recusancy', 42; *The Recusancy Papers of the Meynell Family of North Kilvington, North Riding of Yorkshire 1596–1676, Catholic Record Society*, LVI, Miscellanea (1964), Introduction, xxxvi.

45. *The Recusancy Papers of the Meynell Family*; Aveling, 'Some Aspects of York-shire Catholic Recusant History', 116–20.

46. O'Leary, 'Prisoners in the Clink Prison in 1586', 94–6; O'Leary, 'Prisoners in the Gatehouse', 96–7; O'Leary, 'Recusants in the City of London in 1577': all in *London Recusant*, IV, 2 (1974) 50–3; Edward S. Worrall, 'Some Popish Recusants of the Archdeaconries of Middlesex and St Albans in 1577 and 1601', *London Recusant*, IV, 3 (1974), 85–9; Dickens, 'The Extent and Character of Recusancy in Yorkshire', 42; B.G. Blackwood, 'Plebeian Catholics in the 1640s and 1650s', *Recusant History*, XVIII, 1 (1986), 42–58.

47. For the issues in the dispute, see Bossy, *English Catholic Community*, Chapter 2, and for its origins *The Wisbech Stirs 1595–1598*, ed. P. Renold, *Catholic Record Society*, LI (1958).

48. McGrath, *Papists and Puritans*, 175–8, 184–6, 276–7; Gillian Brennan, 'Papists and Patriotism in Elizabethan England', *Recusant History*, XIX, 1 (1988), 1–15.

49. Joseph B. Gavin, SJ, 'Some Catholic Opinions of King James VI and I', *Recusant History*, X, 5 (1970), 292–303; *Recusant Documents from the Ellesmere Manuscripts, Catholic Record Society*, 1968, 148–9.

50. Mark Nicholls, 'Investigating the Gunpowder Plot', *Recusant History*, XIX, 2 (1988), 140; Dures, *English Catholics 1558–1640*, p. 44.

51. For the terms of the Oath and possible responses to it, see Maurice Lunn, OSB, 'English Benedictines and the Oath of Allegiance 1606–1647', *Recusant History*, X, 3 (1969), 146–63; *Ellesmere MSS, Catholic Record Society*, 1968, 254–5.

52. Timothy H. Watkins, 'King James I Meets John Percy, SJ (25 May 1622)', *Recusant History*, XIX, 2 (1988), 140–54; Josephine Evetts-Secker, 'Jerusalem and Albion: Ralph Buckland's "Seaven Sparks of the Enkindled Soule"', *Recusant History*, XX, 2 (1990), 149–63; Robert V. Caro, SJ, 'William Alabaster: Rhetor, Mediator, Devotional Poet', *Recusant History*, XIX (1988), 155–70.

53. Bossy, *English Catholic Community*, Chapter 3 and p.54; Thomas M. McCoog, SJ, *English and Welsh Jesuits 1555–1650*, Part I: A–F, *Catholic Record Society*, LXXIV (1994), 14–24; Anthony F. Allison, 'Richard Smith's Gallican Backers and Jesuit Opponents. Part III: The Continuation of Controversy 1631–c.1643', *Recusant History*, XX, 2 (1990), 165–206.

54. P.R.P. Knell, 'Notes on some 17th-Century Priests in Essex', *Essex Recusant*, XII, 3 (1970), 100–5; R. G. Dottie, 'John Crosse of Liverpool and Recusancy in Early Seventeenth-Century Lancashire', *Recusant History*, XX, 1 (1990), 31–47; Haigh, 'The Continuity of Catholicism', 184; McCoog, *English and Welsh Jesuits*, Part V, p. 24.

55. Dures, *English Catholics*, p. 73.

56. Glanmor Williams, 'Wales and the Reign of Queen Mary I', *The Welsh History Review*, X (1980–1), 334–58.

57. Williams, 'Wales and the Reigh of Queen Mary I', 334–58.

58. G. Dyfnallt Owen, *Elizabethan Wales: The Social Scene* (Cardiff: University of Wales Press, 1964), pp. 215–21.

59. Glanmor Williams, 'Wales and the Reformation' in Glanmor Williams, *Welsh Reformation Essays* (Cardiff: University of Wales Press, 1967), pp. 20–1, 25;

Dyfnallt Owen, *Elizabethan Wales*, pp. 215–21; A.H. Dodd, *Studies in Stuart Wales* (Cardiff: University of Wales Press, 1952), p. 38; Donald Attwater, *The Penguin Dictionary of Saints* (Harmondsworth, Middlesex: Penguin Books, 1965), p. 345; G. Dyfnallt Owen, *Wales in the Reign of James I* (London: The Boydell Press for the Royal Historical Society, 1988), p. 68; for the Council's strictures on 'superstition' in the veneration of saints, see Tanner (ed.), *Decrees of the Ecumenical Councils*, II, pp. 775–6.

60. Glanmor Williams, 'Wales and the Reformation', 66–79.

61. Williams, 'Wales and the Reformation', pp. 76, 82–5, 95; Howell A. Lloyd, *The Gentry of South-West Wales 1540–1640* (Cardiff: University of Wales Press, 1968), pp. 191–2; Glanmor Williams, *Renewal and Reformation Wales c. 1415–1642* (Oxford and New York: Oxford University Press, 1993), pp. 477–8.

62. Dyfnallt Owen, *Wales in the Reign of James I*, p. 84.

63. J. Gwynfor Jones, 'Caernarvonshire Administration: The Activities of the Justices of the Peace, 1603–1660', *Welsh History Review*, V (1970–1) 13; Glanmor Williams, *Renewal and Reformation*, p. 478; Dyfnallt Owen, *Wales in the Reign of James I*, pp. 99, 110.

2 Catholics in Scotland and Ireland, c. 1558–c. 1640

1. Denis McKay, 'Parish Life in Scotland 1500–1560', *The Innes Review*, X, 2 (1959), 237–67; David McRoberts, 'A Sixteenth-Century Picture of St Bartholomew from Perth', *The Innes Review*, X, 2 (1959), 282–4; Ian B. Cowan, *The Scottish Reformation: Church and Society in Sixteenth-century Scotland* (London: Weidenfeld & Nicolson, 1982), p.2.

2. Jenny Wormald, *Court, Kirk and Community: Scotland 1470–1625* (London: Edward Arnold, 1981), p. 92.

3. Wormaid, *Court, Kirk and Community*, pp. 92–4; Thomas Winning, 'Church Councils in Sixteenth-Century Scotland', *The Innes Review*, X, 2 (1959), 330–1, 336; Gilbert Hill, OFM, Cap., 'The Sermons of John Watson, Canon of Aberdeen', *The Innes Review*, XV, 1 (1964), 3–34; McKay, 'Parish Life', 244; Anthony Ross, OP, 'Libraries of the Scottish Blackfriars', *The Innes Review*, XX, 1 (1969), 20.

4. Ross, 'Libraries of the Scottish Reformation', 244; Winning, 'Church Councils', 336; Wormald, *Court, Kirk and Community*, p. 121. For the political background to and determinants of religious change and the fortunes of Catholicism in Scotland after 1560, see, for example, J.H. Burns, 'The Political Background of the Reformation', *The Innes Review*, X, 2 (1959), esp. 215–36.

5. David McRoberts, 'Material Destruction Caused by the Scottish Reformation', in David McRoberts (ed.), *Essays on the Scottish Reformation* (Glasgow: Burns, 1962), pp. 415–62.

6. For these measures, see, for example, Wormald, *Court, Kirk and Community*, pp. 117 ff.

7. Margaret H.B. Sanderson, 'Catholic Recusancy in Scotland in the Sixteenth Century', *The Innes Review*, XXI, 2 (1970), 88; Anthony Ross, OP, 'Reformation and Repression', *The Innes Review*, X, 2 (1959), 370.

8. Ross, 'Reformation and Repression', 367–8.

9. Ross, 'Reformation and Repression', 268–9; Sanderson, 'Catholic Recusancy', 88.

10. Natalie Zemon Davis, 'The Rites of Violence', *Past and Present*, LIX (1973), 83–4; Cowan, *The Scottish Reformation*, p. 164; Ross, 'Reformation and Repression', 369.

11. Ross, 'Reformation and Repression', 369–70; Sanderson, 'Catholic Recusancy', 89, 90–1, 94; Charles H. Haws, 'The Diocese of Aberdeen and the Reformation', *The Innes Review*, XXII, 2 (1971), 77; *Stirling Presbytery Records 1581–1587* (ed. James Kirk, Edinburgh: Scottish Record Society, 1981), p. 203.

12. Haws, 'The Diocese of Aberdeen and the Reformation', 72–84; David McRoberts, 'The Scottish Catholic Archives 1560–1978', *The Innes Review*, XXVIII, 2 (1977), 61; A.D. Lacaille, 'Notes on a Loch Lomondside Parish', *The Innes Review*, XVI, 2 (1965), 149; Sanderson, 'Catholic Recusancy', 92–6.

13. Sanderson, 'Catholic Recusancy', 96–100.

14. *Abbé Paul MacPherson's History of the Scots College, Rome* (ed. William James Anderson), *The Innes Review*, XII (1961), 9–10.

15. Ross, 'Reformation and Repression', 358, 365; Michael J. Yellowless, 'The Ecclesiastical Establishment of the Diocese of Dunkeld at the Reformation', *The Innes Review.*, XXXVI, 2 (1985), 80–1.

16. John Durkan, 'The Cultural Background in Sixteenth-Century Scotland', *The Innes Review*, X, 2 (1959), 382–439; John Durkan, 'William Murdoch and the Early Jesuit Mission to Scotland', *The Innes Review*, XXXV, 1 (1984), 3–11; *Stirling Presbytery Records 1581–1587*, pp. 80–3, 176, 183, 187.

17. Mary Black Verschuur, 'The Perth Charterhouse in the Sixteenth Century', *The Innes Review*, XXXIX, 1 (1988), 6–9.

18. John Durkan, 'Paisley Abbey in the Sixteenth Century', *The Innes Review*, XXVII, 2 (1976), 110–126.

19. McRoberts, 'Material Destruction', 415–62; Sanderson, 'Catholic Recusancy', 87–94; Richard F. Dell, 'Some Fragments of Medieval Mss in Glasgow City Archives', *The Innes Review*, XVIII, 2 (1967), 117; Ross, 'Reformation and Repression', 355–7, 366–70 ; John Durkan, 'Edinburgh in 1611: Catholic Sympathisers', *The Innes Review*, LX, 2 (1989), 158–61.

20. Brother Kenneth, 'The Popular Literature of the Scottish Reformation', in McRoberts (ed.), *Essays on the Scottish Reformation*, pp. 179–84: for Kennedy and Winzet, see also Gordon Donaldson and Robert S. Morpeth, *Who's Who in Scottish History* (Oxford: Basil Blackwell, 1973), pp. 75–6; Maurice Taylor, 'The Conflicting Doctrines of the Scottish Reformation', in McRoberts (ed.), *Essays on the Scottish Reformation*, pp. 259–73; Ross, 'Reformation and Repression', 365.

21. William James Anderson, 'Rome and Scotland, 1513–1625', in McRoberts (ed.), *Essays on the Scottish Reformation*, pp. 476–7; Sanderson, 'Catholic Recusancy', 87–8; John Durkan, 'William Murdoch and the Early Jesuit Mission in Scotland', *The Innes Review*, 31, 1 (1984), 3–11; Ross, 'Reformation and Repression', p. 373; Haws, 'The Diocese of Aberdeen and the Reformation', 73

22. *Abbé Paul MacPherson's History of the Scots College, Rome*, 9–10.

23. Mark Dilworth, OSB, 'Notes on the Religious Orders, Appendix II: The Schottenklöster at the Reformation', in McRoberts (ed.), *Essays on the Scottish Reformation*, pp. 241–4; Mark Dilworth, OSB, 'The First Scottish Monks in Ratisbon', *The Innes Review*, XVI, 2 (1965), 180–98; Mark Dilworth, OSB, 'Germania Christiana in a seventeenth-century trilogy', *The Innes Review*, XVIII, 2 (1967), 118–40; Mark Dilworth, OSB, 'Ninian Winzet: Some New Material', *The Innes Review*, XXIV, 2 (1973), 125–32.

24. Michael F. Graham, *The Uses of Reform: 'Godly Discipline' and Popular Behavior in Scotland and Beyond, 1560–1610* (Leiden, New York and Cologne: E. J. Bill, 1996), pp. 89-91, and citing Haws, in *ibid.*, p. 89.

25. Sanderson, 'Catholic Recusancy', 91; Ross 'Reformation and Repression', 370–2; John Durkan, 'Care for the Poor: Pre-Reformation Hospitals', *The Innes Review*, X, 2 (1959), 280; Graham, *The Uses of Reform*, pp. 92–3, 113, 143–4, 213.

26. Anderson, 'Rome and Scotland, 1513–1625', 476–7; Brother Kenneth, 'Popular Literature of the Scottish Reformation', 179–84; Ross, 'Reformation and Repression', 365; Taylor, 'Conflicting Doctrines of the Scottish Reformation', 259–73.

27. McRoberts (ed.), *Essays on the Scottish Reformation*, p. xvii; Roman Darowski, 'John Hay and the Origins of Philosophy in Lithuania', *The Innes Review*, XXXI, 1 (1980), 7–15; David McRoberts, 'Scottish Pilgrims to the Holy Land', *The Innes Review*, XX, 1 (1969), 101.

28. Mark Dilworth, OSB, 'Scottish Students at the Collegium Germanicum', *The Innes Review*, XIX, 1 (1968), 15–22; *Abbé Paul McPherson's History of the Scots College, Rome*, 9–24.

29. Anthony Ross, OP, 'Dominicans and Scotland in the Seventeenth Century', *The Innes Review*, XXIII, 1 (1972), 40–7.

30. Ross, 'Dominicans and Scotland', 46; Thomas S. Flynn, OP, *The Irish Dominicans 1536–1641* (Dublin:Four Courts Press, 1993), pp. 285–9.

31. McKay, 'Parish Life in Scotland', 252; A. MacDonnell and D. McRoberts, 'The Mass Stones of Lochaber', *The Innes Review*, XVII, 2 (1966), 77–8.

32. Cowan, *The Scottish Reformation*, p. 169.

33. John Cunningham, 'Church Administration and Organisation', *The Innes Review*, XXIX, 1 (1978), 73–5; Peter F. Anson, *Underground Catholicism in Scotland 1622–1878* (Montrose: Standard Press, 1970), Chapter 1.

34. Frederick M. Jones, CSSR, 'The Counter-Reformation', in Patrick J. Corish (ed.), *A History of Irish Catholicism*, vol. III (Dublin and Melbourne: Gill & Son, 1967), pp.1–28.

35. Jones, 'The Counter-Reformation'; Hiram Morgan, 'The End of Gaelic Ulster: A Thematic Interpretation of Events between 1534 and 1610', *Irish Historical Studies*, XXVI (1988), 27.

36. Nicholas Canny, 'Irish, Scottish and Welsh responses to centralisation. c. 1530–c. 1640', in Alexander Grant and Keith J. Stringer (eds), *Uniting the Kingdom? The Making of British History* (London and New York: Routledge, 1995), p. 150; Colm Lennon, 'The Chantries in the Irish Reformation: The Case of St Anne's Guild, Dublin, 1550–1630', in R.V. Comerford *et al.* (eds), *Religion, Conflict and Coexistence in Ireland. Essays Presented to Monsignor Patrick J. Corish* (Dublin: Gill and Macmillan, 1990), pp. 6–25.

37. Colm Lennon, 'The Rise of Recusancy among the Dublin Patricians, 1580–1613', in W.J. Sheils and Diana Wood (eds), *The Church, Ireland and the Irish* (*Studies in Church History*, XXV, Oxford: Basil Blackwell for the Ecclesiastical History Society, 1989), pp. 123–32; Declan Gaffney, 'The Practice of Religious Controversy in Dublin, 1600–1641', *ibid.*, pp. 145–58.

38. M. K. Ó Murchada, 'Music in Saint Nicholas's Church, Galway 1480–1912', *Journal of the Galway Archaeological and Historical Society*, XLV (1993), 29–30; Brendan Jenning, OFM, 'The Abbey of St Francis', Galway', *Journal of the Galway Archaeological and Historical Society*, XXIII (1947), 101–19.

39. Patrick K. Egan, CC, 'The Augustinian Priory of St Mary Clontuskert O Many', *Journal of the Galway Archaeological and Historical Society*, XXII (1946), 1–14; Kenneth Nicholls, 'A List of the Monasteries in Connacht, 1577', *Journal of the Galway Archaeological and Historical Society*, XXXIII (1972), 28–32; Brendan Jennings, OFM, 'The Chalices and Books of Kilconel Abbey', *Journal of the Galway Archaeological and Historical Society*, XXI (1944), 63–70.

40. Nicholas Canny, 'Rowland White's "Discors touching Ireland"', c.1569', *Irish Historical Studies*, XX (1976–7), 461; Helen Coburn Walshe, 'The rebellion of William Nugent, 1581', in Comerford *et al.* (eds), *Religion, Conflict and Coexistence*, p. 47; Gráinne Henry, 'The emerging identity of an Irish military group in the Spanish Netherlands 1586–1610', in *ibid.*, p.67.

41. Colm Lennon, 'Richard Stanihurst (1547–1618) and Old English Identity', *Irish Historical Studies*, XXI (1978), 121–43.

42. Síle Ní Chinnéide, 'Luke Wadding 1588–1657: Tercentenary Lecture', *Journal of the Galway Archaeological and Historical Society*, XXXI (1954–6), 81–93.

43. Colum Kenny, 'Catholics and the legal profession in Ireland', *Irish Historical Studies*, XXIV (1986), 341–2.

44. Kenny, 'Catholics and the legal profession', 340–8; Colum Kenny, 'The exclusion of catholics from the legal profession in Ireland, 1537–1829', *Irish Historical Studies*, XXV (1987), 337–57.

45. Morgan, 'The end of Gaelic Ulster', 26.

46. Morgan, 'The end of Gaelic Ulster', 8–32.

47. *Calendar of State Papers Domestic: Carew*, vol. II, p. 480 (1577); Frederick M. Jones, CSSR, 'The Spaniards at Kinsale, 1601', *Journal of the Galway Archaeological and Historical Society*, XXI (1944), 1–43; Brendan Jennings, OFM, 'Melchior de Burgos A Connaught Soldier of Fortune in the Low Countries in the Seventeenth Century', *Journal of the Galway Archaeological and Historical Society*, XXIII (1947), 174; Frederick Jones, CSSR, 'James Blake and a Projected Invasion of Galway in 1602', *Journal of the Galway Archaeological and Historical Society*, XXVI (1950), 13; John Davies, *Discovery of the True Causes why Ireland was never Entirely Subdued* (Introduction by John Barry, Shannon, Co Clare: Irish University Press, 1969), p. 284.

48. R.F. Foster, *Modern Ireland 1600–1972* (London: Allen Lane: The Penguin Press, 1988), p. 42; Patrick J. Corish, *The Catholic Community in the Seventeenth and Eighteenth Centuries* (Helicon History of Ireland, Dublin: Helicon, 1981), pp. 29–30; B. Millett, OFM, 'Catalogue of Irish Material in vols 132–139 of the *Scritture Originali riferite nelle congregazioni generali* in Propaganda

Archives', *Collectanea Hibernica Sources for Irish History*, XII (1969), 23–5; Paul Walsh, 'An Account of the Town of Galway', *Journal of the Galway Historical and Archaeological Society*, XLIX (1992), 69–71.

49. Cathaldus Giblin, OFM, 'Catalogue of Irish Interest in the Collection *Nunziatura di Fiandra*', Vatican Archives: part 1, vols 1–50, *Collectanea Hibernica Sources for Irish History*, I (1958), 60–1; B. Millett, OFM, 'Catalogue of Irish Material in Fourteen Volumes of the *Scritture Originali riferite nelle congregazioni generali* in Propaganda Archives', *Collectanea Hibernica*, X (1967), 23–5, *Collectanea Hibernica*, XII, 23–5; Corish, *Catholic Community*, 29–33, 128; Ní Chinnéide, 'Luke Wadding', 87.

50. Corish, *Catholic Community*, p. 35; Flynn, *The Irish Dominicans 1536–1641*, pp. 139–40, 150–1, 239–62; B. Millett, 'Calendar of Volume 1 (1625–68) of the Collection *Scritture referite nei congressi, Irlanda* in Propaganda Archives', *Collectanea Hibernica*, VI and VII (1963–4), 46–7.

51. Corish, *Catholic Community*, pp. 27–8, 34; Ní Chinnéide, 'Luke Wadding', 86.

52. Corish, *Catholic Community*, pp. 34–5; Michael Quane, 'Galway Classical School', *Journal of the Galway Archaeological and Historical Society*, XXXI (1964–5), 16–24.

53. Bartholomew Egan, OFM, 'Notes on the Propaganda Fide Printing-Press and Correspondence concerning Francis Molloy, OFM', *Collectanea Hibernica Sources for Irish History*, II (1959), 115–16; Bernadette Cunningham, 'Geoffrey Keating's *Eochair-Sgiath an Aifrinn* and the Catholic Reformation in Ireland', in Sheils and Wood (eds), *The Church, Ireland and the Irish*, pp. 133–43; Jim Higgins, 'A Fourth Holy Trinity Carving from Galway City', *Journal of the Galway Archaeological and Historical Society*, XLVI (1989–90), 155–8.

54. Gráinne Henry, 'The emerging identity of an Irish military group in the Spanish Netherlands', 53–77; Aidan Clarke, 'The Government of Wentworth, 1632–40, in T.W. Moody, F.X. Martin and F.J. Byrne (eds), *A New History of Ireland* (9 vols, Oxford: The Clarendon Press for the Royal Irish Academy), III (1976), p. 264.

3   Catholics in England and Wales, c. 1640–c. 1740

1. David Mathew, *Catholicism in England: The Portrait of a Minority: Its Culture and Tradition* (3rd edn, London: Eyre & Spottiswoode, 1975), p. 83.

2. Albert J. Loomie, SJ, 'London's Spanish Chapel before and after the Civil War', *Recusant History*, XVIII, 4 (1987), 402–10; M.D.R. Leys, *Catholicism in England 1559–1829: A Social History* (London: Longmans, 1961), p.86; Timothy J. McCann, 'Some Unpublished Accounts of the Martyrdom of Blessed Thomas Bullater, OSFs, in Chichester in 1642', *Recusant History*, XIX, 2 (1988), 179.

3. John Bossy, *The English Catholic Community 1570–1850* (London: Darton, Longman & Todd, 1975), p. 128; Dom Gerard Sitwell, OSB (ed.), *Holy Wisdom or Directions for the Prayer of Contemplation* (Wheathampstead, Herts: Anthony Clarke Books, 1972), pp.111, 157–8; Leys, *Catholicism in England*, p. 84.

4. Leys, *Catholicism in England*, pp. 86–8; J.A. Hilton, *Catholic Lancashire From Reformation to Renewal 1559–1991* (Chichester, W. Sussex: Phillimore, 1994), pp. 34–5.

5. Hilton, *Catholic Lancashire*, pp. 34–5; Michael Mullett, 'Reformation and Renewal, 1450–1690', in Andrew White (ed.), *A History of Lancaster 1193–1993* (Keele, Staffs: Ryburn Publishing/Keele University Press, 1993), p. 71.

6. Hilton, *Catholic Lancashire*, pp. 35–6; P.R. Newman, 'Roman Catholic Royalists: Papist Commanders under Charles I and Charles II, 1640–60', *Recusant History*, XV, 6 (1981), 396–405; C.D. Gilbert, 'The Catholics in Worcestershire 1642–1651', *Recusant History*, XX, 3 (1992), 336–57; Michael Hodgetts, 'The Yates of Harvington, 1631–1696', *Recusant History*, XXII, 2 (1994), 152–81.

7. Mathew, *Catholicism in England*, p. 84; Loomie, 'London's Spanish Chapel', 411.

8. J. Denis McEvilly, 'Worcestershire Entries in Franciscan Registers 1657–1824', *Worcestershire Recusant*, XIII (1969), 10.

9. Bossy, *English Catholic Community*, pp. 62–7; Robert I. Bradley, 'Blacklo and the Counter-Reformation', in Charles H. Carter (ed.), *From the Renaissance to the Counter-Reformation. Essays in Honour of Garrett Mattingly* (London: Jonathan Cape, 1966), p. 365; B.C. Southgate, ' "That Damned Booke": *The Grounds of Obedience and Government* (1655), and the Downfall of Thomas White', *Recusant History*, XVII, 3 (1985), 238–53.

10. For the Declaration of Breda and Charles's 1662 and 1672 Declarations of Indulgence aiming to give effect to it, see J.P. Kenyon, *The Stuart Constitution 1603–1688: Documents and Commentary* (Cambridge: Cambridge University Press, 1966), pp. 357–8, 403–6, 407–8. For Lancashire Catholic numbers, see Hilton, *Catholic Lancashire*, p. 41; some Lancashire statistics from the 1676 Compton Census on non-Anglicans have been supplied by Margaret Panikkar (ed.), *The Compton Census of 1676: The Lancashire Returns* (Wigan: North West Catholic History Society, 1995); Michael Mullett, *James II and English Politics, 1678–1688* (London and New York: Routledge Lancaster Pamphlets, 1994), pp. 6–7; T.A. Birrell, 'William Leslie, Henry Howard and Lord Arlington 1666–67', *Recusant History*, XIX, 4 (1989), 469–83; Bossy, *English Catholic Community*, p. 83.

11. Rev. T. Ellison Gibson (ed.), *Crosby Records A Cavalier's Notebook* (London: Longmans, Green, 1880), p. 211; Kenyon, *The Stuart Constitution*, pp. 451, 453; John Kenyon, *The Popish Plot* (London: Heinemann, 1972), pp. 205–8; Andrew Marvell, *An Account of the Growth of Popery and Arbitrary Government in England* (Amsterdam, 1677, reprinted, with an Introduction by Gâmini Salgâdo, Farnborough: Gregg International, 1971), pp. 6, 11–12 and *passim*.

12. Michael A. Mullett, *John Bunyan in Context* (Keele, Staffs: Keele University Press, 1996), pp. 195–6; Michael Mullett, ' "A Receptacle for Papists and an Assilum": Catholicism and Disorder in Late Seventeenth-Century Wigan', *The Catholic Historical Review*, LXXIII, 3 (1987), 402–3; Mullett, 'Reformation and Renewal'; p. 86; Mullett, *James II*, pp. 40–1.

13. Thomas Jones (ed.), *A Catalogue of the Collection of Tracts for and against Popery (Published in or about the Reign of James II)* part I, *Chetham Society*, vol. XLVIII (1859), *passim*; Judith F. Champ, 'The Franciscan Mission in Birmingham

1657–1824', *Recusant History*, XXI, 1 (1992), 40–3; Marie Rowlands, 'An Inventory of the Chapel of St. Thomas', *Staffordshire Catholic History*, 2 (1962), 27–32; A. M. C. Forster, 'An Outline History of the Catholic Church in North-East England from the Sixteenth Century', *Northern Catholic History*, X (1979), 13, 15; M.A. Mullett, 'Politics and Elections in Lancaster, 1660–1688', *Northern History*, XIX (1983), 78–9; Michael Greenslade, 'Bishop Leyburn at Stafford and Wolverhampton', *Staffordshire Catholic History*, II (1962), 19.

14. Michael Greenslade, 'The Association of Staffordshire Clergy, 1686', *Staffordshire Catholic History*, II (1962), 13–18; Paolo Prodi, 'The Application of the Tridentine Decrees: The Organization of the Diocese of Bologna During the Episcopate of Cardinal Gabriele Paleotti', in Eric Cochrane (ed.), *The Late Italian Renaissance 1525–1630* (London: Macmillan Stratum Series (gen. ed. J.R. Hale), 1970), pp. 227–43.

15. Thomas M. McCoog, SJ, 'Richard Langhorne and the "Nevills of Nevill Holt": A Note', *Recusant History*, XX, 3 (1991), 358–60; Champ, 'The Franciscan Mission in Birmingham', pp. 42–3.

16. Champ, 'The Franciscan Mission'; Michael Mullett, ' "To Dwell Together in Unity": The Search for Agreement in Preston Politics, 1660–1690', *Transactions of the Historic Society of Lancashire and Cheshire*, CXXV (1975), 76–8; T.G. Ward and Leo Warren, *The Manor Mission of Low Furness The Parish of St. Mary of Furness, Ulverston* (Bolton, Greater Manchester: The Catholic Printing Company, 1979), p.17; Mullett, ' "A Receptacle for Papists" ', 406–7; for a summary of penal legislation following James' fall, see Mathew, *Catholicism in England*, pp. 122–3.

17. Mathew, *Catholicism in England*, p. 120; Hodgetts, 'The Yates of Harvington', 172.

18. Anthony Allison, 'The English Augustinian Convent of Our Lady of Syon at Paris: Its Foundation and Struggle for Survival during the first Eighty Years', *Recusant History*, XXI, 4 (1993), 463, 481–2, 484; C.D. van Strien, 'Recusant Houses in the Southern Netherlands as seen by British Tourists, c. 1650–1720', *Recusant History*, XX, 4 (1991), 504, 507.

19. Greenslade, 'Association of Staffordshire Clergy', 13–18.

20. Thomas H. Clancy, SJ, 'Priestly Perseverance in the Old Society of Jesus', *Recusant History*, XIX, 3 (1989), 202–3;. T. Geoffrey Holt, SJ, ' "A College of Jesuits" at Holbeck in Nottinghamshire', *Recusant History*, XIX, 3 (1989), 484–98.

21. Hodgetts, 'The Yates of Harvington', 152–81; Halifax, quoted in Hilton, *Catholic Lancashire*, p. 43; *The Tyldesley Diary: personal records . . . 1712–13–14* (Preston: Hewitson, 1873), pp. 15 ff.

22. Ellison Gibson (ed.), *Crosby Records A Cavalier's Notebook* , p. 133; Rt. Rev. B.C. Foley, *Some People of the Penal Times (Chiefly 1688–1791)* (Lancaster: Cathedral Bookshop, 1991), pp. 120, 174; F. Walker, *Historical Geography of Southwest Lancashire before the Industrial Revolution, Transactions of the Historic Society of Lancashire and Cheshire*, XL (1939), 118–21.

23. Colin M. Haydon, 'Samuel Peploe and Catholicism in Preston,1714', *Recusant History*, XX, 1 (1990), 79; Thomas Ward, *England's Reformation: From the Time of King HENRY VIII, To the End of Oates's Plot, A Poem, in Four Canto's*

(London, Thomas Bickerton, 1716); Walker, *Historical Geography*, pp. 124–5; Hilton, *Catholic Lancashire*, pp. 48–9; L. Gooch, ' "Incarnate Rogues and Vile Jacobites": Silvertop *v.* Cotesworth, 1718–1723', *Recusant History*, XVIII, 3 (1987), 277–81.

24. Walker, *Historical Geography*, p. 127; B. Gordon Blackwood, 'Lancashire Catholics, Protestants and Jacobites', *Recusant History*, XXII,1 (1994), 44–6; Colin Haydon, *Anti-Catholicism in eighteenth-century England, c. 1714–80*: a political and social study (Manchester and New York: Manchester University Press, 1993), p. 106.

25. Haydon, *Anti-Catholicism*, pp. 103–5; Walker, *Historical Geography*, p. 127; Bossy, *English Catholic Community*, p. 287; Haydon, 'Samuel Peploe and Catholicism in Preston', 78–9.

26. Haydon, 'Samuel Peploe', 79.

27. Blackwood, 'Lancashire Catholics, Protestants and Jacobites', 41–59; Marion E. McClintock, *St Thomas the Apostle Claughton-on-Brock: A brief history* (Garstang: Colin Cross, 1997), p. 7; Rt Rev. Brian C. Foley, 'Some Papers of a "Riding Priest" ', *Recusant History*, XIX, 2 (1993), 46–7; (Church Bicentenary Group), *SS. Peter & Paul, Ribchester* (Ribchester: Stydd Lodge Presbytery, 1989), pp. 26–7; Rt Rev. Brian C. Foley, 'A Priest Describes to the Cardinal Prefect of Propaganda his Mission to the Isle of Man, 18 July 1727', *Recusant History*, XXII,1 (1995), 60–2.

28. Blackwood, 'Lancashire Catholics, Protestants and Jacobites', 43–4.

29. Champ, 'The Franciscan Mission in Birmingham', 42–3; Bossy, *English Catholic Community*, p. 284; Eamon Duffy, ' "Poor protestant flies": Conversion to Catholicism in early eighteenth-century England', in Derek Baker (ed.), *Religious Motivation: Biographical and Sociological Problems for the Church Historian, Studies in Church History*, XV (Oxford: Basil Blackwell for the Ecclesiastical History Society, 1978), pp. 292–304; George Every, 'The Catholic Comunity in Walsall 1720–1824', *Recusant History*, XIX, 2 (1993), 31–4.

30. Thomas M. McCoog, SJ, 'Richard Langhorne and the Popish Plot', *Recusant History*, XIX, 4 (1989), 507; Holt, ' "A College of Jesuits" ', 48.

31. Foley, *Some People of the Penal Times*, p. 143; Bossy, *English Catholic Community*, pp. 130, 131,132, 286; F. Blom, J. Blom, F. Korsten and G. Scott, *English Catholic Books 1701–1800: A Bibliography* (Aldershot: Scolar Press; Brookfield, VT: Ashgate Publishing, 1986), pp. 129 ff.; Every, 'Catholic Community in Walsall', 31–4.

32. Foley, *Some People of the Penal Times*, p. 144; J. Anthony Williams (ed.), *Post-Reformation Catholicism in Bath*, vol. I, *Catholic Record Society*, LXV (1995), pp. 45–50.

33. Mathew, *Catholicism in England*, pp. 133–4; C.M. Haydon, 'The Anti-Catholic Activity of the SPG, c. 1698–1740', *Recusant History*, XVIII, 4 (1987), 418–21.

34. Haydon, *Anti-Catholicism*, p. 124; Eamon Duffy, ' "Englishmen in vaine": Roman Catholic allegiance to George I', in Stuart Mews (ed.), *Religion and National Identity: Studies in Church History*, XVII (Oxford: Basil Blackwell for the Ecclesiastical History Society, 1982), pp. 345–65.

35. Haydon, *Anti-Catholicism*, pp. 124–6; Mathew, *Catholicism in England*, p. 126

36. Haydon, *Anti-Catholicism*, pp. 128–9; Foley, *Some People of the Penal Times*, p.140.
37. Foley, *Some People of the Penal Days*, pp. 140,144.
38. Philip Jenkins, '"A Welsh Lancashire"? Monmouthshire Catholics in the Eighteenth Century', *Recusant History*, XV, 3 (1980), 186–7; see also Geraint H. Jenkins, *Literature, Religion and Society in Wales, 1660–1730* (Cardiff: University of Wales Press for the History and Law Committees of the Board of Celtic Studies, 1978), p. 189.
39. Philip Jenkins, 'Anti-Popery on the Welsh Marches in the Seventeenth Century', *Historical Journal*, XXIII (1980), 275–93; Philip Jenkins, '"A Welsh Lancashire"?', 176–9; John R. Guy, 'Eighteenth-Century Gwent Catholics', *Recusant History*, XVI,1 (1982), 78–88.
40. Guy, 'Eighteenth-Century Gwent Catholics', 78–88; Jenkins, '"A Welsh Lancashire"?', 178–9.
41. Jenkins, '"A Welsh Lancashire"?', 181–3; Guy, 'Eighteenth-Century Gwent Catholics', 83–4.
42. Guy, 'Eighteenth-Century Gwent Catholics', 78–88 ; Jenkins, *Literature, Religion and Society*, pp. 47–8, 56, 116, 190.
43. Jenkins, '"A Welsh Lancashire"?', 178; Jenkins, *Literature, Religion and Society*, pp. 195–7; Philip Jenkins, 'Old and New Catholics in Stuart Wales: The Carne Family of Glamorgan', *Recusant History*, XVII, 4 (1985), 362–71.

4 Catholics in Scotland and Ireland, c. 1640–c. 1745

1. Maurice Lee, Jr, *The Road to Revolution Scotland under Charles I, 1625–37* (Urbana and Chicago, IL: University of Chicago Press, 1985), pp. 10–11, 62–3, 196–7; Keith M. Brown, *Kingdom or Province? Scotland and the Regal Union, 1603–1715* (London: Macmillan, 1993), pp. 72–3, 122–3; Margaret Steele, 'The "Politick Christian": The theological background to the National Covenant', in John Morrill (ed.), *The Scottish National Covenant in its British Context* (Edinburgh: Edinburgh University Press, 1990), p. 35; Peter Donald, *An Uncounselled King Charles I and the Scottish Troubles, 1637–1641* (Cambridge Studies in Early Modern British History, eds, Anthony Fletcher *et al.*, Cambridge, New York and Melbourne: Cambridge University Press, 1990), pp. 131–2; 179–92; F. D. Dow, *Cromwellian Scotland 1651–1660* (Edinburgh: John Donald, 1979), p. 205.
2. Anthony Ross, OP, 'Dominicans and Scotland in the Seventeenth Century', *The Innes Review*, 23, 1 (1972), 63; Wendy Doran, 'Bishop Thomas Nicholson: First Vicar-Apostolic 1695–1718', *The Innes Review*, XXXIX, 2 (1988), 109–17; Mark Dilworth, OSB, 'The Scottish Mission in 1688–1689', *The Innes Review*, XX, 1 (1969), 71.
3. Roderick Macdonald, 'The Catholic Gaidhealtachd', *The Innes Review*, XXIX (1978), 57–60; John Cunningham, 'Church and Administrative Organisation: 1878–1978', *The Innes Review*, XXIX (1978), 75: Nicholson was appointed under the supervision of a prefecture apostolic, answerable to Propaganda Fide.

4. Ross, 'Dominicans and Scotland', 47–53.

5. Ross, 'Dominicans and Scotland', 54–6

6. Alexander S. MacWilliam, 'The Jesuit Mission in Upper Deeside, 1671–1737', *The Innes Review*, XXIII, 1 (1972), 37.

7. MacWilliam, 'The Jesuit Mission', 22, 25.

8. MacWilliam, 'The Jesuit Mission', 26–7, 35, 37.

9. MacWilliam, 'The Jesuit Mission', 26–35.

10. MacWilliam, 'The Jesuit Mission'; Joseph Rickaby, *The Spiritual Exercises of St. Ignatius Loyola Spanish and English With a Continuous Commentary* (London: Burnes & Oates, 1915), p. 189.

11. Alasdair Roberts, 'Gregor McGregor (1681–1740) and the Highland Problem in the Scottish Catholic Mission', *The Innes Review*, XXXIX, 2 (1988), 84–94.

12. Roberts, 'Gregor McGregor', 84, 90, 92–4.

13. Roberts, 'Gregor McGregor', 84–104.

14. Doran, 'Bishop Thomas Nicholson', 129

15. James F. McMillan, 'Jansenists and Anti-Jansenists in Eighteenth-Century Scotland: The *Unigenitus* Quarrels on the Scottish Catholic Mission, 1732–1746', *The Innes Review*, XXXIX, 1 (1988), 12–13, 15–16, 25–6, 39–40; James F. McMillan, 'Thomas Innes and "Unigenitus"', *The Innes Review*, XXXIII (1982), 23–30.

16. David McRoberts, 'The Rosary in Scotland', *The Innes Review*, XXIII, 1 (1972), 81–6; Ross, 'Dominicans in Scotland', 41, 57–8.

17. Alasdair Roberts, 'Catholic Marriage in Eighteenth-Century Scotland', *The Innes Review*, XXXIV, 1 (1983), 10, 12.

18. Roberts, 'Catholic Marriage', 13.

19. Alasdair R. B. Roberts, 'The Role of Women in Scottish Catholic Survival', *Scottish Historical Review*, LXX, 2 (1991), 133–6

20. Roberts, 'The Role of Women', 146–53.

21. Roberts, 'The Role of Women', 143–9

22. Peter F. Anson, *Underground Catholicism in Scotland 1622–1878* (Montrose: Standard Press, 1970), pp. 113–14.

23. *The Annals of Loch Cé. A Chronicle of Irish Affairs from AD 1014 to AD 1590* (ed. and trans. William M. Hennessy, 2 vols, London: Longmans, 1871), II, pp. 517–8. For the background to this period, see the recent works by Thomas Bartlett, *The Fall and Rise of the Irish Nation: the Catholic Question, 1690–1830* (Dublin: Gill and Macmillan, 1992) and by Sean J. Connolly, *Law and Power: The Making of Protestant Ireland, 1660–1760* (Oxford: Clarendon, 1992).

24. Donal F. Cregan, 'The Social and Cultural Background of a Counter-Reformation Episcopate, 1618–60', in Art Cosgrove and Donal McCartney (eds), *Studies in Irish History Presented to Owen Dudley Edwards* (Dublin: University College, 1979), pp. 88–9, 91–2; Thomas S. Flynn, OP, *The Irish Dominicans 1536–1641* (Dublin: Four Courts Press, 1993), pp. 163–9, 176. For further illustration of the seventeenth-century Irish familiarity with both traditional Celtic and Renaissance European culture, see the career of the Spanish-trained papal diplomat, Dominic O'Daly, from a Kerry bardic background to which 'Europe was never remote': Sr Benvenuta

MacCurtain, 'An Irish Agent of the Counter-Reformation, Dominic O'Daly', *Irish Historical Studies*, XV (1966–7), 391–406.

25. Cregan, 'Social and Cultural Background', pp. 90–5, 102–4, 107, 109–11, 114–15, 117; Patrick J. Corish, *The Catholic Community in the Seventeenth and Eighteenth Centuries* (Dublin: Helicon, 1981), pp. 63–4.

26. Keith J. Lindley, 'The impact of the 1641 rebellion upon England and Wales, 1641–5', *Irish Historical Studies*, XVIII (1972–3), 155–8; Aidan Clarke, 'The 1641 Rebellion and anti-popery in Ireland', in Brian Mac-Cuarta, SJ, *Ulster 1641: Aspects of the Rising* (Belfast: Queen's University Institution of Irish Studies, 1993), pp. 139–57; Jacqueline Hill, '1641 and the Quest for Catholic Emancipation, 1691–1829', in *ibid.*, p. 161; T. C. Barnard, 'The Uses of 23 October 1641 and Irish Protestant Celebrations', *English Historical Review*, CVI (1991), 889–920; J. G. Simms, 'John Toland (c 1670–1722), a Donegal Heretic', in David Hayton and Gerard O'Brien (eds), *War and Politics in Ireland, 1649–1730* (London and Ronceverte, WV: The Hambledon Press, 1986), p. 42.

27. John Lowe, 'Charles I and the Confederation of Kilkenny', *Irish Historical Studies*, XIV (1964–5), 5–6; Corish, *The Catholic Community*, p. 44; John T. Gilbert (ed.), *A Contemporary History of Affairs in Ireland, from 1641 to 1652* (Dublin: Irish Archaeological and Celtic Society, 1879), vol. I, Part II, p. 712; Francis X. Martin, OSA, ' "Obstinate" Skerrett, Missionary in Virginia, the West Indies and England', *The Journal of the Galway Archaeological and Historical Society*, XXXV (1976), 20; *Historical Manuscripts Commission: Ormonde* (1885), pp. 496–9.

28. J. G. Simms, 'Cromwell's Siege of Waterford in 1649' in Hayton and O'Brien (eds), *War and Politics in Ireland*, pp. 11–12; Lowe, 'Charles I and the Confederation of Kilkenny', 8; *A Contemporary History of Affairs in Ireland*, vol. III, Part II, p. 261; Corish, *The Catholic Community*, pp. 48–9.

29. Corish, *The Catholic Community*, pp. 53–4; Thomas Bartlett, 'The O'Haras of Annaghmore, c. 1600–c. 1800: Survival or Revival', *Irish Economic and Social History*, IX (1982), 34–5; Karl S. Bottigheimer, 'The restoration land settlement: a structural view', *Irish Historical Studies*, XVIII (1972–3), 1–2, 21; *Calendar of State Papers Domestic, Charles II, vol. II, 1666–1669*, p. 556; L. J. Arnold, 'The Irish court of claims of 1663', *Irish Historical Review*, XXIV (1984–5), 427.

30. Benignus Millett, OFM, 'Calendar of Volume 1 (1625–68) of the Collection *Scritture referite nei congressi, Irlanda*, in Propaganda Archives', *Collectanea Hibernica, Sources for Irish History*, nos 6 & 7 (1963–4), 20–3, 29–31; Corish, *Catholic Community*, pp. 55–6, 68; *Dictionary of National Biography*, vol. XV, p. 1328; *Historical Manuscripts Commission: Ormonde*, pp. 174, 344; J. R. Western, *Monarchy and Revolution. The English State in the 1680s* (London: Blandford Press, 1972), p. 150; J. G. Simms, 'Dublin in 1685', in Hayton and O'Brien (eds), *War and Politics in Ireland*, p. 61; Celestine Murphy, 'The Wexford Catholic Community in the late seventeenth century', in R. V. Comerford, Mary Cullen, Jacqueline R. Hill and Colm Lennon (eds), *Religion, Conflict and Coexistence in Ireland: Essays Presented to Monsignor Patrick J. Corish* (Dublin: Gill and Macmillan, 1990), pp. 78–81, 84–6.

31. Murphy, 'The Wexford Catholic Community', pp. 86–7, 93; Simms, 'Dublin in 1685', pp. 54–5, 58, 63, 78–9, 81.

32. John Miller, 'Thomas Sheridan (1646–1712) and his "Narrative"', *Irish Historical Studies*, XX (1976–7), 115–17; Patrick Kelly, '"A light to the blind": the voice of the dispossessed elite in the generation after the defeat at Limerick', *Irish Historical Studies*, XXIV, 9 (1984–5), 43; Western, *Monarchy and Revolution*, p. 153.

33. Western, *Monarchy and Revolution*; J. G. Simms, 'The Jacobite Parliament of 1689', in Hayton and O'Brien (eds), *War and Politics in Ireland*, pp. 65–81.

34. Murphy, 'Wexford Catholic Community', 89–90; J. G. Simms, 'Williamite Peace Tactics, 1690–1', in Hayton and O'Brien (eds), *War and Politics in Ireland*, pp. 181–201; J. G. Simms, 'The Treaty of Limerick', in *ibid.*, pp. 203–24 and esp. 205.

35. J. G. Simms, 'The Bishops' Banishment Act of 1697', *Irish Historical Studies*, XVII (1970–1), 185–99; *Historical Manuscripts Commission: Ormonde*, p. 174.

36. D. W. Hayton, 'From Barbarian to Burlesque: English Images of the Irish c. 1600–1750', *Irish Economic and Social History*, XV (1988), 14–15; Murphy, 'Wexford Catholic Community', pp. 79–80, 90–5; Corish, *The Catholic Community*, p. 71.

37. Hayton, 'From Barbarian to Burlesque', 13; William Edward Hartpole Lecky, *A History of Ireland in the Eighteenth Century* (5 vols, London: Longmans, Green & Co., 1892), I, p. 141; J. G. Simms, 'The Making of a Penal Law (2 Anne, c. 6), 1703–4', in Hayton and O'Brien (eds), *War and Politics in Ireland*, pp. 273–6; J. G. Simms, 'Irish Catholics and the Parliamentary Franchise, 1692–1728', in *ibid.*, pp. 233–4; J. G. Simms, 'The Irish Parliament of 1713', in *ibid.*, p. 277.

38. Murphy, 'Wexford Catholic Community', pp. 97–8; *Calendar of State Papers Domestic, Anne*, vol. II, 1703–4, p. 24; James Mitchell, 'The Tholsel at Galway (1639–1822)', *Journal of the Galway Archaeological and Historical Society*, XXXV (1976), 81; Raymond Hughes, 'A Galway Election List of 1727', *ibid.*, 105–28.

39. Hughes, 'A Galway Election List', 113–28; J. L. McCracken, 'The ecclesiastical structure, 1714–60', in T. W. Moody and W. E. Vaughan (eds), *A New History of Ireland 1691–1800* (9 vols, Oxford: Clarendon, 1986), IV, pp. 95–6; Corish, *Catholic Community*, pp. 90–1.

40. Corish, *Catholic Community*, pp. 76, 78–80, 82–3, 86–7; Lecky, *A History of Ireland*, I, pp. 265–8; *Ireland in the Stuart Papers: Correspondence and Documents of Irish interest from the Stuart Papers in the Royal Archives, Windsor Castle, vol. I: 1719–42* (Dublin: Four Courts Press, 1995), pp. 150–1.

41. Lecky, *History of Ireland*, I, pp. 264, 267; McCracken, 'Ecclesiastical structure', p. 96.

42. Daniel Gahan, 'Religion and land-tenure in eighteenth-century Ireland: tenancy in the south-east', in Comerford *et al.* (eds), *Religion, Conflict and Coexistence*, pp. 99–117; Thomas Bartlett, 'The O'Haras of Annaghmore c. 1600–c. 1800: Survival or Revival', 34–52; Bartlett, *The Fall and Rise of the Irish Nation*, quoted in Jim Smyth, 'The Making and Undoing of a Confessional State: Ireland, 1660–1829', *Journal of Ecclesiastical History*, XLIV (1993), 510.

5   Catholics in England and Wales, c.1745–c.1829

1. For background, see W. J. Sheils, 'Catholicism from the Reformation to the
    Relief Acts', in Sheridan Gilley and W. J. Sheils (eds), *A History of Religion in
    Britain: Practice and Belief from Pre-Roman Times to the Present* (Oxford and
    Cambridge, MA: Blackwell, 1994), pp. 248–51, and Sheridan Gilley, 'The
    Roman Catholic Church in England, 1780–1940', in *ibid.*, pp. 346–51.
2. J. Derek Holmes, 'Aspects of Nineteenth-Century Catholicism in England',
    in G.T. Bradley (ed.), *Yorkshire Catholics: Essays presented to the Right Reverend
    William Gordon Wheeler, MA, DD, on the occasion of his retirement as Bishop of
    Leeds* (Leeds: Leeds Diocesan Occasional Publications, no. 1,1985), p. 26;
    for Pugin, his exaltation of medieval architecture and his denigration of
    classical forms, see Sheridan Gilley, 'The Roman Catholic Church in Eng-
    land, 1780–1940', pp. 352–3. (If Victorian Catholics tended to be dismissive
    about the zeal of their Hanoverian forebears, the eighteenth-century priest
    Joseph Berington was convinced that he lived in an age of English Catholic
    decadence, and Bishop Challoner himself was pessimistic over 'the great
    decay of piety and religion amongst a great part of our Catholics': Mon-
    signor Anthony Stark, *Bishop Challoner His Life and Times* (London: The
    Guild of Our Lady of Ransom, n.d.), p. 24.)
3. Kevin MacGrath, *Catholicism in Devon and Cornwall 1767* (Buckfast Abbey,
    Devon: Buckfast Abbey Publications, 1960), pp. 2, 4, 5; Stewart Foster, 'A
    Miracle at Glastonbury', *South West Catholic History*, III (1985), 3–6.
4. W. J. Sheils, 'Catholicism from the Reformation to the Relief Acts', pp. 248–
    51; Stark, 'Bishop Challoner', p. 25.
5. G. Holt, SJ, 'Croxteth–Gillmoss: The Development of a Mission', *North West
    Catholic History*, XXII (1995), 1–8.
6. J. F. Giblin, *The Anderton Family of Birchley* (Formby: Print Origination, 1993),
    pp. 6–8, 21; J.F. Giblin, *The Gerard Family of Bryn and Ince and the Parish of SS
    Oswald and Edmund in Ashton-in-Makerfield* (Formby: Print Origination,
    1990), pp. 1, 18; Marion E. McClintock, *St Thomas the Apostle, Claughton-on-
    Brock: a brief history* (Garstang: Colin Cross, 1994), pp. 9, 13; Rt Rev. B.C.
    Foley, 'Ann Fenwick née Benison (1724–1777) Heiress, Foundress of
    Hornby Mission', in B.C. Foley, *Some People of the Penal Times (Chiefly 1688–
    1791)* (Lancaster: Cathedral Bookshop, 1991), pp. 27, 33, 34;
7. Gilley, 'The Roman Catholic Church, 1780–1940', p.348; B.C. Foley,
    'Robert Edward, Ninth Lord Petre of Thorndon in Essex', in Foley, *Some
    People of the Penal Times*, pp. 105–18; Nigel Abercrombie, 'The First Relief
    Act', in Eamon Duffy (ed.), *Challoner and His Church A Catholic Bishop in
    Georgian England* (London: Darton, Longman & Todd, 1981), pp. 185–6.
8. Philip Caraman, SJ, 'Wardour Chapel', *South Western Catholic History*, III
    (1985), 25–31.
9. J. Anthony Williams, 'Change or Decay? The Provincial Laity 1691–1781',
    in Duffy (ed.), *Challoner and His Church*, pp. 43–4; Betty Strudwick, 'The
    Darrells of Calehill', *Kent Recusant History*, IV (1980), 89–92.
10. R.R. Sellman, 'Father Darbyshire's Journal 1726–1757', *South Western Cath-
    olic History*, I (1983) 32–3; see also Dominic Bellenger, 'People and Places I:

Father Darbyshire', *South Western Catholic History*, II (1984), 4; and Edw. S. Worrall, 'Watching Lord Petre. I', *Essex Recusant*, VII (1965), 42–3.

11. Worrall, 'Watching Lord Petre', 40–3; Colin Haydon, *Anti-Catholicism in eighteenth-century England, c. 1714–80: a political and social study* (Manchester and New York: Manchester University Press, 1993), *passim*; David Mathew, *Catholicism in England 1535–1935. Portrait of a Minority: Its Culture and Tradition* (London: Catholic Book Club, 1938), p. 141; Charles Butler, *Historical Memoirs of the English, Irish, and Scottish Catholics, Since the Reformation* (4 vols, 3rd edn, London: John Murray, 1822), III, pp. 275–8.

12. J.A. Hilton, 'The Case of Wigan: Catholic Congregationalism in the Age of Revolution', *North West Catholic History*, X (1983), 1–7: see also John Bossy, *The English Catholic Community 1570–1850* (London: Darton, Longman & Todd, 1975), pp. 303–5, 339, 346, 351.

13. Leo Warren, *A Short History of St. Wilfird's Church Preston* (Preston: Mather Bros, 1972), pp. 3, 13, 16; Holmes, 'Aspects of Nineteenth-Century Catholicism', pp. 30–1.

14. Bryan Little, 'Tensions in Trenchard Street: The Bristol Cause,1829–1847', *South Western Catholic History*, III (1985), 19–24.

15. J. Anthony Williams (ed.), *Post-Reformation Catholicism in Bath* (2 vols, London: Catholic Record Society, vol. LXV [1975]), I, pp. 66–9.

16. Williams (ed.), *Post-Reformation Catholicism*, pp. 70 ff. (with statistics)

17. 'Notes and Queries', *Kent Recusant History*, X, XI (1983–4), 204–5; Bernard W. Kelly, *Historical Notes on English Catholic Missions* (London: Kegan Paul, Trench, Trübner & Co., 1907, reprinted, London: Michael Gandy, 1995), 447; V.J. L. Fontana, 'Portsmouth and the Origins of the Catholic Chaplaincies', *South Western Catholic History*, VIII (1990), 3–4.

18. Fontana, 'Portsmouth and the Origins of Catholic Chaplaincies'; Christopher Buckingham, 'The Dover Mission (1)', *Kent Recusant History*, IV (1980), 83–4.

19. Dominic Bellenger, 'The French Exiled Clergy in Reading', *South Western Catholic History*, II (1984), 22; D.T.J. Bellenger, 'The French Exiled Clergy in England and National identity, 1790–1815', in Stuart Mews (ed.), *Religion and National Identity... (Studies in Church History*, XVIII, Oxford: Basil Blackwell, 1982), p. 400; Rev. David Quinlan, *The Whitby Catholics (640–1957)* (2nd edn, Farnworth: Catholic Printing Co., 1965, pp. 14–18. In Whitby a 'circulating Catholic library' was also established.

20. Bellenger, 'French Exiled Clergy in Reading', 22–31; MacGrath, *Catholicism in Devon and Cornwall 1767*, p. 5.

21. Dominic Bellenger, 'People and Places I: Etienne Chapon', *South Western Catholic History*, II (1984), 3–4; MacGrath, *Catholicism in Devon and Cornwall 1767*, p. 5; Sister Mildred Murray Sinclair, OSB, 'The Nuns Go West', *South West Catholic History*, III (1985), 36; Warren, *St. Wilfrid's Church Preston*, p. 12; Margaret J. Mason, 'Nuns of the Jerningham Letters: Elizabeth Jerningham (1727–1807) and Frances Henrietta Jerningham (1725–1824), Augustinian Canonesses of Bruges', *Recusant History*, XXII, 3 (1995), 352–3. Nuns were regarded as exotics even in strongly Catholic rural Lancashire: when the agricultural improving squire Dicconson of Wrightington told his coachman to collect nuns from Wigan for transfer to Wrightington,

the coachman's question to another servant, 'What are nuns?', elicited the reply, 'I don't know. Some new sort of potato perhaps.': J.A. Hilton, *Catholic Lancashire From Reformation to Renewal 1559–1991* (Chichester, W. Susses: Phillimore, 1994), p. 83.

22. T.E. Muir, *Stonyhurst College 1593–1993* (London: James and James,1992), pp. 70 ff.; Michael Sharratt, 'The Origin and Growth of the Ushaw Library', *Northern Catholic History*, XXIV (1986), 22–34.

23. Holmes, 'Aspects of Nineteenth-Century Catholicism', p. 29; Cardinal Basil Hume, Forward to Eamon Duffy (ed.), *Challoner and His Church*, p.ix.

24. Mathew, *Catholicism in England*, p. 143; Bossy, *The English Catholic Community*, p. 310.

25. *The Canons and Decrees of the Council of Trent* (ed. and trans H. J. Schroeder, OP (Rockford, IL: TAN Books, 1978), pp. 46–7, 49, 60–1, 162, 164–5, 226, 232; Eamon Duffy, 'Richard Challoner 1691–1781: A Memoir', in Duffy (ed.), *Challoner and His Church*, pp. 1–26; Stark, *Bishop Challoner*, pp. 21–2.

26. Patrick O'Donovan, *The Venerable Bishop Richard Challoner Sometime Vicar Apostolic of the London District* (London: Westminster Cathedral, 1981), p. 17; Bossy, *English Catholic Community*, pp. 369–70; Bishop Challoner, *The Garden of the Soul: A Manual of Spiritual Exercises and Instructions for Christians who, living in the World, aspire to Devotion* (Burns & Oates edn, London, n.d.), pp. 73–4; Thomas a Kempis, *The Imitation of Christ*, quoted in Michael Mullett, *Popular Culture and Popular Protest in Late Medieval and Early Modern Europe* (London: Croom Helm, 1987), p. 47.

27. Saint Francis de Sales, *Introduction to the Devout Life* (ed. and trans. Allan Ross, London: Burns Oates & Washbourne, 1950), p.18; Challoner, *The Garden of the Soul*, pp. 40ff., 95, 103; Richard Luckett, 'Richard Challoner: The Devotional Writer', in Duffy (ed.), *Challoner and His Church*, pp. 82, 87: Challoner also radically simplified the recondite English of the Douai Bible – Stark, *Bishop Challoner*, p. 19; John Bossy, 'Catholic Lancashire in the Eighteenth Century', in John Bossy and Peter Jupp (eds), *Essays Presented to Michael Roberts* (Belfast: Blackstaff Press, 1976), p. 56.

28. *Canons and Decrees of Trent* (ed. Schroeder), p. 197; *The Garden of the Soul*, pp. 95, 103; for Charles Wesley's hymn, see Michael A. Mullett, *John Bunyan in Context* (Keele, Staffs: Keele University Press, 1996), p.141.

29. David Butler, *Methodists and Papists: John Wesley and the Catholic Church in the Eighteenth Century* (London: Darton, Longman & Todd, 1995), pp. 70–81; *Canons and Decrees of Trent* (ed. Schroeder), p. 33; Challoner, *The Garden of the Soul*, pp. 5, 18, 94, 92, 153.

30. Challoner, *The Garden of the soul*, pp. 10–11, 31, 6; Marie Rowlands, 'The Education and Piety of Catholics in Staffordshire in the 18th Century', *Recusant History*, X, 2(1969), 76.

31. Rowlands, 'Education and Piety of Catholics', 66–7; Mathew, *Catholicism in England*, pp. 152, 90.

32. Rowlands, 'Education and Piety of Catholics', 67–9; Bossy, 'Catholic Lancashire', pp. 64–5; *Canons and Decrees of Trent* (ed. Schroeder), p. 77; Challoner, *The Garden of the Soul*, p. 248.

33. Rowlands, 'Education and Piety of Catholics', 77–8; Challoner, *The Garden of the Soul*, pp. 213, 219–30.
34. Rowlands, 'Education and Piety of Catholics', 68–9; Bossy, 'Catholic Lancashire', pp. 64–5; Stark, *Bishop Challoner*, p. 31.
35. Stark, *Bishop Challoner*, p. 74; Rowlands, 'Education and Piety of Catholics', 71–6; Bossy, 'Catholic Lancashire', p. 65.
36. Rowlands, 'Education and Piety of Catholics', 72–5.
37. Erasmus Saunders (1721), quoted in Philip Jenkins, *A History of Modern Wales 1536–1990* (London: Longman, 1992), p. 112.
38. John Hobson Matthews (ed.), 'Reputed Papists in the Diocese of St David's, 1767', *Catholic Record Society*, Miscellanea II (1906), pp. 303–4; Jenkins, *History of Modern Wales*, p. 115; John Hobson Matthews (ed.), 'Some Records of the Monmouth Mission', *Catholic Record Society*, Miscellanea VII (1911), pp. 131–2; [Thomas Murphy], *The Position of Catholics in England and Wales During the Last Two Centuries* (London: Burns & Oates, 1892), pp. 62–3; J.H. Matthews (ed.), 'Catholic Mission Registers of Perthîr', *Catholic Record Society*, Miscellanea I (1905), pp. 271–2; John Hobson Matthews (ed.), 'The Old Registers of the Catholic Mission of Llanarth in the County of Monmouth', *Catholic Record Society*, Miscellanea II (1906), pp. 144–80; M.J. Dowden, 'A Disputed Inheritance: The Tredegar Estates in the Eighteenth Century', *Welsh Historical Review*, XVI (1992–3), 36–46.
39. Paul Hook (ed.), 'Catholic Registers of Holywell, Flintshire, 1698–1829', *Catholic Record Society*, Miscellanea III (1906), pp. 104–34.

6   Catholics in Scotland and Ireland, c.1745–c.1829

1. William James Anderson (ed.), 'Abbé Paul McPherson's History of the Scots College, Rome', *The Innes Review*, XII (1961), 4, 136; Mark Dilworth, OSB, 'Scottish Supplement to the Necrology', *The Innes Review*, XV, 2 (1964), 171–81; William James Anderson, 'Father Gallus Robertson's New Testament', *The Innes Review*, XVII, 1 (1966), 54–5; Reginald C. Fuller, *Alexander Geddes 1737–1802: A Pioneer of Biblical Criticism* (Sheffield: The Almond Press, 1984), reviewed in *The Innes Review*, (1985); F. Forbes and W. J. Anderson, 'Clergy Lists of the Highland District, 1732–1828', *The Innes Review*, XVII, 2 (1966), 136–40, 147–9; Charles Burns, 'Additions to the *Fondo Missioni* Handlist', *The Innes Review*, XXXIII (1982), 32.
2. Peter F. Anson, *Underground Catholicism in Scotland 1622–1878* (Montrose: Standard Press, 1970), pp. 201–3; David McRoberts, 'The Rosary in Scotland', *The Innes Review*, XXIII, 1 (1972), 85–6.
3. Anson, *Underground Catholicism*, p. 204.
4. Anson, *Underground Catholicism*, pp. 211–12; William James Anderson, 'David Downie and the "Friends of the People"', *The Innes Review*, XVI, 2 (1965), 165–179
5. Antony Ross, OP, 'Three Antiquaries: General Hutton, Bishop Geddes and the Earl of Buchan', *The Innes Review*, XV, 2 (1964), 122–39; Bernard Aspinwall, 'Some Aspects of Scotland and the Catholic Revival in the Early Nineteenth Century', *The Innes Review*, XXVI, 1 (1975), 3–19.

6. Ross, 'Three Antiquaries', 136; Ian A. Muirhead, 'Catholic Emancipation in Scotland: The Debate and the Aftermath Part Two', *The Innes Review*, XXIV, 2 (1973), 103–20.
7. Roderick Mcdonald, 'The Highland District in 1764', *The Innes Review*, XV, 2 (1964), 140–50; F. Forbes and W.J. Anderson, 'Clergy Lists of the Highland District, 1732–1828', 131; Noel Macdonald Wilby, 'The "Encrease of Popery" in the Highlands 1714–1747', *The Innes Review*, XVII (1966), 106.
8. Wilby, 'The "Encrease of Popery"' 112–14.
9. Wilby, 'The "Encrease of Popery"', 91; the tabulated figures have been compiled on the basis of Anderson, 'Father Gallus Robertson's Edition of the New Testament', 50; Macdonald, 'The Highland District in 1764', 150; and Roderick Macdonald, 'Catholics in the Highlands in the 1760s', *The Innes Review*, XVI, 2 (1965), 218–20.
10. Margaret M. McKay (ed.), *The Rev. Dr John Walker's Report on the Hebrides of 1764 and 1771* (Edinburgh: John Donald, 1980), pp. 18, 85: I am grateful to my friend Angus Winchester for pointing out this source to me and for kindly lending me his copy; Macdonald, 'Catholics in the Highlands in the 1760s', 218; Mary McHugh, 'The Religious Condition of the Highlands and Islands in the Mid-Eighteenth Century', *The Innes Review*, XXXV, 1 (1984), 12–3, 20; Macdonald, 'The Highland District in 1764', 150; Forbes and Anderson, 'Clergy Lists of the Highland District', 131; Anderson, *Underground Catholicism*, p. 117.
11. Forbes and Anderson, 'Clergy Lists of the Highland District', 134, 136–7, 152; Roderick Mcdonald, 'The Catholic Gaidhealtachd', *The Innes Review*, XXIX (1978), 60; for Colin Campbell, see above pp. 112.
12. Forbes and Anderson, 'Clergy Lists of the Highland District', 132–43; Macdonald, 'The Highland District in 1764', 147–50; Macdonald, 'The Catholic Gaidhealtachd', 58–61.
13. W.J. Anderson, 'The Edinburgh Highland Chapel and the Rev. Robert Menzies', *The Innes Review*, XVII (1966), 197–8.
14. Macdonald, 'The Catholic Gaidhealtachd', 57–8, 60; Anson, *Underground Catholicism*, pp. 111, 113, 163–4, 207–8, 241.
15. W.J. Anderson, 'Ecumenism in Ardnamurchan, 1790', *The Innes Review*, XVII, 2 (1966), 188–92; Macdonald, 'The Catholic Gaidhealtachd', 60–1; Thomas A. Fitzpatrick, 'Catholic Education in Glasgow, Lanarkshire and South-West Scotland before 1872', *The Innes Review*, XXXVI, 2 (1985), 86; Alexander MacWilliam, 'Catholic Dundee: 1787 to 1836', *The Innes Review*, XVII,2 (1967), 76; Christine Johnson, 'Secular Clergy of the Lowland District 1732–1829', *The Innes Review*, XXXIV, 2 (1983), 66–87.
16. Johnson, 'Secular Clergy', 66–87; Alasdair Roberts, 'Catholic Baptismal Registers in the City of Aberdeen, 1782–1876', *The Innes Review*, XXXI, 1 (1980), 17–25; Anson, *Underground Catholicism*, pp. 229, 250–1.
17. Wilby, 'The "Encrease of Popery"', 113; Anderson, 'The Edinburgh Highland Chapel and the Rev. Robert Menzies', 195–8.
18. Anson, *Underground Catholicism*, p. 198; James M. Lawlor, 'Benefactors of the Early Glasgow Mission: 1793 and 1797', *The Innes Review*, XXXV, 1 (1984), 22–3; Fitzpatrick, 'Catholic Education in Glasgow, Lanarkshire and South-West Scotland', 86–7.

19. Lawlor, 'Benefactors of the Early Glasgow Mission', 23–32.
20. Fitzpatrick, 'Catholic Education in Glasgow', 86–7.
21. MacWilliam, 'Catholic Dundee: 1787 to 1836', 75–87; David F. Ward, 'The Dundee Mission in 1804', *The Innes Review*, XXII, 1 (1971), 46–7.
22. Cathaldus Giblin, OFM, 'Catalogue of Materials of Irish Interest in the Collection *Nunziatura di Fiandra*, Vatican Archives: part 6, vols 133–5 Gg', *Collectanea Hibernica, Sources for Irish History*, X (1967), p. 99; Gearóid Ó Tuathaigh, *Ireland before the Famine 1794–1848* (Dublin: Gill and Macmillan, 1990), p. 43.
23. R. B. McDowell, 'The Age of the United Irishmen: Revolution and the Union', in T.W. Moody and W.E. Vaughan (eds), *The New History of Ireland IV 1691–1800* (Oxford: Clarendon, 1986), pp. 339–73, and esp. p. 355; J.C. Beckett, *The Making of Modern Ireland 1603–1923* (London: Faber & Faber, 1966), pp. 261–7, and esp. p. 265; Donal A. Kerr, 'Under the Union Flag: The Catholic church in Ireland, 1800–1870', in *Ireland after the Union: Proceedings of the Royal Irish Academy and the British Academy, London 1986* (Introduction by Lord Blake, Oxford: Oxford University Press for the British Academy, 1989), pp. 23, 26
24. See Emmett Larkin, 'The Devotional Revolution in Ireland 1850–1870', *American Historical Review*, LXXVII, 3 (1972), 625–52 ; see also the discussion in John Newsinger, 'The Catholic Church in Nineteenth-Century Ireland', *European History Quarterly*, XXV, 2 (1995), 247–67.
25. Newsinger, 'The Catholic Church in Nineteenth-Century Ireland', 247–67; Patrick K. Egan, 'Progress and Suppression of the United Irishmen in the Western Counties', *Journal of the Galway Archaeological and Historical* Society, XXV, 3 and 4 (1954), 105; Thomas Bartlett, *The Fall and Rise of the Irish Nation. The Catholic Question 1690–1830* (Dublin: Gill & Macmillan,1992), p. 312; Constantia Maxwell (ed.), Arthur Young, *A Tour in Ireland With General Observations on the Present State of that Kingdom Made in the years 1776, 1777 and 1778* (Cambridge: Cambridge University Press, 1925), pp. 194–5.
26. Bartlett, *The Fall and Rise of the Irish Nation*, p. 312; Ludwig Bieler, 'O Sullivan Beare's *Patricia Decas*: A Modern Irish Adaptation', *Journal of the Galway Archaeological and Historical Society*, XXII,1 and 2 (1946), 19–33.
27. Norman P. Tanner, SJ (ed.), *Decrees of the Ecumenical Councils* (2 vols, London, and Washington, DC: Sheed & Ward and Georgeton University Press, 1990), II, p. 679; Anon., *Letters from the Irish Highlands* (London: John Murray, 1825), pp. 121–2; Síle Ní Chinnéide, 'A Frenchman's Tour of Connacht in 1791', *Journal of the Galway Archaeological and Historical Society*, XXXV (1976), 57. Spontaneous lay 'canonisation', free of the careful, clerically-controlled procedures required by the Counter-Reformation Church (see Peter Burke, 'How to Be a Counter-Reformation Saint', in Kaspar von Greyerz (ed.), *Religion and Society in Early Modern Europe*, London, Boston and Sydney: George Allen & Unwin with the German Historical Insitute, 1984, pp. 45–55) remained for some time part of the unregulated Irish devotional scene, as with the cult of Fr Nugent in County Limerick, at whose grave in 1813 his followers consumed soil mixed with holy well water: *Letters from the Irish Highlands*, pp. 114–15.

28. *Letters from the Irish Highlands*, p.121; Ní Chinnéide, 'A Frenchman's Tour', 57; Michael P. Carroll, *Veiled Threats: The Logic of Popular Catholicism in Italy* (Baltimore, MD and London: Johns Hopkins University Press, 1996), p. 75.

29. Patrick J. Corish, *The Irish Catholic Experience: A Historical Survey* (Dublin: Gill and Macmillan, 1985), pp.130–6; Bartlett, *The Fall and Rise of the Irish Nation*, 312; Mark Tierney, OSB, 'A Short-Title Calendar of the Papers of Archbishop James Butler II in Archbishop's House, Thurles: Part 2, 1787–91', *Collectanea Hibernica, Sources for Irish History*, XX (1978), pp. 94–5; for the confraternities in the Counter Reformation, see John Bossy, 'The Counter-Reformation and the People of Catholic Europe', *Past and Present*, XLVII (1970), 58–60.

30. Newsinger, 'The Catholic Church in Nineteenth-Century Ireland', 250, 252–3, 255; William P. Burke, *The Irish Priests in the Penal Times (1660–1760). From the State Papers* (Waterford: Author, 1912), pp. 307–8.

31. Burke, *The Irish Priests in the Penal Times*; Síle Ní Cinnéide, 'Coquebert de Montbret's Impressions of Galway City and County in the Year 1791', *Journal of the Galway Archaeological and Historical Society*, XXV, 1 and 2 (1952), 12; H. Fenning, 'The Library of a Preacher of Drogheda: John Donnelly, O.P. (d. 1748), *Collectanea Hibernica, Sources for Irish History*, XVIII, XIX (1976–7), p. 25.

32. B. Millett, OFM, 'Catalogue of Irish Material in Vols. 123–131 of the *Scritture originali nelle congregazioni generale* in Propaganda Archives', *Collectanea Hibernica, Sources for Irish History*, XI (1968), pp. 7–35; Corish, *The Irish Catholic Experience*, p. 158; Tanner (ed.), *Decrees of the Ecumenical Councils*, II, p. 761: 'provincial councils for the control of conduct, correction of abuses, settling disputes and other matters allowed by the sacred canon, are to be restored'.

33. Tanner (ed.), *Decrees of the Ecumenical Councils*: 'Diocesan synods ... should be held every year and attendance at these is obligatory on all'; Mark Tierney, OSB, 'A Short-Title Calendar of the papers of Archbishop James Butler II in Archbishop's House, Thurles; Part 1, 1764–80', *Collectanea Hibernica, Sources for Irish History*, XVIII, XIX (1976–7), pp. 124–5.

34. For the Council of Trent's extensive and detailed requirements for the scrutiny and education of candidates for the priesthood, see Tanner (ed), *Decrees of the Ecumenical Councils*, II, pp. 744–53; for Trent on the dignity of bishops – 'made by the Holy Spirit *rulers of the church of God*' – *ibid.*, pp. 743–4; James Mitchell, 'Laurence Nihell, Bishop of Kilfenora and Kilmacduagh, 1726–1795', *Journal of the Galway Archaeological and Historical Society*, XXXIV (1974–5), pp. 80–1; for Borromean reform, see, for example,: Robert Trisco, 'Carlo Borromeo and the Council of Trent: the Question of Reform', in John M. Headley and John B. Tomaro (eds), *San Carlo Borromeo: Catholic Reform and Ecclesiastical Politics in the Second Half of the Sixteenth Century* (Washington, DC: The Folger Shakespeare Library, London and Toronto: Associated University Presses, 1988), pp. 47–84; Agostino Borromeo, 'Archbishop Carlo Borromeo and the Ecclesiastical Policy of Philip II in the State of Milan' (including the cardinals' 'restoration of episcopal functions to their fullest extent ... full and uninhibited exercise of the jurisdictional rights invested in the archiepiscopal see'), in *ibid.*, pp. 85–111; and Adriano Pros-

peri, 'Clerics and Laymen in the Work of Carlo Borromeo', in *ibid.*, pp. 112–38.

35. Robert Muchembled, 'Lay Judges and the Acculturation of the Masses (France and the Southern Low Countries, Sixteenth to Eighteenth Centuries)', in von Greyerz (ed.) *Religion and Society in Early Modern Europe*, pp. 56–65; Hugh Fanning,OP, 'Some Eighteenth-Century Broadsides', *Collectanea Hibernica Sources for Irish History*, XII (1969), p. 56.

36. Hugh Fanning, OP, 'The Journey of James Lyons from Rome to Sligo, 1763–65', *Collectanea Hibernica Sources for Irish History*, XI (1968), pp. 107–8.

37. James Butler, *A Justification of the Tenets of the Roman Catholic Religion*, 1787, in James Mitchell, 'Laurence Nihell', 71; Tierney, 'A Short-Title Calendar of Archbishop Butler's Papers', 2, pp. 75, 94; Thomas E. Hachey, Joseph M. Hernon, Jr, and Lawrence J. McCaffrey, *The Irish Experience* (revised edn, Armonk, NY and London: M.E. Sharpe, 1996), p. 47.

38. Tanner (ed.), *Decrees of the Ecumenical Councils*, II, pp. 776–84; Mitchell, 'Laurence Nihell', 80–1; Padráig Ó Súilleabháin, OFM, 'Documents Relating to Wexford Priory and Parish 1730–98', *Collectanea Hibernica Sources for Irish History*, VIII (1965), p. 115; Cathaldus Giblin, OFM, 'Ten Documents Relating to Irish Diocesan Affairs 1740–1784', *Collectanea Hibernica Sources for Irish History*, XX (1978), pp. 75–6; Tierney, 'A Short Title Calendar of Archbishop Butler's Papers', 2, p. 95.

39. H. Fenning, OP, 'Some Problems of the Irish Mission, 1733–1774', *Collectanea Hibernica Sources for Irish History*, VIII (1965), pp. 78–80, 90–3; Giblin, 'Ten Documents Relating to Irish Diocesan Affairs', pp. 79–80, 81–6; Brian Jennings, OFM, 'The Abbey of St Francis, Galway', *Journal of the Galway Archaeological and Historical Society*, XXII, 3 and 4 (1947), 101–19; Burke, *The Irish Priests in the Penal Times*, pp. 307–8; Ó Súillebháin, 'Documents Relating to Wexford Friary', pp. 110–28.

40. Fenning, 'Some Problems of the Irish Mission', pp. 92–100.

41. Tierney, 'A Short-Title Calendar of Archbishop Butler's Papers', 2, p.89; Newsinger, ' The Catholic Church in Ireland', p. 259.

42. Martin Brenan, *Schools of Kildare and Leighlin AD 1775–1835* (Dublin: M.H. Gill, 1935), pp. 23–7; for the *O Salutaris Hostia*, 'one of the most popular and long-lived of devotional inventions', see John Bossy, *Christianity in the West 1400–1700* (Oxford and New York: Oxford University Press, 1985), p. 69.

43. Pádraig Ó Súilleabháin, OFM, 'Sidelights on the Irish Church, 1811–38', *Collectanea Hibernica Sources for Irish History*, IX (1966), p. 75.

44. Mitchell, 'Laurence Nihell', 77; Brenan, *Schools of Kildare and Leighlin*, pp. 67–9; Corish, *Irish Catholic Experience*, p.160.

INDEX

Gother, John, 92–3, 157, 162
Gouda, Legate de, 46, 49
Grattan, Henry, 181
Gray, Marie, 117
Greenock, 179
Grindal, Archbishop, 13, 15
Gunpowder Conspiracy, 24, 74, 203
Gunther, family of, 98, 99

Haddington, 44
Hamilton, Abbot Jerome, 43
Hamilton, Abbot, John, 47
Hamilton, Archbishop, 34–5, 42
Hamilton, Archibald, 46
Hammersmith, 151
Harris, 54
Hartburn, Richard, 13
Hawarden, Dr, 85
Hay, Bishop, Vicar Apostolic, 166, 167, 177, 178
Hay, John, S.J., 42, 46, 50, 206
Haydock, George Leo, 150
Heneage, Elizabeth, 141
Hengrave Hall, Suffolk, 151
Henry VIII, 11, 55
Hepburn, James Bonaventure, 50
Herbert, family of, 163–4
Herefordshire, 163
Herries, Lord, 40
Hertfordshire, 21
Hesketh
  family of, 87
  James, 141
Highlands and Islands, ix, 40, 52–4, 105, 106–14, 166, 170–6, 177, 219–220
Hobbes, Thomas, 75–6
Holden, Henry, 75–6
Holdforth, Joseph, 146
Holme Pierrepoint, 84
Holy Orders, 187
Holyrood Abbey, 48
Holyrood House, 44, 167
Holywell, 29, 31, 85, 96, 101, 164, 219
Hoogstraten, 82
Hornby, Lancs, 142–3, 160

Hornyold, Bishop, Vicar Apostolic, 161,162
Hughes, John, 100
Huntly, earls, marquises and family, dukes of Gordon, 40, 44, 46–7, 102, 176, 177
  Lady, 118
Hutton, George Henry, 168

Imitation of Christ, 7, 155, 175, 195, 200, 218
Innes, John, 118
Innes, Thomas, 114, 168, 213
Inverness, 44
Inns of Court, 21, 61, 202
Ireland, ix, 28, 30, 52, 55–68, 102, 105,119–37, 180,196, 197, 198
  popular religion in, 183–6
  Tridentine bishops in, 120–3,182–3, 213–14
Irish College, Paris, 192
Irish Rebellion, 1641, 70, 123–4, 214
Islay, 53, 54
Italy, 4, 222

James duke of York, 76–7
  and Exclusion, 78–9
James IV, 34
James VI and I, 19, 20, 23, 24, 25, 29, 30, 45, 61, 102, 203, 204
James VII and II, 79, 81, 82, 99, 103–4, 106, 115, 118, 129–30, 131, 162, 209
Jansenism
  in Scotland, 112–14, 118, 119, 166, 213
  in Ireland, 123
Jerningham, family of, 94, 217
Jerusalem, 50–1
Jesuits (Society of Jesus), 3, 4, 5, 6, 9, 10, 14, 22, 23, 26, 28, 40, 42, 45, 46, 49, 50, 51, 52, 56, 58, 61, 62, 65, 68, 72, 77, 81, 83–4, 85, 92, 97, 98, 99, 103, 104, 105, 106–10, 113, 117–18, 124, 126, 141, 152, 154, 164, 166, 170, 173, 202, 203, 205, 210, 213